FLEXIBLE CAPITALISM

EASA Series

Published in Association with the European Association of Social Anthropologists (EASA)
Series Editor: Eeva Berglund, Helsinki University

Social anthropology in Europe is growing, and the variety of work being done is expanding. This series is intended to present the best of the work produced by members of the EASA, both in monographs and in edited collections. The studies in this series describe societies, processes, and institutions around the world and are intended for both scholarly and student readership.

FLEXIBLE CAPITALISM

Exchange and Ambiguity at Work

Edited by Jens Kjaerulff

berghahn
NEW YORK • OXFORD
www.berghahnbooks.com

Published in 2015 by
Berghahn Books
www.berghahnbooks.com

©2015, 2018 Jens Kjaerulff
First paperback edition published in 2018

Library of Congress Cataloging-in-Publication Data
Flexible capitalism: exchange and ambiguity at work / edited by
Jens Kjaerulff.
    pages cm. -- (EASA series; 25)
    Includes bibliographical references and index.
    ISBN 978-1-78238-615-5 (hardback) -- ISBN 978-1-78920-
073-7 (paperback) -- ISBN 978-1-78238-616-2 (ebook) 1. Work
environment--Social aspects. 2. Adaptability (Psychology)
3. Interpersonal relations. 4. Capitalism--Social aspects.
I. Kjaerulff, Jens.
  HD6955.F585 2015
  331.2--dc23

                                                    2014033555

British Library Cataloguing in Publication Data
A catalogue record for this book is available from the British Library

ISBN: 978-1-78238-615-5 (hardback)
ISBN: 978-1-78920-073-7 (paperback)
ISBN: 978-1-78238-616-2 (ebook)

Contents

Acknowledgements

This volume has been long in the making. Early in the process, Jakob Krause-Jensen was my collaborator. As the project gradually took firmer shape, however, Jakob regrettably had to withdraw due to too many other commitments. I want in the first instance to acknowledge Jakob's considerable share in conceptualizing the project and getting it underway. Daniel Miller and Susan Wright also offered generous input at this early stage of the project.

The leap from project to book owes much to James G. Carrier. In his capacity as editor for the book series of the European Association of Social Anthropologists (EASA), James suggested that we converted our ideas into a book proposal for the EASA series. Ever since, James has been immensely helpful and encouraging, through what turned out to be a long and challenging process. The biggest thank you of all must surely go to James.

In my effort towards assembling the collection and shaping the project I have also benefited from exchanges with a number of other colleagues, only some of whom can be listed here. During a temporary lectureship I held in social anthropology at the University of Manchester, Chris Gregory and Karen Sykes were very generous with their time and attention to my queries extending from the project. For pointed commentary on draft versions of my introduction, I thank Hannah Knox, Jakob Krause-Jensen, Keir Martin, Susana Narotzky, Patrick Neveling, Karen Sykes and Louise Takeda. Acknowledgements also go to Berghahn's anonymous readers and editorial staff, who at different stages provided shrewd feedback. Shortcomings of course are owing to me.

Last, I want to acknowledge some less direct but profound influences underlying my own involvement in the project. Ton Otto's exemplary mentorship during my PhD years helped shape my continued interest in 'work' as a topic of anthropological enquiry. While this volume was taking shape I earned some basic but compelling lessons on work, of a kind too easily glossed over, which ought to be part of any curriculum. For these I humbly express my gratitude, in particular to Fraser, Ian, Jake, Jeff, Martin, Paul, Trevor, Tylor, and my clever friend Todd Francoeur. My parents' hard work has meant more for me than I know. I dedicate my part of the effort with this volume to Erling Kjaerulff and Kirsten Kjaerulff.

Jens Kjaerulff

Copenhagen, 2014

Introduction

Jens Kjaerulff

This volume is concerned with the social aspects of 'work', under-stood broadly as the practice of paid labour, in market environments which in recent decades have received attention under banners such as 'flexible capitalism' (Sennett 1998) and 'flexible accumulation' (Harvey 1990). At this level of discourse, we refer in the first instance to 'flexible capitalism' simply as an umbrella label for the general field in which the collection's enquiry is set, rather than a more strictly defined analytic or empirical notion. What sets the volume apart from the wider literature on the topic is its anthropological approach to work as a matter of exchange, and to empirical enquiry about work thus conceived through fieldwork in settings variously qualifying as part of flexible capitalism. From the perspective of anthropology, exchange is not confined straightforwardly to economic transactions. Rather, exchange amounts to a 'total' phenomenon, as Mauss (1990) famously put it, appreciated in light of the fuller contexts to which fieldwork gives access. A key focus through much anthropological enquiry on exchange has been the ways in which transactions serve as vehicles for 'making and breaking' relations, that is, as modes of (re) producing and transforming the quality of sociality (e.g. Malinowski 1961; Lévi-Strauss 1969; Bourdieu 1977; Strathern 1988). In light of this legacy, it is striking that the practice of work in contemporary 'flexible' settings has remained largely unexplored from this per-spective, because the wider literature on such work has converged on a concern falling squarely within its scope of enquiry. This is the concern with the detrimental impact of flexible capitalism on social relations and morality, hinted at for example in the title of Sennett's seminal book, *The Corrosion of Character* (Sennett 1998). From the perspective of anthropological scholarship on exchange, this kind of concern has long been familiar, even if it has gained new force in recent decades. One might say, to use Polanyi's well-known term, that social life in contemporary work regimes appears forever more 'disembedded' (Polanyi 2001), or to paraphrase Marx (1990), that it appears to reach forever more 'alienating commodity forms'. What this familiarity suggests, however, is that the current concern may be partly shaped by what Maurer has called a 'Western folk theory' (Maurer 2006: 19), a teleological view pivoting on an essentialist 'gift/commodity' divide, according to which contemporary Western worlds are liable to consolidate themselves ever more firmly in the latter realm (e.g. Bloch and Parry 1989; Carrier 1995; cf. Macfarlane 1993). The view 'comes full circle' through selective descriptive renderings informed by, and in turn confirming, the stereotype (cf. Carrier 1995: 97). What is thereby obscured is a reality of economic practice comprising a more entangled and ambiguous mix of 'gift and commodity' exchange, in which relationships not only decline but simultaneously proliferate. It is this more complex reality of flexible capitalist work practice, and in particular the emergence of new forms of sociality through it, which is the volume's focus. The volume's title, *Flexible Capitalism*, alludes to this focus through a pun on the touted notion of flexibility, conventionally associated with contemporary capitalism as a distinguishing managerial and organizational trope. The title invokes this conventional association, but it simultaneously hints at the volume's approach to contemporary capitalist work practice as a 'flexible', that is, ambiguous matter of exchange and sociality exceeding the commodity form.

At one level, the volume aims to contribute to wider interdisciplinary literature by introducing a perspective which may shift the terms of enquiry. Contemporary economic practice is a subject deservedly attracting the attention of many scholars and students of various disciplinary backgrounds, whom we hope to engage. Anthropological exchange theory on the other hand is a specialized domain of expertise even within anthropology. In consideration of a wider uninitiated readership, part of this introduction therefore outlines the legacy of anthropological exchange theory, including that of the 'gift/commodity' distinction. What this perspective contributes is an alternative framework for approaching the social implications of flexible capitalism. Where wider enquiry has tended to be conceptually cast in terms of grander and culturally biased tropes such as 'society' (reflected in the commonplace notions of post-industrial, network or risk society), anthropological exchange theory is rooted in an enquiry into the dynamics through which sociality, in a more open and basic sense, is forged (e.g. Strathern 1988; cf. Long and Moore 2013). The collection thus aims to convince a wider readership that an anthropologically informed perspective on exchange provides a way of deepening and extending our understanding of the dynamics of sociality at work in flexible capitalism, by introducing some of this perspective's core analytical notions, and by engaging these notions in empirical contexts of contemporary 'flexible' work practice. Substantially, the volume's chapters contribute to this wider literature by exploring and documenting how, across diverse settings of contemporary flexible capitalist work, 'gift-like' moralities and socialities proliferate in, and even sustain, the kind of intensified commoditization that more widely has been touted as tearing social relations apart.

At another level, the volume is intended more specifically as a contribution to anthropological literatures, both on work and on exchange. Considering how central a part work is of many people's lives, there is a sense in which anthropologists have been remarkably inattentive to the subject. It is concisely captured in a passage from a recent book by Spittler, a German anthropologist who specializes in the study of work. He observes that while one might 'expect the subject of work to be as important a topic in anthropology as, for instance, exchange, magic [or] marriage . . . this is not the case . . . [T]here are only a few theoretically oriented anthropological monographs and collections of articles in English' (Spittler 2008: 11). The catch here is theory. Anthropologists have long paid attention to work, understood in the widest sense of how people wrest a living from their environments, as an element in attending to social life more broadly. There have, in fact, also been a fair number of anthropologists writing on work in the narrower sense of paid employment (see e.g. Nash 1998; Ortiz 2002). But there has hardly been a level of marked consensus within anthropology as to what work 'means' or comprises, or in terms of how to theoretically approach it, sufficing to clearly distinguish an 'anthropological' approach to work (cf. e.g. Sahlins 1972; Wallman 1979; Collins and Gimenez 1990; Ortiz 1994; Spittler 2001; Procoli 2004; Durrenberger and Marti 2006). Instead, the growing number of anthropologists taking an interest in contemporary work practices in recent years have, to a degree that contrasts with the study of other anthropological topics, such as exchange, magic and marriage, looked for theoretical inspiration elsewhere, such as from political economy (e.g. Roseberry 1988), the sociology of work (e.g. Burawoy 1979; Thompson 1989) and cultural studies (e.g. Willis 1977; du Gay 1996). While interesting and insightful research has ensued, an effect has been to reinforce a lack of common ground among anthropologists as to what questions and ideas about work and its contemporary transformations are worth pursuing. Against this background, our collection begins to explore an approach to sociality in a keenly debated contemporary work regime, drawing on a distinct and rich anthropological legacy. The formulation 'at work' in the volume's subtitle thus alludes to more than its focus on work in flexible capitalist settings. It highlights its specific approach to such work as *practice*, that is, the practice of *exchange* in the encompassing anthropological understanding. Paid work is by definition an exchange of money for a service, but as the volume's chapters demonstrate, transactions in the context of paid work exceed the economic aspects underlying this definition. It is the significance of these wider transactions in flexible capitalist settings which the volume's distinct anthropological orientation helps to investigate, and which the volume's chapters converge on teasing out.

By the same token, the volume also contributes to the anthropological literature on exchange by introducing work in flexible capitalist settings as a focus worth more sustained attention. It is curious that, while Marx's writings on labour (understood as a commodity) retrospectively have become adopted as an important legacy in more recent anthropological exchange theory – not least via Gregory's *Gifts and Commodities* (1982), considered further below – practices of work in contemporary flexible settings have remained largely ignored in this more recent body of exchange theory. This is in contrast with the attention devoted to other novel commodity forms that have emerged in recent decades in the realm of 'property', which have provided a focus for innovative enquiry, in significant measure building on the legacy of anthropological studies of exchange (see e.g. Hirsch 2010). One might say that a key element explored here has been the 'disambiguating' efforts that go into the creation of new kinds of property, which from this perspective are seen as inherently comprising 'fractal' relations (e.g. Strathern 1991; cf. Law 1999). Property claims are recursively conceived in terms of ownership relations. Yet the 'substance' of potential property is simultaneously and variously 'related' more widely – for example to communities of scholars and informants, in the case of intellectual property to which anthropological institutions might lay claim (see

Strathern 1999: 173–75) – so that claims to property require a wider network of relations to be 'cut' (Strathern 1996; Hirsch 2010). Some studies broadly falling within this recent thrust of enquiry do focus on contexts of paid work, but mainly attend to the 'cutting', such as the audit exercises that reduce work practice to entities that lend themselves to quantitative measures and exchanges (e.g. Strathern 2000). However, less attention has been devoted to the substance of flexible capitalist work in terms of the continued significance of the broader exchanges, moralities and relations that exceed the commodity form. It is here the emphasis lies, in the studies collected in this volume. As its subtitle suggests, such exchanges and relations are 'at work' in ambiguous ways. At the more obvious level, they remain central to the practice of paid work, yet they also remain outside its conception as economic practice. In its own right, such dynamics are hardly novel to the anthropological exchange perspective. What deserves renewed attention, however, is the ways such exchanges and relations proliferate, and in turn how such ambiguities 'work out' in the wake of the structural changes which have come to define flexible capitalism. It is here our collection concentrates the focus.

Flexible Capitalism

Flexible capitalism is not of one piece. It is in the first instance an expression, used among other umbrella phrases to collectively designate dimensions of economic practice that have emerged (roughly) since the 1970s, contrasted with a recent past of, for example, 'industrial' or 'Fordist' capitalism. Other expressions put to similar use include 'new', 'late', 'disorganized' and 'fast' capitalism. While 'flexibility' has become an emblematic concept, it must be made clear at the outset that it is a somewhat nebulous notion. In some contemporary economic contexts it is used for more particular effects (analytically as well as empirically); in others, it is used interchangeably with synonyms such as 'adaptability' and 'versatility'; while in yet other contexts clearly affected by dimensions falling within the rubric of 'flexible capitalism', the concept of flexibility itself is rarely used. This disparity is reflected in the collection, where the concept of flexibility itself figures more prominently in some chapters, and less so in others. It must be emphasized, therefore, that the concept, or its etymology or social life per se, is not the focus of this volume (in such regard, see for example Martin 1994).

For the sake of overview, the trajectory and distinguishing features of what is framed as 'flexible capitalism' may be characterized, in rather general terms, in the following way. The late 1960s and early 1970s saw the postwar boom of Euro-American economies grind to a halt, and inflation rise to a point where the Nixon administration decided to detach the US dollar from the gold standard, thus allowing for a greater measure of fiscal flexibility (e.g. Gregory 1997: 265–96; McMichael 1998). In slightly delayed parallel with this development, liberal market ideology surged to new prominence on the political scene (see e.g. Harvey 2005), not only in Europe and America but also in Latin America, Asia and later Eastern Europe, as a number of states in these areas found new enthusiasm for expanding market economy. Coupled with various technological advances during the same period, most conspicuously in the fields of computing and communication infrastructure (see e.g. Castells 1996), these developments expanded and opened up new markets, and above all enabled new kinds of market dynamics and engagements. Malleability in the realm of economic abstraction took on a more tangible life of its own, as the science of economics grew more powerful across the political spectrum and in economic practice (Carrier and Miller 1998). A greater dispersal of investment, production and recruitment of labour allowed for greater flexibility in terms of the accumulation of capital, the production process and the organization of labour (see e.g. Harvey 1990: 141–72). Product design and production processes came to entail higher measures of 'flexible specialization' (Piore and Sabel 1984), such as in terms of 'tailor-made' and 'just-in-time' production, and so at the level of the skills and tasks involved. New flexible affiliations with the labour market emerged, as 'subcontracting', along with 'network' and global 'follow-the-sun' production, became more prevalent (see e.g. Castells 1996; Felstead and Jewson 1999).

These developments have attracted considerable attention in the social sciences over the last three decades, and a number of prominent scholars have linked the emergence of this diffuse but pervasive regime of economic practice to broader social and cultural transformations. To mention just a few examples, Harvey's seminal excursus on 'flexible accumulation' was part of his wider exploration of 'the condition of postmodernity' (Harvey 1990). Beck saw the contours of a 'risk society' emerge from the volatile environments that followed the demise of stable forms of work organization (e.g. Beck 1992). Castells wrote of the 'rise of the network society' (Castells 1996), while Sennett outlined how the 'new flexible capitalism' undermined work as a source of identity (Sennett 1998). In a similar vein, as Boholm observes, a 'central thought' in works by Giddens and Bauman has been that, as 'the market assume[s] novel structural features . . . traditional social relationships, groupings and identities erode' (Boholm 2003: 157). In turn, other scholars have taken such views for granted as fact, adopting them as 'axioms' when approaching contemporary change (Baca 2005: 39). In a more comprehensive review, Strangleman indeed points to a 'trend' in contemporary mainstream scholarship on work (Strangleman 2007). This trend consists in a shared lament of 'loss' (ibid.: 88), a lament that 'the kind of economy that could provide a measure of stability for some through a "job for life" is no longer possible' (ibid.: 87), and that contemporary economic practice entails 'a process of individualisation and fragmentation which spans the workplace and the wider communities in which individuals live' (ibid.: 88).

While the aim of this collection is to move beyond this wider discourse of 'loss', it must be emphasized that the aim is not to promote an uncritical approach, let alone a defence of neoliberal infatuations with flexibilization. Indeed, there is an important place for this kind of discourse as a device for bringing wider critical attention to the social dimensions of contemporary economic transformations (cf. Maurer 2006: 17). To appreciate this, it is useful to briefly consider a longer trajectory of what is arguably one of the main effects of the features listed above as particular to 'flexible' capitalism. This effect fundamentally resembles the kind of abstraction which for Marx distinguished and enabled conventional capitalist exploitation – a point acknowledged by Harvey (1990: 186–97). Although Marx did not put it this way, one might say that it was the abstraction of value (reflected in and mediated by the prevalent use of modern money) which made value 'flexible' enough to be treated as an entity in its own right, that is, to be extracted, circulated and accumulated as capital. In essence, there is much to suggest that this kind of abstraction has in recent decades reached yet more extreme levels in the guise of flexibility, partially spurred by what Marx saw as the inherent capitalist need for the continuous expansion of value extraction (cf. e.g. Harvey, ibid.; Carrier and Miller 1998). One thing that the wider discourse on 'loss' helps bring out of the dark then, if not necessarily into focus, are contemporary practices of exploitation, even if they are more commonly cast in the more approachable and evocative terms of declining social relations. But this is also where the 'Western folk theory' alluded to above begins to act its part, so that, for example, past circumstances of industrial and colonial exploitation ironically come to serve as images of ostensibly more benign forms of sociality that are now lost (Strangleman 2007; Neveling, this volume). Concisely stated, the widely prevailing and intuitively compelling stereotype (also entertained within anthropology) that 'gift-like situations' are essentially benign, while 'commodity-like situations' are essentially malign, is both the strength and limitation of the 'folk theory'. The wider discourse on 'loss' is of course reinforced by a related stereotype, which sees 'work-like situations' as all about commodities. There is no doubt that exploitation and powers of capital continue to shape capitalist practice to an effect where those who mostly benefit in monetary terms are few, or that such power also operates at intimate levels (e.g. Burawoy 1982; du Gay 1996; Pongratz and Voss 2003). Moreover, as we will see below, it is not that 'gift' exchange is lacking dimensions of power, calculation or exploitation. But there is more to the practice of flexible capitalist work, and the image conjured in the wider discourse on 'loss', to an effect where all that is significant boils down to power and exploitation to the detriment of sociality, seems overly simplistic. And whereas such dimensions have by now been rather well traversed, the simultaneous proliferation of sociality has so far received little attention. Concentrating on the latter dimension does in this way not amount to denying or belittling the malign aspects of flexible capitalism; rather, it is a quest for understanding a part of a more complex picture, which on closer inspection seems empirically compelling.

The volume's chapters are all based on fieldwork in settings which in different ways exhibit features highlighted as distinctive of flexible capitalism in the wider literature, although as stressed above, these features are not consistently conceived in terms of 'flexibility'. Most explicit in this regard is the chapter by Garsten, a comparative study based on three different pieces of fieldwork, making concrete how flexibility is a multiple phenomenon. In Garsten's chapter, one setting concerns flexibility at the level of employment among temporary staff; in another, flexibility is what is required in the context of frequent organizational change; while in the third case, flexibility in terms of social roles is entailed in traversing an extensive network across different organizations. Two chapters, those by Cross and Neveling, are based on fieldwork in formally designated settings of 'offshore' production. Here, flexibility occurs in the first instance in terms of the organization of global production vis-à-vis local regulations. In the two settings considered in Narotzky's chapter, flexibility also occurs in terms of global production, respectively related to increasingly open and competitive markets in agriculture as a result of EU market integration, and to subcontracting in shoe manufacturing.

In Cross's chapter, 'flexible specialization' at the level of skills is also at issue, as it is in a different way in the chapter by Knox, based on fieldwork among 'knowledge workers' in the (global) ICT and media industry. Wood's chapter examines a work environment in North America's booming oil and gas sector shaped by fiscal flexibilities in the realm of speculative finance capital; Grétarsdóttir's chapter considers a case of aggressive export promotion through flexible transnational networks and identities; while Kjaerulff's chapter is based on fieldwork among people working from their homes via the internet, where flexible work time is at issue. In different ways then, all the chapters engage with practices of work in environments affected by features highlighted in the wider literature as distinctive of flexible capitalism. As this terse listing suggests, the chapters cover overlapping features of flexible capitalism that can be somewhat hard to meaningfully segregate. Yet, the chapters converge in documenting a more complex situation than is commonly portrayed of the social entailments of such work. It is in order to appreciate the 'workings' of this more complex picture that anthropological exchange theory is useful.

Work, Exchange, Ambiguity

Exchange is a key dimension of the practice of work. Understood in the modern colloquial and generic sense of paid labour, any activity may be considered 'work', so long as the person undertaking that activity does so in exchange for money (cf. Marx 1973: 100–108; Godelier 1980). In this, exchange (of labour for money) is a defining criterion of the modern conception of work. People may also undertake the same activity without receiving a money payment for doing it. While this does not qualify as work in a formal modern sense, it may be considered work of a more informal kind, such as 'housework'. Underlying this more informal notion of work is a social dimension, a social contract about the division of labour, which again suggests a fundamental dimension of exchange in work, also in this broader sense. This dimension of work is found in all human societies, and has been subject to enquiry for a long time in the social sciences.

Anthropological studies of exchange have not focused narrowly on modern formal work in its own right (but see e.g. Carrier 1992; Mollona 2005; Spittler 2009), which is arguably a reason they remain somewhat overlooked in mainstream scholarship on work. On the other hand, enquiry about the social aspects of exchange more broadly, as they are entailed in notions such as 'housework', has been particularly developed in anthropology. It is in part this attention to the intricate social dimensions of exchange which distinguishes anthropological from other approaches to exchange, prevalent in academic disciplines such as sociology and economics (e.g. Carrier 1991; Hann and Hart 2011).

Anthropological approaches to exchange vary considerably, but they may be said to broadly share some additional features. First, exchange is understood in a wide sense, ranging from exchanges of objects and even people in some cases, to exchanges of more ephemeral entities such as words and gestures in others. Second, anthropological approaches often see, or at least invoke, exchanges as concrete events of ongoing 'process' in terms of which cultural life and social relations are (re)created and changed, events which in turn also reflect a much wider spectrum of cultural and social life than granted in sociology and economics.

While most approaches to exchange in anthropology reflect some measure of these features, a distinction is commonly made between what has respectively been called 'collectivist' or 'holistic' orientations on the one hand, and 'individualistic' or 'transactionalist' ones on the other (e.g. Ekeh 1974; Kapferer 1976; cf. Carrier 1991; Graeber 2001: 23–47; Macfarlane 1993). The latter, to different degrees, share aspects of approaches to exchange in sociology and economics, in that individual reasoning, and sometimes also a rationality of a presumed universal individualist kind, is perceived as underlying exchange activity. While focused on social life in a wider sense than is common at least in economics, such approaches have often proved limited, for example, in their appreciation of cultural dimensions, at least from the perspective of anthropology. On the other hand, some versions of such approaches pay keener attention to the actual 'process' aspects in terms of which events of exchange are often invoked, than is generally the case with more holistic orientations (e.g. Barth 1981, 1989). According to convention in anthropology, these individualist orientations are sometimes also classified 'formalist', following a distinction made in the 1950s considered further below (see also Kjaerulff, this volume). But the legacy of this orientation goes further back, notably to works of Simmel and Weber (Barnard 2000: 80–98) and to strands of phenomenology.

In contrast to what is sometimes the case among anthropologists, this volume does not treat holistic and individualistic orientations as fundamentally incompatible. Indeed, the divide between them may not be as clear-cut as it is often made out to be, and a theme explored in the volume and detailed below, may be said to turn on the simultaneous coexistence of both individual pursuit and social considerations as motivating factors in exchange. However, it is particularly the holistic orientation which is associated with anthropological exchange theory (e.g. Carrier 1991), and which forms the point of departure for this book.

From a historical perspective, two scholars in particular have inspired this orientation, and they are used in what follows to frame the volume's approach. One is the Austrian-born economic historian Karl Polanyi (1886–1964), and the other is the French sociologist Marcel Mauss (1872–1950). Both Polanyi's and Mauss's writings on exchange were in part inspired by empirical anthropological studies of exchange in so-called primitive societies. These included studies of ceremonial exchange in Melanesia and on North America's north-west coast (respectively by Malinowski and Boas), where items such as seashells and blankets were exchanged on special occasions (known respectively as *kula* and potlatch), involving complex dynamics of prestige. In such societies, 'economic' exchange did not appear as segregated from other forms of exchange, as seemed to be the case in monetized economies. It is not least this dimension which has comprised the 'holistic' impetus in so-called holistic exchange orientations.

Polanyi and 'the Great Transformation'

The term 'embeddedness', invoked earlier, reflects this holistic orientation, and is commonly attributed to Polanyi's celebrated book *The Great Transformation* (Polanyi 2001). Originally published in 1944, the book is a historical account of what Polanyi saw as a fundamental shift in the relation between society and economy over the centuries prior to his lifetime (see also Isaac 2005; Hann and Hart 2009). Drawing on anthropological and historical studies, Polanyi argued that economic practice prior to agrarian capitalism had been 'embedded' (Polanyi, 2001: 60) in more widely prevailing patterns of social organization. He distinguished different patterns, and corresponding principles of exchange, in terms of which economic practice unfolded (ibid.: 45–58). The principle of reciprocity (reciprocal exchange) was dominant in so-called primitive societies, where social relations were conceived of in terms of clans and extended kinship, such as Malinowski had described it in his research on Melanesia. Exchange of prestigious seashells and marriage partners between members of two specific clans were accompanied by exchanges of other items used to sustain a livelihood between the same two clans, thus comprising what might be called an 'economy' consisting of exchanges between those clans, as well as within them along lines of perceived relatedness (such as matrilineal descent). A different principle of exchange, 'redistribution' (ibid.), was predominant in so-called archaic societies, where a more centralized and stratified organization of social relations prevailed. Here, items such as food – paid as rent for land use to a feudal elite, for example – were redistributed 'for use and consumption mainly to the nonproducing part of the population' (ibid.: 54), thus comprising an economic system underpinned by this wider form of social organization.

Polanyi's main focus, however, was on the emergence and development of market exchange as the predominant form in modern economies, where food and labour are simply bought and sold for money. Polanyi linked this development to yet a distinct principle of exchange, that of barter, which he saw as underlying early forms of market trade, and as existing simultaneously with other principles of exchange in clan-based and feudal societies, albeit it was peripheral to these in terms of economic importance. But in contrast to Adam Smith's famous claim about mankind's intrinsic 'propensity to truck and barter', Polanyi did not see barter as a straightforward or natural precursor to capitalist economic practice (Polanyi 2001: 59–70; see also Humphrey and Hugh-Jones 1992). Rather, drawing mainly on historical material from England, his hunch was that modern capitalist markets had emerged (in tandem with the consolidation of state power) through a deliberate and partially state-enforced promotion of market exchange across a radically expanded canvas: in geographical terms, in terms of volume of commodities produced and exchanged, and in terms of numbers of people affected. In the latter regard, Polanyi outlined how a poverty-ridden and socially uprooted population emerged and was shaped as part of this process, an element that was essential for modern industrial production (and states), which depended on it for labour power (Polanyi 2001: 35 ff).

The 'great transformation', then, consisted for Polanyi in the fundamental shift this development entailed in terms of the relation between social organization and economic practice. As he famously observed: 'the control of the economic system by the market is of overwhelming consequence to the whole organization of society: it means no less than the running of society as an adjunct to the market. Instead of [the] economy being embedded in social relations, social relations are embedded in the economic system' (ibid.: 60).

Polanyi used the term 'embeddedness' in a descriptive rather than a strictly analytical sense, but the concept became emblematic for the holistic approach to economic practice that he subsequently staked out. In a later publication (Polanyi 1957), seminal in the development of economic anthropology as a disciplinary specialization, Polanyi reformulated what he saw as distinctive about his approach. Distinguishing two meanings of the term 'economic', a 'substantive' and a 'formal' one, and two corresponding approaches to enquiry, he held that the substantive approach (which he promoted) was based on empirical investigation, whereas the formal one (pursued in mainstream economics, and by some anthropologists) was based only on logic (ibid.: 243–50). A main point Polanyi made with the distinction was that the two meanings had been conflated because of the extent to which formal economics had been institutionalized empirically in modern market economies (cf. Miller 1998). Extending from this point, he advocated approaching economic practice as a matter of what he called 'instituted process'. The process aspect was conceived of as the movement of items (between hands, and through space); the institutional aspect consisted of the social circumstances upon which such movement rely, to in fact function as an economy (Polanyi 1957: 243–50). For Polanyi, this institutional dimension in large measure extended from the patterns of social organization he had outlined in *The Great Transformation*.

In the heated debate that ensued between scholars of substantivist and formalist orientations, George Dalton – the main substantivist spokesman after Polanyi's death in 1964 – conceded that the formalist approach was more appropriate for understanding modern market economies, leaving the substantivists mainly to focus on other kinds of economic practice (Isaac 2005: 20–21). Isaac observes that Polanyi would likely have been 'deeply shocked' by this (ibid.), as Dalton thereby undermined Polanyi's comparative ambition of also examining modern economies in terms of embeddedness or 'instituted process'. This reorientation stymied the impact of Polanyi's holistic orientation on the study of modern market economies (ibid.).

More recently, Polanyi's notion of 'embeddedness' has been taken in new analytical directions (e.g. Granovetter 1985; Callon 1998; cf. Barry and Slater 2002, Beckert 2009). But it was the patterns of social organization and the corresponding principles of exchange which analytically comprised the more substantial lead, both in Polanyi's work and in the subsequent developments it inspired in economic anthropology, which are an important part of the holistic approaches' legacy (Gregory 2009; Hann and Hart 2011: 55–71).

In the context of our approach to flexible capitalism, the continued relevance of Polanyi's work and the studies of exchange it inspired is in the first instance in terms of the focus on embedded economic practice that was brought to the context of transforming market dynamics. Extending this spirit of Polanyi's enquiry, the volume's chapters thus concur on suggesting that a core feature of flexible capitalism turns precisely on its continued wider embeddedness, even if the configuration of this embeddedness (capitalism as 'instituted process', following Polanyi's later conceptualization) may be undergoing transformation. Paraphrasing a succinct formulation in Narotzky's chapter (this volume), our collection demonstrates how contemporary 'flexible' procurement of profit works, 'not so much through disembedding the economy from other social relations and value realms, but rather through pervasively embedding capitalist objectives in all spheres of responsibility ... the accumulation of surplus value hinges on not fully commoditizing the labour force'.

At the same time, an instructive shortcoming of Polanyi's approach (accentuated by Dalton's version of it) is its underlying evolutionary outlook. This is reflected in the grand narrative of *The Great Transformation*, where different 'types' of societies are seen to represent stages in a grand evolution of economic practice. A similar mind-set (the 'Western folk theory' mentioned above) has effectively informed approaches to transforming economic practice more broadly (Bloch and Parry 1989; Carrier 1995; Macfarlane 1993; Maurer 2006). From the perspective developed in this volume, the vocabulary of 'eras', 'ages' and 'isms' often deployed in the context of flexible capitalism is suggestive (see also Strangleman 2007). It is in part to move beyond this limitation that the chapters draw on the legacy from the other key historical figure in anthropological exchange theory, Marcel Mauss.

Mauss and 'the Gift'

The inspiration that stems from Mauss in the development of anthropological perspectives on exchange has arguably been more profound, and had a more lasting impact than is the case with that of Polanyi. It has also resulted in a more diverse range of theoretical perspectives, owing more to various influential interpretations of Mauss's scholarship than to Mauss's writings in their own right (e.g. Hart 2007). It is therefore more accurate to speak of 'Maussian approaches' (Carrier 1991), which in different ways relate to aspects of Mauss's writings, above all his famous essay *The Gift* (Mauss 1990), originally published in French in 1925. In what follows, a few key elements in this essay are considered, and then developed with reference to two more recent Maussian orientations.

Like Polanyi (and drawing on several of the same anthropological sources), Mauss's interest in so-called primitive exchange was rooted in an evolutionary outlook. But as will be apparent below, Mauss believed exchange in some respects resembling market trade had been more prevalent in primitive forms of exchange than Polanyi allowed for. Mauss saw exchange in primitive and archaic societies as 'total social phenomena', as he called it (ibid.: 3), simultaneously entailing religious, juridical, moral, aesthetic and economic dimensions. In other words, 'the economic' dimension of such exchange (here in quotation marks as it was not clearly segregated), had a range of entailments reflecting a wider 'social contract', which in Mauss's view had been 'hidden' (ibid.: 4) by modern laissez-faire market ideology. Underlying the project in *The Gift* was a polemical engagement with intellectual and ideological traditions which saw political and military power as a precondition for peaceful trade, restraining humanity's presumed natural acquisitive and self-interested propensity. Mauss, in contrast, wanted to explore exchange as an inherently moral and social activity, that is, one that is not dependent on a social contract apart from exchange, but where that activity is the very foundation and source of social relations (Sahlins 1972: 149–83; Graeber 2001: 152–55). This is reflected in his main question in *The Gift*: 'what rule . . . compels the gift that has been received to be obligatorily reciprocated' (Mauss 1990: 3).

A famous lead for Mauss was an anthropological account which in his reading suggested that gifts exchanged among the Maori remained entangled with their donors. Gifts were perceived to contain a 'spirit' which, although gifts were given voluntarily on the face of it, compelled a return gift to the donor. This spirit not only reflected social relationships, but literally took part in them, and more prestigious exchange items could even have 'personal' names (ibid.: 24). The 'spirit of the gift' also reflected and evoked wider ontological (that is, cosmic, social and moral) orders, in terms of which exchanges and social relations were conceived. Exchanges of gifts were thus instrumental in creating and maintaining these orders, and Mauss traced these dimensions of exchange using a considerable range of anthropological and philological sources. He especially concentrated on what he called 'agonistic' or competitive gift exchange, epitomized by the so-called potlatch found on North America's north-west coast. He elevated this to a general form of exchange that he argued existed in many places, and he further argued that this form reflected something like the acquisitive dimensions of modern market exchange while retaining the social and moral dimensions apparently lacking in the latter (e.g. ibid.: 75). On the one hand, such exchanges were displays of lavish and apparently generous giving; on the other, they were marked by underlying interests and competition, both motivated and contained in terms of wider social, cosmic and moral considerations (ibid.).

It is these wider and ambiguous dimensions of exchange, including 'economic' exchange, which have subsequently comprised a major focus of so-called Maussian approaches. While the chapters in the volume draw on a broader range of such approaches, a few key works and conceptual distinctions will be considered here.

Gregory on Gifts and Commodities

A conceptual distinction often invoked in more recent Maussian orientations is that between 'gifts' and 'commodities'. By extension this distinction is also applied to forms of exchange (gift exchange and commodity exchange), and to types of social relationships and moralities (gift and commodity relations and moralities). The distinction is commonly attributed to a landmark study by Gregory, entitled *Gifts and Commodities* (Gregory 1982; cf. Sahlins 1972: 185–277). Broadly speaking, this book had two aims. Firstly, drawing on the one hand on Lévi-Strauss's anthropological study of kinship structures and marriage exchange (Lévi-Strauss 1969), itself partly inspired by Mauss's *The Gift*, and on Marx's seminal contributions to political economy (Marx 1990) on the other, Gregory developed a synthesis that expanded the scope of the 'Maussian' orientation considerably, both analytically and in terms of the empirical realms to which it could usefully be applied. This dimension has subsequently been both widely acclaimed and critically engaged. The second aim of *Gifts and Commodities* was to show that, in postcolonial Papua New Guinea (PNG), both forms of exchange prevailed simultaneously, if in ambiguous ways. This second ambition of the book has been both overlooked and misunderstood (e.g. Gregory 1997: 47–48), but it is important in the context of our approach to flexible capitalism, which is why it is highlighted here.

Gregory contrasted gift and commodity exchange by saying that where gift exchange is the exchange of 'inalienable things between transactors who are in a state of reciprocal dependence', commodity exchange is the exchange of 'alienable things between transactors, who are in a state of reciprocal independence' (Gregory 1982: 12). While the conceptual distinction is clear, Gregory intended it as a tool for understanding complex practices of exchange in PNG, which involved both gift and commodity elements. Among other things, he showed how land used for postcolonial commodity production continued to belong to clans rather than to individual owners, and how commodity production was, as a result and in considerable measure, underpinned by and sustaining a wider system of gift-exchange that had proliferated in postcolonial times. At issue was not only the material sustenance and 'reproduction' of clans and labour power (ibid.: 112–65), but also an intricate system of prestige competition. Prestige was achieved by inflicting gift debts on gift recipients by means of lavish gifts, the availability of which was in turn related to the production and exchange of commodities (ibid.: 166–209). Gregory showed how in some cases even money (in the form of modern banknotes) served as gifts (ibid.: 187–91). Where this 'gift-money' was given as a sacrifice to God, the gift was in fact 'alienated' and provided, in the shape of banknotes, a basis for the accumulation of capital in the system of commodity exchange from which the banknotes originated (Gregory 1980). An important thrust of Gregory's book was thus that the conceptual distinction between gifts and commodities was useful for understanding practices that were complex and ambiguous matters, simultaneously involving both gift and commodity elements.

It may be helpful at this point to briefly illustrate some of what the gift/commodity distinction implies in the context of work through a concrete and simple example. One way of doing so is to relate it to Marx's distinction between 'use value' and 'exchange value'. As is clear from the opening chapter of *Capital*, Marx saw the distinguishing feature of a commodity as its exchange value, set apart from the same item's use value (Marx 1990: 125–77). Referring to an example credited to Aristotle (Gregory 1994: 912; Marx 1904: 19), a pair of shoes may be said to have use value, in that they protect the feet. Shoes may also have exchange value, in that they can be exchanged for different items judged to be of equivalent value as far as that transaction is concerned. Use value then is concrete and is measured in quality: how well shoes protect the feet. Exchange value, on the other hand, is abstract and is measured in quantity: a given number of shoes may be exchanged for a given number of items of any other kind judged to be of equivalent exchange value. Or, the shoes may simply be exchanged for a quantity of money, the measure in terms of which exchange value is commonly expressed. From this perspective, money is the commodity par excellence, in that its use value *is* its exchange value.

Marx claimed to be the first among political economists to point out that work too had both use value and exchange value (Marx 1990: 132), and these two dimensions of work are of course in part what is entailed in the contrast between housework and paid labour, mentioned above. The notion of housework may cover a number of activities, such as cleaning, cooking, or child minding. As housework, such activities are of concrete use, they have qualitative value for people in a household who in some measure share or 'exchange' such tasks, as part of a wider endeavour of caring for each other. Their performance further reflect and produce the quality of those social relations (cf. e.g. ibid.: 168–71). As an example, 'mother's cooking' is (at least according to a saying) unique. Following Gregory's formulation, such exchanges of housework may be said to amount to exchanges of 'inalienable things between transactors who are in a state of reciprocal dependence'; that is, to gift exchange in an expanded analytical sense. As paid work, on the other hand, the exact same activities may be exchanged as commodities between anyone who wants to sell or buy them, irrespective of their lack of social relation otherwise. This form of exchange in turn contributes to producing a corresponding 'commodity relation' of independence.

The point however, is that the practice of paid work is a more complex and ambiguous matter, where these two dimensions are at issue simultaneously. Marx developed the distinction between work's use and exchange value precisely to interrogate the implications of such ambiguity. He concentrated in particular on bringing out the exploitation and alienation exercised by reducing the use value of work to its exchange value. Taussig captures this by saying that, in Marx's view, 'what the capitalist acquires in buying the commodity of labour power as an exchange-value is the right to deploy the use-value of labour as the intelligent and creative capacity of human beings to produce more use-values than those that are reconverted into commodities as the wage' (Taussig 1980: 26). Extending from this formulation, one might say that, from the perspective of Gregory's synthesis of Marx and Mauss, part of the use value at issue (beyond what is counted as exchange value), is the rather basic cultural and social (that is, 'intelligent and creative') capacities which indeed enable humans to engage collectively in concrete practices of paid work at all, and such capacities are in no small measure produced and deployed as 'gifts' (cf. Gregory 1982: 29–35). This perspective in turn entails appreciating what sort of use value paid work might have as conceived by those who practice it, in terms of their engagements in wider social relationships and cultural schemes. It is in part to elucidate such dimensions to the practice of paid work that the gift/commodity distinction is useful.

Several chapters in this collection invoke the distinction, but they concentrate in particular on 'gift' dimensions in the work practices under consideration. Extending from the orientation outlined here, this does not amount to contradicting or trivializing the escalated commoditization or the 'cutting of networks' more commonly highlighted in literature on contemporary capitalist exchange. Rather, the essays add to such perspectives by exploring how the 'flexibilization' of such exchange seems accompanied, even sustained, by a simultaneous (if subtle) proliferation of gift dimensions, through which new forms of sociality arise. Cross's chapter (this volume), for example, examines an Indian setting of flexible offshore production, where hidden exchanges among employees on the shop floor of literal gift items and of work favours across divides of task specialization not only enhance cooperation and production, but also foster new relations across traditional divides of gender and caste that otherwise prevail in this Indian environment. Paraphrasing Martin (this volume), the approach thus allows the contributors to collectively demonstrate how, 'far from simply removing sociality from workplaces, "flexibilization" leads in many contexts to its intensification'.

Bloch and Parry on the Short and Long Term

While several of the volume's chapters invoke or build on the gift/commodity distinction, others engage a related conceptual framework turning on a distinction between 'short-term' and 'long-term' transactional and moral orders. The distinction was developed in a seminal collection of essays edited by Parry and Bloch, entitled *Money and the Morality of Exchange* (Parry and Bloch 1989). Focused specifically on exchanges involving modern money, this volume is relevant for ours in part because we focus on a particular and prevalent kind of monetary exchange, that is, paid work.

In the introduction to the volume, Bloch and Parry (1989) develop a critique of the prevalent idea that modern monetary exchange undermines morality and social relationships, as reflected in Polanyi's thesis about 'the great transformation' and indeed in the 'Western folk theory' mentioned above (see also Maurer 2006). The volume's ethnographic chapters suggest a more complex picture, by showing that exchanges involving money vary enormously in terms of how they are informed and assessed. Where the chapters converge is in terms of a unity which, in Bloch and Parry's words,

> is to be found neither in the meanings attributed to money nor in the moral evaluation of particular types of exchange, but rather in the way the totality of transactions form a general pattern which is part of the reproduction of social and ideological systems concerned with a time-scale far longer than the individual life. (Bloch and Parry 1989: 1)

It is this totality they conceive of in terms of a relationship between the long and short term. For Bloch and Parry, short-term transactions and moralities concern individual and often acquisitive activities, whereas long-term transactions and moralities are concerned with 'the reproduction of social and cosmic order' (ibid.: 2), that is, the kinds ontological orders (broadly conceived) also touched on above in the context of Mauss.

To appreciate the distinction, it is important to understand that the place of monetary exchanges within this scheme cannot be taken for granted. The chapters in Parry and Bloch's volume amply illustrate how monetary exchanges can be both of a short- and long-term nature even 'within one society', as it were. But whether monetary exchanges in their own right are of a short- or long-term nature (or both), the two domains prevail as distinct in all societies. Bloch and Parry suggest that this is because their coexistence constitutes:

> a symbolic resolution of the problem posed by the fact that transcenden-tal social and symbolic structures must both depend on, and negate, the transient individual . . . If the long-term cycle is not to be reduced to the transient world of the individual, they must be kept separate . . . But if the long term is to be sustained by the creativity and vitality of the short-term cycle, they must also be related. (ibid.: 26)

Bloch and Parry's approach is interesting in the context of our volume for several reasons, two of which are highlighted here. First, transformations associated with flexible capitalism are often held to affect dimensions of temporality. Yet much has been made of this connection in the literature we take issue with in terms of sweeping generalizations. In a critical review, Wajcman rhetorically sums this up by saying that the idea of 'time-space compression' coined by Harvey (1990) has become 'a constant theme in mainstream sociological accounts of post-modern society' (Wajcman 2008: 59). One example is Sennett who, presumably unfamiliar with Parry and Bloch's volume, observes that a key question 'posed by the new flexible capitalism' is how 'long-term goals [can] be pursued in an economy devoted to the short term' (Sennett 1998: 10). Sennett's answer is essentially that the long term becomes completely overtaken by the short term (cf. e.g. Adam 2006; Eriksen 2001). Parry and Bloch's approach, on the other hand, seems an interesting way to explore the question, if in a manner different to that of Sennett. Neveling's contribution (this volume), for example, draws on and adds new dimensions to Bloch and Parry's distinction by showing that 'the long term' in Mauritius has a long historical trajectory closely related to colonial trade. Developing his argument in part as a critique of Bloch and Parry, Neveling shows that the pursuit of long-term goals entails a measure of uncertainty (commonly associated with the short term, as Sennett sees it), which has long been part of the experience of working in Mauritius. From this perspective, continuity with the past, more than radical rupture, is what distinguishes contemporary flexible capitalist practice in Mauritius.

Secondly, one may wonder why Bloch and Parry's arguments about the simultaneous and ambiguous coexistence of the short and long term became so widely acknowledged (though see Maurer 2006), while Gregory's similar argument about commodity and gift exchange did not, as touched on above. A possible reason for the different reception might have to do with their respective ethnographic objects of study: exotic exchanges of various kinds in PNG in Gregory's case, versus monetary exchange, on the surface of things so universally familiar (like work), in Bloch and Parry's. The merit of Bloch and Parry's perspective with regard to the manner in which it complements Gregory's is the way it traverses highly different cultural settings. This drives home, more convincingly perhaps than Gregory's focus on PNG, the *general* importance of the *specific* social, cultural and historical dimensions that underlie exchange, which is also this volume's focus (cf. Joyce 1987). In the context of our focus on work for example, Weber's famous study of 'the Protestant ethic' (Weber 1958) may seem a wonderful case study of paid work as a long-term transactional order and morality. In its own right it is. Yet, as Joyce observes in his introduction to an interesting collection of historical studies of paid work, Weber's thesis has too often been invoked in impressionistic fashion as 'a single, monolithic ethic' (Joyce 1987: 4), disregarding cultural and social diversity across the Protestant realm. Where Gregory's approach complements that of Bloch and Parry is in the way its combined focus on concrete objects, exchanges and relationships in fact helps direct ethnographic attention to such cultural and historical specifics in contexts of paid work. Again, Neveling's contribution (this volume), with its combined

historical and ethnographic focus on Mauritian sugar and textile production and trade, and on gender relations, is an excellent point in
case.

Outline of the Book

The preceding sections on flexible capitalism and approaches to
exchange in anthropology are intended as a general introduction to
the volume's subject matter and theoretical orientation. The sections
have not attempted a more thorough review of either subject. The
works considered above are widely acknowledged contributions
to the anthropology of exchange, yet they have also been critiqued
on different accounts. Some chapters in this volume draw on these
works, others extend from them by drawing on related exchange orientations, while yet other chapters engage critically with elements
considered in the above. What in the first instance unites the chapters
is the way practices of paid work in contexts of flexible capitalism
are interrogated in terms of this general theoretical orientation on
the basis of anthropological fieldwork. The chapters are all based on
fieldwork in settings which in different ways comprise features highlighted as distinctive of flexible capitalism in the wider literature on
that subject. Where this literature has emphasized (what we concep-
tualize as) commodity and short-term entailments of such features,
the chapters converge on exploring work practice in such settings as a
more ambiguous matter, for example by highlighting the place of gift
and long-term dimensions in such practice.

As the volume aims at reaching a broad readership, the empirical chapters are at one level organized with readers in mind whose
knowledge of anthropological exchange theory at the outset is limited
to what has been outlined above. The first two empirical chapters (by
Cross, Grétarsdóttir) examine examples of gift exchange to explore
the significance of gift relations and moralities in flexible capitalist
work practice. The third chapter (Garsten) engages both the 'short/
long term' and the 'commodity/gift' distinctions through a comparative enquiry about social relations in three different settings
of flexible work. The fourth chapter (Wood) complicates the commodity conception of labour and capital by interrogating practices
where constructs in investment finance are exchanged as partial payments for labour. In the fifth chapter (Knox), a distinction between
'inalienable and alienable objects' is introduced (extending from that
between gift and commodity) to enquire about knowledge and skills

as ambiguous entities of exchange, while the sixth chapter (Narotzky) develops the concept of 'reciprocity' by drawing on literatures on respectively moral and political economy, its aim being to interrogate ambiguities pertaining to notions of value. The two chapters which then follow focus on different temporal dimensions of exchange. The seventh chapter (Neveling) is a historically informed engagement with long-term aspects of work, critiquing certain aspects of Bloch and Parry's framing of the concept, while the eighth chapter (Kjaerulff) draws on so-called 'individualistic' exchange orientations, where uncertainty related to the passing of time in exchange has been highlighted as a core dimension. This organization of the book does not reflect a progression in terms of the subtlety of arguments, but it does reflect an ambition to funnel uninitiated readers along, as the chapters progressively engage with more dimensions of exchange theory not considered in this introduction.

At another level, the volume's empirical chapters are organized in terms of overlaps with regard to substantial focus. The first three chapters (by Cross, Grétarsdóttir, Garsten) converge on exploring the proliferation of social relations through exchanges and in terms of moral discourses of very different kinds, which they demonstrate are instrumental for the practice of work, yet exceed economic rationality.

The opening chapter by Cross is set in a Belgian-owned, on-demand diamond-processing factory in southern India, located in what is known as a free trade zone (also known as export processing zones; see Neveling, this volume). Such zones, where strictures to economic competition in terms of taxes, wages and legislation are deliberately eased to attract foreign-based production, have proliferated in recent decades, and become icons of the kind of offshore production often highlighted as a core feature of global flexible capitalism. Another distinguishing feature of this diamond-processing factory is that the craft of diamond cutting, as practised in Belgium, is here broken down into a series of smaller tasks, which are then distributed among a greater number of employees than is the case in Belgium. This kind of 'flexible specialization' facilitates both the transfer and dispersal of production, and the control of it in offshore settings. As Cross notes, most discussions of such settings have primarily focused on the increased commoditization and alienation they facilitate. Yet, what Cross found in the course of his fieldwork was a developed and complex pattern of social relations sustained by exchanges of gift items such food and consumer goods, both among employees and between employees and managers. The argument Cross pursues is that the competitiveness of this offshore manufacturing plant (in terms of efficiency and cost, for example) in fact depends upon the kinds of gift exchanges and relations that he documents. He shows how this has to do with the social circumstances of such work, both with respect to the local Indian context and in the context of shop-floor action and interaction. In the former regard, the factory is seen among Indian employees as a space relatively free of social restrictions in terms of caste and gender, an important factor both in attracting labour power and in facilitating the building of social relations within the plant. In the latter regard, relations between less experienced staff on the one hand, and more experienced and managerial staff on the other, are 'smoothed' by the frequent exchanges of gifts, in ways that variously enhance production efficiency. Moreover, flirting relations between male and female workers underpinned by gift exchanges help them cope with the intensity of the factory's production regime. Cross's chapter thus demonstrates that gift relations are critical for high rates of productivity: workers are dependent on the latter for secure wages, and high rates of productivity are of course central to the company's rationale for pursuing offshore production in the first place.

Where Cross's focus is a relatively circumscribed ethnographic setting, the following chapter examines a more dispersed but spectacular case of gift exchange, aimed at fostering expanded business networks. The context for Grétarsdóttir's chapter is the neoliberal turn that has marked Icelandic political and economic life over the past couple of decades. Grétarsdóttir's chapter centres on how efforts to 'put Iceland on the map of global business' have also comprised pursuits at the level of social and cultural engineering on the part of the Icelandic government. An imagined 'Viking' past has thus been invoked in imagining contemporary Icelandic identity as transnational and entrepreneurial, well beyond the shores of Iceland. Qualities seen as important from the perspective of neoliberal business ideology have in this way been promoted in terms and ways that far exceed a conventional commodity exchange rationale. Grétarsdóttir's focus is the circumstances of the ceremonial giving of a gift by the state of Iceland to the state of Canada in the year 2000, commemorating the millennium of the alleged first 'Icelandic' immigrants to North America. The gift in question is a piece of art, a sculpture based on a legend from the Icelandic Sagas about a woman and her son, to whom she (according to legend) gave birth while on a journey to the New World; hence the title of the artwork, *The First White Mother in America*. Like supremely inalienable gifts described in the literature on gift exchange, the sculpture has rich and intricate evocative potential. Grétarsdóttir demonstrates what this entails, as she describes how the gift donation and the sculpture's narrative aids the mobilization of ethnic (Icelandic-Canadian) networks, which serve as concrete conduits for Icelandic business pursuits in Canada, while simultaneously giving participants a sense of social efficacy and ethnic pride as they volunteer time and effort to develop them. More than showing how 'flexible' notions of nationality and nation-states continue to play a role in neoliberal economic practice, Grétarsdóttir argues that the gift of the sculpture, as well as the 'gift relations' pursued in the Icelandic-Canadian volunteer networks considered, bear resemblance to aspects of gift exchange discussed in Melanesian contexts, where gift giving and the development of gift relations serve as ways of spreading 'fame' and of achieving social efficacy (see Munn 1986).

The following chapter by Garsten draws on fieldwork conducted in three different settings over the course of Garsten's research career. Contrasting the organization and practice of work among clients of temporary staffing agencies ('temps'), employees of Apple Computer and experts working for so-called 'think tanks', Garsten shows how flexibility amounts to various things, and the chapter examines the dynamics between the organization and practice of flexible work across this diverse material. Drawing on Turner (1967), Garsten suggests that flexible work has 'liminal' dimensions, in that it denies many structural features of work while simultaneously opening up new configurations of work relationships, which are critical for work performance. Garsten explores this ambiguous character of flexible work in terms of what she calls 'an economy of connection'. In one way, the flexible forms of work considered all accentuate commodity qualities and short-term moralities. 'Temps' work in a social periphery, as replacement for other staff and in various locations; Apple Computer staff experience frequent restructuring and are moved about within the organization to keep it versatile in the fast-paced computing industry; and because 'think-tankers' collect and produce information by consulting with a large number of agencies, they too traverse a social periphery, although of a more prestigious kind than is the case for 'temps'. Yet, Garsten shows that in practice, investing in social relations is critical for continued performance across such economic environments. Precisely because of the tenuous character of such work, connections become critical. Temps care in particular about the quality of their relations with assignment coordinators, and actively cultivate long term relations with them; Apple Computer staff pursue long-term relations with colleagues both within the company and beyond it to be able to maintain working networks despite, or even because of, frequent organizational changes; and think-tankers are dependent on an array of connections in their pursuit of specialized and reliable information. Garsten suggests that these relations are more 'gift-like' than the flexible environments might suggest, but also that such relations amount to investments in connections in an expanded economic sense, similar to the relations developed through strategic gift exchange in the kinds of exotic settings anthropologists have traditionally studied. Both Apple staff and think-tankers, for instance, may obtain highly valued insider information from strategically well-placed sources, but only if the latter trust that the former can offer valuable information in return at some later point in time. By exploring flexible work's 'liminal' dimensions, Garsten thus demonstrates that, in practice, longer-term relations are creatively pursued through gift-like exchanges, partly in response to the ways in which short-term and commodity aspects of work relations are accentuated at the level of flexible organization.

Taken together, the three first chapters thus demonstrate that gift exchange and gift relations proliferate in flexible capitalist practice, in ways which serve to underpin the exchange of commodities and capital accumulation. As Garsten observes in her chapter (see also Martin, this volume), the very contingency of work that is highlighted more widely as a defining characteristic of flexible capitalism, may in fact foster more 'transactional' ways of cultivating relations in work contexts. However, gift exchange and relations are here, as these chapters also collectively bring out, neither to be conceived in simple terms of an altruistic mind-set, nor in narrow terms of calculated gain. As with Mauss's examples of agonistic gift exchange, such exchanges and relations are better conceived of as 'interested' in a broad sense. Whether in terms of flirting or paternalistic gift relations (Cross), ethnic nostalgia and 'fame' (Grétarsdóttir) or in terms of 'expert distinction' across institutional divides (Garsten), there is an 'economy of connection' at work (in Garsten's words), concerned with durable long-term relations conceived in various moral terms, which simultaneously serve as an underlying and ambiguous premise for pursuits of gain in the narrower monetary sense. What these chapters collectively underscore is thus the diverse ways that diverse kinds of sociality come to flourish in, and underpin, the practice of work in flexible capitalist settings. The chapters by Cross and Grétarsdóttir also highlight wider but specific historical and cultural dimensions which shape such work, dimensions which are variously brought in focus throughout the volume (see esp. Narotzky, Neveling, this volume), but are often ignored in the wider literature on the subject (see e.g. Baca 2005).

Where the volume's first three chapters in the first instance bring out the proliferation of gift relations and the ways they bolster commodity exchange, the three following chapters by Wood, Knox and Narotzky, take a blurring of the distinction between gift and commodity (and corresponding relations and moralities) as their point of departure. Knox suggests one significance of this ambiguity lies in the way workers are able to reclaim the kind of reciprocal ties seemingly erased in flexible capitalist work contexts. Wood explores how tokens of finance capital serve use-value functions and as spectacles of worth, fostering commitment to work and underpinning longer-term outlooks. Narotzky in turn emphasizes how such ambiguity helps accentuate the exploitation of use value lodged in reciprocal relations.

Wood's chapter is set in the Canadian province of Alberta, a major centre of North America's booming oil and gas sector, both in terms of resource extraction and associated speculative finance. As Wood notes, whereas the world of flexible capitalist finance (such as the trading of derivatives on Wall Street) has in recent years been consolidated as an important domain of ethnographic enquiry, less attention has been devoted to the kind of 'financialization of work' in corporate offices that is the focus of this chapter. Wood concentrates on junior energy corporations seeking financing for the purpose of short-term value creation for shareholders. For such junior corporations, Alberta's recent energy boom has been marked by accelerated merger and acquisition activity, where employees, along with oil and gas assets, often circulate between one corporation and another. In order to attract labour to the kind of short-term contracts this corporate environment affords, junior companies tend to offer stock options as part of their employees' compensation packages, thus promising a chance to earn equity and unevenly share in the corporation's production of surplus value. In this way, workers' labour is exchanged only partly for wages, and partly for optioned capital. Wood's ethnography is focused on the ambiguous nature of this kind of exchange as it works in practice. On the one hand it constitutes workers as direct participants in market exchange of financial energy-related commodities. On the other hand the exchange of work for optioned capital also comprises gift-like expectations of returns affecting long-term outlooks and the sense of social worth.

The tension is brought to a peak during the takeover events which the chapter investigates, where one company is absorbed by another, and the ambiguous value of stock options is realized. Not only is an employee's share (or loss) in terms of earned surplus value measured out; so is the employee's use value (as a labourer) in the process of negotiating a new contract with the acquiring company, a process where an existing option package may be substituted for a new one that mirrors an employee's future deemed worth in the spectacle of finance capital. Wood argues that options and work in this setting thus comprise forms of contested value underpinning social worth, as reflected in employees' ambivalence over the risky business of work that hinges on periodic windfalls that accrue from corporate takeovers in the energy market.

The empirical context of Knox's chapter is the information and communication technology (ICT) sector in the United Kingdom around the turn of the millennium. ICT developments and their implications for capitalist practice have been widely touted, to a point where knowledge and ICTs have achieved a status as icons of 'the new economy' (e.g. Woolgar 2002). Knox considers the significance of this hyperbole through a focus on notions of skills and knowledge invoked in the ethnographic setting of a business initiative in Manchester called MediaNet. MediaNet aims at stimulating economic growth by fostering the Manchester region's development as a hub for the creation of so-called 'new media'. In concrete terms of national and EU policy and funding, the wider discourse on knowledge and ICTs tangibly frames the project. MediaNet first pursued its goals, referring to policy documents rehearsing this discourse, by attempting to facilitate the sharing and circulation of skilled knowledge across different professional specializations involved in the production of new media. As the project unfolded, however, this approach fell short of engaging the project's envisioned participants, and was abandoned in favour of different strategies, resonating in different ways with the same policy documents. Eventually, MediaNet aimed at simply functioning as a broker in the labour market for those who already possessed the relevant conjuncture of skills, as opposed to facilitating the sharing of those skills. Drawing on Weiner's (1992) distinction between alienable and inalienable possessions (which extends from the commodity/ gift distinction), Knox suggests that MediaNet's initial approach relied on framing skills and knowledge as alienable entities to be circulated devoid of context and attachment for general economic prosperity. In the subsequent approach, skills and knowledge were effectively imagined as inalienable and embedded in particular persons and social relations. MediaNet's task then became framed as one of matching already skilled personnel with 'market needs' for the benefit of a public in the Manchester region (rather than merely for profit in a general sense), now imagined as a locality against a wider and precarious global situation invoked in policy documents. Knox shows how, underlying this development, the discourse on the economic significance of knowledge and ICTs continued to serve as an important resource for framing MediaNet's undertakings, simultaneously being co-opted and subverted in contests over the in/alienable value of knowledge and skills. What Knox's informants particularly underscored was the importance of workers' capacities for adjustment in the face of shifting market demands, that is, their 'potential' for continuous learning and creativity as (effectively) inalienable qualities, lodged in wider reciprocal relations such as on-line communities of computing expertise (cf. Kelty 2008). One might say that the use value of labour (that is, the 'intelligent and creative capacity of human beings' in Taussig's formulation, quoted above), here becomes highlighted ethnographically precisely in terms the wider social ties it entails. Knox argues that what we can discern in this ethnographic emphasis on workers' 'potential' as lodged in reciprocal ties is a reworking of public forms, through which people recover some of the sociality seemingly erased in economic and political practices where skills and knowledge are assumed to function simply as alienable commodities.

The ethnographic focus of Narotzky's chapter is two settings in Spain, each of which in their different way has been exposed to wider conjectures of recent economic transformation. One concerns agriculture in rural Catalonia, the other shoe manufacturing in the region of Vega Baja, in the region of Valencia. In both settings, Narotzky suggests globalizing market dynamics have accentuated ambiguities pertaining to value, conceived as economic value on the one hand and moral value on the other. To develop her analysis, Narotzky draws on discussions in moral and political economy, and on the history of labour relations in the regions, to show how notions of economic and moral value have a history of entanglement. In the context of multi-generation family farms in rural Catalonia, known as *casa*, contracts between family members that specify mutual obligations of unpaid work transfers comprise 'reproductive' work such as care for the farm's oldest and youngest generations. Inheritance of the farm as an economic means of sustaining a livelihood has in turn been conditioned on such work, conceived as a 'payoff of love', as Narotzky puts it. Value has in this way had simultaneous economic and moral dimensions for a long time, but the ambiguity has in recent decades taken on new significance. Whereas earlier the farm's economic viability was assessed in terms of its capacity to sustain household reproduction, it is now being cast more in terms of 'market viability', and its capacity to sustain an urban lifestyle. The sense of reciprocal moral obligation underpinning farming operations in the region has concomitantly become more susceptible to evaluations in terms of 'market value'. In the context of shoe manufacturing in Vega Baja, Narotzky outlines similar developments accentuating the ambiguity of value. Since the 1970s, large-scale factory production of shoes has in large measure been replaced by subcontracting networks, which in turn have proliferated in the Vega Baja area. An effect has been that reciprocal (kinship and neighbourhood) relations underpinned by a sense of moral obligation (a 'traffic of favours' as Narotzky puts it) have come to play a key role in the production of footwear here. Market volatility and dynamics in the global footwear industry there-fore have a range of repercussions in the region at the level of recip-rocal relations. Such relations are increasingly perceived as 'part of' the market, hence the accentuated ambiguity pertaining to notions of economic and moral value here. Narotzky's argument is that, while such ambiguity is not particularly novel, it is being exploited in new ways, as moral values underpinning reciprocal obligations increas-ingly become a source of value extraction in the economic sense: use value is being converted in new ways into surplus value. Against the wider literature on flexible capitalism, but complementing this vol-ume's general thrust, Narotzky thus suggests that flexible capitalist exploitation in fact hinges on not fully commoditizing the labour force.

Where these three chapters overlap is not so much at the level of social 'outcomes', as they highlight respectively the persistence of long term outlooks and social worth (Wood), reciprocal rela-tions (Knox) and their exploitation (Narotzky). Their overlap is more in terms of bringing ambiguities into focus on which such outcomes hinge, as they work out across different scales of inter-action and imagination. Narotzky concentrates her argument in this regard at the analytical level. 'Exploitation' (understood as the extraction of surplus value) requires paying attention to value as an abstract entity from the perspective of wider scale market exchange, the conventional domain of political economy approaches. Moral economy approaches on the other hand have underscored a lack of 'emic' appreciation of such abstract dynamics, and explored how the perception of distinct realms of value came about historically in reaction to experiences of exploitation. Narotzky's hunch is that the present circumstances of transformation require a simultaneous focus on both levels so as to appreciate the dynamics of exploitation on the one hand, and on the other the experience of blurred value realms. Knox concentrates in this regard on what in Tsing's phrase might be conceived as practices of 'scale-making' (Tsing 2000). This is most obviously at issue in MediaNet's shifting attempts to frame the significance of its pursuits with reference to policy documents, serving as scale-making devices. These documents allowed MediaNet to accentuate the project's significance in terms of different regional and global scales of community and market relations and exchange, despite the documents' wanting framing (as it turned out) of skills and knowledge as alienable entities. Yet, Knox's chapter also brings out how different scale-making devices (such as on-line forums) simultaneously made reciprocal exchange recognizable as such, more broadly among an emergent self-conscious public of ICT knowledge workers. Conceived as an artefact of scale making, this new public is in part accentuated also by the scale-making effects of aforementioned policy documents. Such productive overlaps – what Tsing conceives as 'contingent articulations' (ibid.: 119 ff.) – hinge on the ambiguous quality of entities exchanged across different scales of interaction and imagination, and the relations and moralities involved. Similar dynamics are at work in Wood's chapter, where constructs of speculative finance capital serve as ambiguous scale-making devices. The dramatic performance that for Tsing distinguishes economic scale making (indeed Tsing [ibid.] draws on examples from Alberta's resource finance sector), is in Wood's analysis played out in terms of the value of labour. Following Graeber (2001: 49–89), one could say that the social 'importance of actions' – that is, the value of work in the broadest sense – for Wood's corporate employees becomes dramatized not only at the time of contract negotiations in terms of option packages, but at an everyday level through more mundane spectacles, ranging from various fantastical news broadcasts focused on Alberta's place in the economy (cf. Tsing 2000) to the stock tickers that Wood notes could usually be seen on employees' computer screens. As Wood shows, such spectacles ambiguously underpin longer-term outlooks and a sense of social worth, even if the work contract's more tangible returns at a further remove are uncertain. Taken together, these chapters thus suggest how ambiguities pertaining to value and exchange as they work out across different scales of interaction and imagination can not only enhance exploitation, but simultaneously constitute a canvas in terms of which to frame new inalienable forms of sociality and identity. Such dynamics have been brought out in various idioms in exchange-related literature (e.g. Graeber 2001), and they are also at issue in other contributions to the volume, though at the level of argument the emphasis in these chapters lies elsewhere. In Grétarsdóttir's chapter they can thus be discerned in ethnic terms, in Martin's chapter in terms of tradition (*kastom*), while in Neveling's and to an extent in Garsten's chapter it is in terms of temporal horizons.

The next two chapters partially overlap in terms of their engagement with temporal entailments of exchange in flexible capitalist practice. As Munn observed in a famous review essay, as an 'inescapable dimension of all aspects of social experience and practice', temporality 'frequently fragments into all the other dimensions and topics anthropologists deal with' (Munn 1992: 93). In this vein, temporality has often figured as a more underlying or superficially engaged element in literature on exchange and in that on flexible capitalism. Some temporal dimensions of flexible capitalist work are brought out for more sustained consideration in these two contributions.

Neveling's chapter simultaneously engages two such dimensions, one being the widely entertained Occidentalist assumption that flexible capitalism constitutes a radical historical break with earlier forms of capitalist practice (cf. Carrier 1995). Neveling confronts this assumption by exploring important historical continuities between colonial labour regimes and contemporary flexible labour in offshore production. The setting of Neveling's chapter resembles that considered by Cross, albeit in the context of Mauritius, which Neveling investigates, the notion export processing zones (EPZs) prevails. Where Cross mainly concentrates on the practice and significance of gift exchange on the factory shop floor, Neveling develops his arguments through a combined ethnographic and historical perspective on economic practice in Mauritius, from the colonial incorporation of the island into the global sugar industry in the nineteenth century to the time when EPZs became established in the 1970s. Such a combined ethnographic and historical approach is rare in research on flexible capitalist practice, and it allows an empirically rich basis for Neveling's critique. The trajectory of capitalist practice in Mauritius shows that many of the ills now attributed to flexible capitalism are not particularly novel. Vulnerabilities to wider global trade, and related insecurities of work and beyond, were familiar to people in Mauritius long before the introduction of EPZs. Neveling shows that attempts to cope with such circumstances are hardly novel either, and the latter provides his leverage for developing two related points on the second dimension of temporality considered in the chapter. The first point (according with Bloch and Parry's argument) is that work in capitalist settings should not necessarily be interpreted as a short-term moral engagement or transactional pattern. Neveling indicates that work from the perspective of Mauritian workers, also in contemporary EPZ settings, may be understood in terms of long-term moralities and transactional cycles. Neveling's fascinating account of ghost attacks and exorcism on factory shop floors, and his critical engagement with Ong's account of similar phenomena in Malaysia (Ong 1987), serve to underscore how work indeed involves long-term horizons of existential proportions, not only lying ahead in a worker's life time, but also going back to the concrete colonial context that Neveling considers, which has shaped Mauritian cultural outlooks and social relations. The second point Neveling argues on this basis (against Bloch and Parry), is that the notion of long-term moralities and transactional cycles is often confounded with notions of firm structure and stability, indeed even in Bloch and Parry's famous introductory chapter (Bloch and Parry 1989). This allows for false dichotomies, between an ostensibly stable past and unstable present, for example, which underlie not only literature on flexible capitalism, but also a good few anthropological conceptions of exchange, cast in terms of stable gift and unstable commodity relations. Neveling's argument here is that long-term morality and transactions should be understood more as something to strive for, which requires deliberation and action, and which does not necessarily 'work out'.

Kjaerulff's chapter complements and extends the second point developed in Neveling's chapter, although from a different theoretical perspective. The chapter critically engages the prevalent rationale that flexible work produces a heightened sense of risk and uncertainty, and suggests that a reverse causality may also be at work. Here, uncertainty as a more basic dimension of living fosters a proliferation of the kind of flexible work which is the chapter's empirical focus. Kjaerulff develops his argument by juxtaposing a careful examination of Sennett's famous book *The Corrosion of Character* (Sennett 1998), and his research in rural Denmark among people practising flexible work via the internet from their homes, work known as 'teleworking'. He concentrates on the way Sennett develops his key analytical notion of 'routine' in the historical context of industrial work to show that Sennett's argument here bears implicit affinity to a body of more 'individualistic' exchange-oriented theory (e.g. Berger and Luckmann 1966; Bourdieu 1977). This body of theory has highlighted the place of routines and agency in cultural change and reproduction, along with the temporal and representational dimensions of exchange. What Kjaerulff notes is that this theoretical affinity becomes strikingly absent when Sennett turns to the ostensible demise of routines and rise of uncertainty in contexts of flexible capitalism. Drawing on this body of theory and on his telework research, Kjaerulff then develops an expanded conception of uncertainty and flexibility. The kind of temporal dimensions of exchange famously discussed by Bourdieu (1977) imply that something like 'uncertainty' is an inherent predicament of living (cf. Garsten's, Wood's and Knox's arguments in this volume, respectively about 'liminality', 'meantime', and 'potential'). Kjaerulff suggests this predicament may account for a finding brought out by his research, namely that telework unfolds not only as straightforward 'active' engagements, but also as more symbolic ones, turning on ICTs ambiguous potentials. The latter, he argues, may serve to achieve what he conceives of as a measure of 'flexibility' against socially reinforced ideals of work and family, which his informants regularly found compromised. As with 'uncertainty', Kjaerulff suggests such symbolic practices of 'flexibility' are familiar from the wider exchange-oriented literature, here commonly cast as a matter of representation and performance (e.g. Bourdieu 1977). From this perspective, he argues that, in trying to cope with a kind of uncertainty that has long prevailed, new means of creating flexibility afforded by telework are added to familiar ones, and as such teleworking is embraced as an asset.

Through different theoretical routes, Neveling and Kjaerulff thus challenge connected elements underlying a widely entertained idea, namely that flexible capitalism entails a 'great transformation' in terms of temporality (e.g. Harvey 1990; Sennett 1998; Eriksen 2001; Adam 2006). Through their exploration of the dynamic and normative dimensions of the 'long term' understood as historically situated ideals, the realization of which cannot be taken for granted in lived experience, these chapters also demonstrate the merit in moving beyond the conception of an entrenched divide between collectivistic and individualistic approaches in anthropological exchange theory. The 'long term' from this perspective bears affinity to notions of 'tradition' as discussed in another rich body of anthropological literature (see e.g. Otto and Pedersen 2005), allowing for a different understanding of the 'nostalgic' lament (Strangleman 2007) of flexible capitalism's detrimental effects.

In an afterword, Martin considers some wider significances of the collection from the perspective of two 'end points' which can be said to frame it. One is the recent global financial crisis; the other is Melanesian ethnography, which has been particularly influential in the development of anthropological exchange theory.

Concluding Introductory Remarks

Against a wider trend in mainstream literature on flexible capitalism, this volume explores a more complex picture. In the context of paid work, where change has been a core theme of debate, it interrogates dimensions of contemporary social changes along with continuities which have received limited attention. The chapters converge in suggesting that sociality proliferates in flexible capitalism, in ways which simultaneously sustain work regimes more conventionally seen as simply tearing social relations apart. By exploring the conjunction of anthropological fieldwork and exchange theory in this context, an aim of the volume is to introduce a wider readership to a promising direction for further inquiry. In the comprehensive literature review cited above, the sociologist of work Tim Strangleman (2007) not only identifies the 'trend' which our volume aims to move beyond. He also suggests a need for a reorientation of research within this field of study, both theoretically and methodologically in terms of situated qualitative empirical studies of contemporary practices of work. The collection of essays presented here outlines the contours of a way in which such a reorientation might be focused. In as much as the practice of paid work remains at heart a practice of exchange, we hope to convince a broad audience that this volume is only just a beginning; that is, that an anthropological approach to empirical enquiry on exchange has much to contribute to further research on work in flexible capitalism. Given this ambition of the book, it is pertinent to end this introduction by also alerting the reader to a possible limitation when attempting this approach, all the more since 'ethnography' (divorced from anthropology) in recent years has become increasingly embraced across a broad interdisciplinary canvas as a 'method'. To the extent that ethnography is taken to offer an empirically richer picture from 'the native's point of view', and that picture in turn is accepted as the whole picture, it can lead to a kind of reductionist approach which is no less problematic than the kind this volume aims to move beyond, whether executed within or beyond the discipline of anthropology (see e.g. Kapferer 2005; Carrier 2012). It is for this reason that the legacy of anthropological enquiry on exchange has been emphasized in the above as an important resource for the kind of approach which this volume aims to advance. At least part of that legacy is not quite as alien to an interdisciplinary readership as the framing of it here might suggest, as the references above to Polanyi, Marx and Durkheim's close collaborator Mauss amply indicate. On the other hand, an anthropologically informed engagement with the kinds of issues brought in focus in this book may in fact be close to the spirit in which such foundational social scientists carried out their enquiries around a century ago.

References

Adam, B. 2006. 'Time', *Theory, Culture and Society* 23(2/3): 119–126.

Baca, G. 2005. 'Legends of Fordism: Between Myth, History, and Foregone Conclusions', in B. Kapferer (ed.), *The Retreat of the Social: The Rise and Rise of Reductionism*. Oxford: Berghahn Books, pp. 31–46.

Barnard, A. 2000. *History and Theory in Anthropology*. Cambridge: Cambridge University Press.

Barry, A., and D. Slater. 2002. 'Introduction: the Technological Economy', *Economy and Society* 31(2): 175–193.

Barth, F. 1981. 'Models Reconsidered', in *Process and Form in Social Life: Selected Essays*, Vol. 1. London: Routledge and Kegan Paul, pp. 76–104.

——— 1989. 'The Analysis of Culture in Complex Societies', *Ethnos* 54(3/4): 120–142.

Beck, U. 1992. *Risk Society: Towards a New Modernity*. London: Sage.

Beckert, J. 2009. 'The Great Transformation of Embeddedness: Karl Polanyi and the New Economic Sociology', in C. Hann and K. Hart (eds), *Market and Society: The Great Transformation Today*. Cambridge: Cambridge University Press, pp. 38–55.

Berger, P.L., and T. Luckmann. 1966. *The Social Construction of Reality: A Treatise in the Sociology of Knowledge*. New York: Doubleday.

Bloch, M., and J. Parry. 1989. 'Introduction: Money and the Morality of Exchange', in J. Parry and M. Bloch (eds), *Money and the Morality of Exchange*. Cambridge: Cambridge University Press, pp. 1–32.

Boholm, A. 2003. 'Situated Risk: An Introduction', *Ethnos* 68(2): 157–158.

Bourdieu, P. 1977. *Outline of a Theory of Practice*. Cambridge: Cambridge University Press.

Burawoy, M. 1979. 'The Anthropology of Industrial Work', *Annual Review of Anthropology* 8: 231–266.

——— 1982. *Manufacturing Consent*. Chicago: University of Chicago Press.

Callon, M. 1998. 'Introduction: The Embeddedness of Economic Markets in Economics', in M. Callon (ed.), *The Laws of the Markets*. Oxford: Blackwell, pp. 1–57.

Carrier, J. G. 1991. 'Gifts, Commodities, and Social Relations: A Maussian View of Exchange', *Sociological Forum* 6(1): 119–136.

——— 1992. 'Emerging Alienation in Production: A Maussian History', *Man* 27(3): 539–558.

——— 1995. 'Maussian Occidentalism: Gift and Commodity Systems', in J. Carrier (ed.), *Occidentalism: Images of the West*. Oxford: Clarendon Press, pp. 85–108.

——— (2012). 'The Trouble with Class', *European Journal of Sociology* 53: 263–84.

Carrier, J.G., and D. Miller (eds). 1998. *Virtualism: A New Political Economy*. Oxford: Berg.

Castells, M. 1996. *The Rise of the Network Society*. Oxford: Blackwell.

Collins, J.L., and M. Gimenez (eds). 1990. *Work Without Wages: Comparative Studies of Domestic Labor and Self-employment*. Albany: State University of New York Press.

du Gay, P. 1996. *Consumption and Identity at Work*. London: Sage.

Durrenberger, E., and J. Marti (eds). 2006. *Labor in Cross-cultural Perspective*. New York: AltaMira Press.

Ekeh, P. 1974. *Social Exchange Theory: The Two Traditions*. London: Heinemann.

Eriksen, T.H. 2001. *Tyranny of the Moment: Fast and Slow Time in the Information Age*. London: Pluto Press.

Felstead, A., and N. Jewson (eds). 1999. *Global Trends in Flexible Labor*. London: Macmillian.

Godelier, M. 1980. 'Work and its Representations: A Research Proposal', *History Workshop Journal* 10: 164–174.

Graeber, D. 2001. *Toward an Anthropological Theory of Value: The False Coin of Our Own Dreams*. New York: Palgrave.

Granovetter, M. 1985. 'Economic Action and Social Structure: The Problem of Embeddedness', *American Journal of Sociology* 91(3): 481–510.

Gregory, C. 1980. 'Gifts to Men and Gifts to God: Gift Exchange and Capital Accumulation in Contemporary Papua', *Man* 15(4): 626–652.

——— 1982. *Gifts and Commodities*. London: Academic Press.

——— 1994. 'Exchange and Reciprocity', in T. Ingold (ed.), *Companion Encyclopedia of Anthropology*. London: Routledge, pp. 911–939.

——— 1997. *Savage Money: The Anthropology and Politics of Commodity Exchange*. Amsterdam: Harwood Academic.

——— 2009. 'Whatever Happened to Householding?' in C. Hann and K. Hart (eds), *Market and Society: The Great Transformation Today*. Cambridge: Cambridge University Press, pp. 133–159.

Hann, C., and K. Hart (eds). 2009. *Market and Society: The Great Transformation Today*. Cambridge, Cambridge University Press.

————— 2011. *Economic Anthropology: History, Ethnography, Critique.* Cambridge: Polity.

Hart, K. 2007. 'Marcel Mauss: In Pursuit of the Whole', *Comparative Studies in Society and History* 49(2): 473–485.

Harvey, D. 1990. *The Condition of Postmodernity: An Enquiry into the Origins of Cultural Change.* Oxford: Blackwell.

————— 2005. *A Brief History of Neoliberalism.* Oxford: Oxford University Press.

Hirsch, E. 2010. 'Property and Persons: New Forms and Contests in the Era of Neoliberalism', *Annual Review of Anthropology* 39(1): 347–360.

Humphrey, C., and S. Hugh-Jones. 1992. 'Introduction: Barter, Exchange and Value', in C. Humphrey and S. Hugh-Jones (eds), *Barter, Exchange and Value: An Anthropological Approach.* Cambridge: Cambridge University Press, pp. 1–20.

Isaac, B. 2005. 'Karl Polanyi', in J.G. Carrier (ed.), *A Handbook of Economic Anthropology.* Cheltenham: Edward Elgar Publishing, pp. 14–25.

Joyce, P. 1987. 'The Historical Meanings of Work: An Introduction', in P. Joyce (ed.), *The Historical Meanings of Work.* Cambridge: Cambridge University Press, pp. 1–30.

Kapferer, B. 1976. 'Introduction: Transactional Models Reconsidered', in B. Kapferer (ed.), *Transaction and Meaning: Directions in the Anthropology of Exchange and Symbolic Behavior.* Philadelphia: Institute for the Study of Human Issues, pp. 1–22.

————— 2005. 'Introduction: The Social Construction of Reductionist Thought and Practice', in B. Kapferer (ed.), *The Retreat of the Social: The Rise and Rise of Reductionism.* Oxford: Berghahn Books, pp. 1–18.

Kelty, C.M. 2008. *Two Bits: The Cultural Significance of Free Software.* Durham, NC: Duke University Press.

Law, J. 1999. 'After ANT: Complexity, Naming and Topology', in J. Law and J. Hassard (eds), *Actor Network Theory and After.* Oxford: Blackwell, pp. 1–14.

Lévi-Strauss, C. 1969 [1949]. *The Elementary Structures of Kinship.* London: Eyre and Spottiswoode.

Long, N., and H.L. Moore. 2013. 'Introduction: Sociality's New Directions', in N. Long and H.L. Moore (eds), *Sociality: New Directions.* Oxford: Berghahn, pp. 1–24.

McMichael, P. 1998. 'Development and Structural Adjustment', in J.G. Carrier and D. Miller (eds), *Virtualism: A New Political Economy.* Oxford: Berg, pp. 95–116.

Macfarlane, A. 1993. 'Louis Dumont and the Origins of Individualism', *Cambridge Anthropology* 16(1): 1–28.

Malinowski, B. 1961 [1922]. *Argonauts of the Western Pacific.* New York: Dutton.

Martin, E. 1994. *Flexible Bodies: Tracking Immunity in American Culture from the Days of Polio to the Age of AIDS.* Boston: Beacon Press.

Marx, K. 1904 [1859]. *A Contribution to the Critique of Political Economy*. Chicago: Charles H. Kerr and Company.

——— 1973. *Grundrisse*. Harmondsworth: Penguin.

——— 1990 [1867]. *Capital*, Vol. 1. London: Penguin.

Maurer, B. 2006. 'The Anthropology of Money', *Annual Review of Anthropology* 35: 15–36.

Mauss, M. 1990 [1925]. *The Gift: The Form and Reason for Exchange in Archaic Societies*, trans. W.D. Halls. London: Routledge.

Miller, D. 1998. 'Conclusion: A Theory of Virtualism', in J.G. Carrier and D. Miller (eds), *Virtualism: A New Political Economy*. Oxford: Berg, pp. 187–215.

Mollona, M. 2005. 'Gifts of Labour: Steel Production and Technological Imagination in an Area of Urban Deprivation, Sheffield, UK', *Critique of Anthropology* 25(2): 177–198.

Munn, N.D. 1986. *The Fame of Gawa: A Symbolic Study of Value Transformation in a Massim (Papua New Guinea) Society*. Durham, NC: Duke University Press.

——— 1992. 'The Cultural Anthropology of Time: A Critical Essay', *Annual Review of Anthropology* 21: 93–123.

Nash, J. 1998. 'Twenty Years of the Anthropology of Work: Changes in the State of the World and the State of the Arts', *Anthropology of Work Review* 18(4): 1–6.

Ong, A. 1987. *Spirits of Resistance and Capitalist Discipline: Factory Women in Malaysia*. Albany: State University of New York Press.

Ortiz, S. 1994. 'Work, the Division of Labour and Co-operation', in T. Ingold (ed.), *Companion Encyclopedia of Anthropology*. London: Routledge, pp. 891–910.

——— 2002. 'Laboring in the Factories and in the Fields', *Annual Review of Anthropology* 31(1): 395–417.

Otto, T., and P. Pedersen. 2005. 'Disentangling Traditions: Culture, Agency and Power', in T. Otto and P. Pedersen (eds), *Tradition and Agency: Tracing Cultural Continuity and Invention*. Aarhus: Aarhus University Press, pp. 11–49.

Parry, J., and M. Bloch (eds). 1989. *Money and the Morality of Exchange*. Cambridge: Cambridge University Press.

Piore, M.J., and C.F. Sabel. 1984. *The Second Industrial Divide: Possibilities for Prosperity*. New York: Basic Books.

Polanyi, K. 1957. 'The Economy as Instituted Process', in K. Polanyi, C. Arensberg, and H. Pearson (eds), *Trade and Market in the Early Empires: Economies in History and Theory*. New York: Free Press, pp. 243–270.

——— 2001 [1944]. *The Great Transformation*. Boston: Beacon Press.

Pongratz, H., and G. Voss. 2003. 'From Employee to "Entreployee": Towards a "Self-Entrepreneurial" Work Force?' *Concepts and Transformation* 8(3): 239–254.

Procoli, A. (ed.). 2004. *Workers and Narratives of Survival in Europe: The Management of Precariousness at the End of the Twentieth Century*. Albany: State University of New York Press.

Roseberry, W. 1988. 'Political Economy', *Annual Review of Anthropology* 17: 161–185.

Sahlins, M. 1972. *Stone Age Economics*. New York: Aldine de Gruyter.

Sennett, R. 1998. *The Corrosion of Character: The Personal Consequences of Work in the New Capitalism*. New York: Norton.

Spittler, G. 2001. 'Work: Anthropological Aspects', in E. Neil, J. Smelser and P.B. Baltes (eds), *International Encyclopedia of the Social and Behavioral Sciences*. Oxford: Pergamon, pp. 16565–16569.

——— 2008. *Founders of the Anthropology of Work*. Berlin: LIT Verlag.

——— 2009. 'Contesting The Great Transformation: Work in Comparative Perspective', in C. Hann and K. Hart (eds), *Market and Society: The Great Transformation Today*. Cambridge: Cambridge University Press, pp. 160–174.

Strangleman, T. 2007. 'The Nostalgia for Permanence at Work? The End of Work and its Commentators', *Sociological Review* 55(1): 81–103.

Strathern, M. 1988. *The Gender of the Gift: Problems with Women and Problems with Society in Melanesia*. Berkeley: University of California Press.

——— 1991. *Partial Connections*. Savage, MD: Rowman and Littlefield.

——— 1996. 'Cutting the Network', *Journal of the Royal Anthropological Institute* 2(3): 517–535.

——— 1999. 'Potential Property: Intellectual Rights and Property in Persons', in *Property, Substance and Effect: Anthropological Essays on Persons and Things*. London: Athlone Press, pp. 161–178.

Strathern, M. (ed.). 2000. *Audit Cultures: Anthropological Studies in Accountability, Ethics and the Academy*. London, Routledge.

Taussig, M. 1980. *The Devil and Commodity Fetishism in South America*. Chapel Hill: University of North Carolina Press.

Thompson, P. 1989. *The Nature of Work: An Introduction to Debates on the Labour Process*. London: Macmillan.

Tsing, A.L. 2000. 'Inside the Economy of Appearances', *Public Culture* 12(1): 115–144.

Turner, V. 1967. 'Betwixt and Between: The Liminal Period in Rites de Passage', in *The Forest of Symbols: Aspects of Ndembu Ritual*. Ithaca, NY: Cornell University Press, pp. 93–111.

Wajcman, J. 2008. 'Life in the Fast Lane? Towards a Sociology of Technology and Time', *British Journal of Sociology* 59(1): 56–77.

Wallman, S. (ed.). 1979. *Social Anthropology of Work*. London: Academic Press.

Weber, M. 1958. *The Protestant Ethic and the Spirit of Capitalism*. New York: Scribner.

Weiner, A.B. 1992. *Inalienable Possessions: The Paradox of Keeping-while-Giving*. Berkeley: University of California Press.

Willis, P. 1977. *Learning to Labour: How Working Class Kids get Working Class Jobs*. Aldershot: Gower.

Woolgar, S. 2002. 'Five Rules of Virtuality', in S. Woolgar (ed.), *Virtual Society? Technology, Cyberbole, Reality*. Oxford: Oxford University Press, pp. 1–22.

1

Everybody Gives
Gifts in the Global Factory

Jamie Cross

Sitting on the floor of his rented two-roomed house one Sunday afternoon in November 2009, 32-year-old Prakash, Worldwide Diamonds' oldest employee, played with his six-month-old daughter and reflected on thirteen years of factory labour. Prakash had joined the company in its first batch of seventy-five new recruits in September 1997. I had known him since my first day on the 'A-shift', when I had been told to sit alongside him and learn how to hold, touch and look at a rough diamond. During that time he had never been slow to criticize the company, to lambaste its wage regimes, its systems of control or the intensity with which it required people to work. But when I now asked why he had never left the factory, he put the factory's shop-floor gift economy squarely at the heart of his explanation.

> Worldwide Diamonds' workers are really good: everybody gives! People will always bring you little things at work and if there is some event, no matter if is something small or something big, if somebody gets married or somebody has died, everybody will give something. Whether it is one hundred rupees or thirty rupees, they will give whatever they can, but everybody will give something. You can't find those kind of relationships everywhere. I've been thinking of leaving that factory for so long, so why am I still there? My relations keep me there, that's why.

'Everybody gives!' It was an exacting phrase. The conclusion Prakash drew from it, 'my relations keep me there', suggested that he understood these exchanges to have powerful social effects, and that these effects bound him to the workplace. As Prakash recognized, gift giving did not just reveal ties and relationships on the factory floor but constituted the very mechanism through which these relationships were created.

This chapter asks what we should make of the gifts that were given between workers and their managers on the floor of a massive offshore manufacturing unit in South India. Such exchanges appear anomalous in the ethnography of global manufacturing, yet here they underpinned the organization of hyper-intensive or post-Fordist production processes. Following diverse acts of giving, this chapter explores how these transactions constituted the performative and relational grounds on which workers came to know themselves and sought to shape the world around them. Like other chapters in this volume, it extends our anthropology of capitalism by examining the multiple modalities of exchange through which flexibility is achieved.

The Hidden Abodes of Global Manufacturing

At the end of 2004, I was granted open ethnographic access to a large subcontracting unit for the global diamond industry in Andhra Pradesh, South India. The factory in question, Worldwide Diamonds, occupied several thousand square feet inside the state's first free trade zone. The zone itself was spread across 350 acres of flat scrubland, and was surrounded by an eight-foot high perimeter wall topped with broken glass. Since the 1970s, zones like this one have played a crucial role in the globalization of production, creating capitalist enclaves across South and South-East Asia that are free from state regulation. These have become vital spaces for the diffusion of just-in-time inventory systems, total-quality-control mechanisms and hyper-efficient models of workspace organization, which David Harvey (1990, 2005) has identified as the cornerstones of flexibility in large-scale capitalist production processes, and which have made informality and precariousness an integral part of many global commodity chains (Burawoy 1985; Ross 2009; Tsing 2009; Cross 2010).

The zone in which Worldwide Diamonds operates is located midway between Andhra Pradesh's industrial port of Vizag (Visakhapatnam), a heavily polluted and densely populated city of over 1.5 million people, and the rural sugar trading town of Annakapalle. In 2005, Worldwide Diamonds employed a Telugu-speaking workforce of approximately 1,200 people. Most of these workers were aged between eighteen and twenty-four, roughly 70 per cent of them were men and all were native to this region of coastal Andhra Pradesh. The zone offered no accommodation, and factory workers lived with their families in caste-segregated villages across a semi-rural, peri-urban hinterland or in housing colonies along the busy highway that cuts through the region. On the factory floor, this labour force was managed by a group of young Indians, recent graduates with degrees in engineering, business or human resources. They, in turn, were overseen by a small number of European expatriates, English, Belgian and Israeli men, who had been posted here to oversee production processes to train workers in specialized diamond cutting and polishing techniques. Some of these men had worked in the diamond industry since they were young apprentices, and had witnessed the industry's transformation as production shifted from European workshops to sites of low-cost sub-contracted manufacturing in South and South-East Asia.

Work in Worldwide Diamonds was poorly paid and chronically insecure. For their first year, a new recruit was expected to work for a stipend of 1,200 rupees (US$15) per month, after which they entered a piece-rate wage regime that might earn them up to $40 per month, equivalent to the rates of day labour in the local construction industry. The formal employment contracts that workers' signed with the company were rendered essentially meaningless by the company's hire-and-fire policy. Workers who were deemed unproductive could be summarily expelled from the workplace, and those who attempted to organize colleagues in protest at working conditions with the support of a local communist trade union were either blacklisted or sacked. In 2002, the intimidation of union organizers here had made the factory a cause célèbre for Indian unionists and, in a test case, it was investigated by the UN's International Labour Organization.

In January 2005, I joined 120 other people on the 6 AM TO 2 PM 'A-shift' in the Preparation Department, where rough diamonds began their transformation into polished gemstones. In the tradition of industrial ethnography (e.g. Burawoy 1982; Blim 1992; Prentice 2008), I secured the permission of managers to become a participant in rather than just an observer of labour processes. As I have described in more detail elsewhere (Cross 2011a, 2011b, 2014), over the course of 2005 I was trained to become a competent and productive machine operator, learning to handle single-spindle machines, semi-automatic bruiting machines, rotating scaifes and hand-held tangs, and eventually able to cut and polish rough diamonds into a basic round shape, give them eight basic facets, a smooth, flat table and their sharp pointed culet.

As I was taught to corner, bruit and block rough diamonds, I came to understand that a complex economy of non-monetary and non-monetized transactions was flourishing on the shop floor. The 'underlife' (Goffman 1961) of this global factory involved a host of transactions that were not encompassed by what we might call the wage-labour economy or commodity exchange. Workers gave away items of homemade food, brand-name sweets and chocolates, hand-crafted art pieces, blessed temple food and decorative or ornamental consumer goods to other workers and to their monitors, supervisors and managers, and they spoke of giving their labour to the company.

These acts of giving criss-crossed the factory floor, with different aims and effects. Like transactions described by others in this volume (e.g. Grétarsdóttir, Narotzky, Wood) these were ambivalent exchanges. Some transactions took place without any immediate expectation of a return or any explicit agreement about one, in ways that created, transformed, cultivated and nourished relationships of friendship and care, solidarity and mutual aid. Other transactions were more transparently interested or instrumental attempts to gain favour or foster relations of patronage, clientage and service. In some exchanges, we might discern what Garsten (this volume) calls an economy of connection, but in others we can discern what might be called an economy of 'detachment', with the gift establishing a separation or division of giver from receiver (Strathern 1991: 588; Cross 2011a, 2013).

Some exchanges took place between people who identified themselves as members of the same caste community, while others took place between members of caste communities that have, historically, maintained prohibitions on exchange. Some took place between co-workers, people who occupied positions of equality in the factory hierarchy, while other exchanges took place between workers and their managers, people who occupied differential positions of power, control and authority. Such transactions offer a vivid illustration that what anthropologists call 'the gift' is never a unitary category, and that gifts can be animated by what David Graeber (2011) calls different moral or transactional logics, significantly 'co-operation', 'reciprocal exchange' and 'hierarchy'.

What should we make of such transactions on the floor of today's global sweatshops? The 'hidden abode of production' into which Karl Marx (1990) descended to examine exchanges between the owners of capital and the bearers of labour power still lies beneath the surface of anthropological theorizing about gift exchange. Marcel Mauss's essay on the gift (Mauss 1966) was written partially in response to Marxist political economy, the anthropologist deploying ethnological material in a tone that was nostalgic and utopian to describe societies in which the market was not the main medium of human relations and in which the objects of exchange did not inevitably become alienable, quantifiable commodities (Graeber 2001; Coleman 2004). Chris Gregory's influential post-Maussian approach (Gregory 1982, 1997) distilled the essence of gift and commodity exchange into separate, analytically distinct and seemingly incompatible regimes of value (Caliskan and Callon 2009), and many anthropologies and geographies of labour in global factories have perpetuated this sharp distinction between spheres of commodity and gift exchange.

The kinds of transactions that I encountered on the floor of Worldwide Diamonds, however, appear anomalous in ethnographic accounts of industrial work at similar sites of global manufacturing in China, Malaysia, Indonesia, Thailand, Mexico and Sri Lanka (Ong 1987; Wolf 1992; Lynch 1999; Mills 1999; Hewamanne 2003; Salzinger 2003; Wright 2006). In this literature, the precarious labour contracts between workers and supply-chain capitalists in the world's economic zones epitomize the short-term transactional orders that Gregory described as belonging to the sphere of commodity exchange (Gregory 1982, 1997). Indeed, most discussions of exchange in export manufacturing zones are primarily concerned with the commoditization of labour, which is often understood to reach some kind of contemporary apotheosis in these spaces (cf. Neveling, this volume). In China's economic zones, for example, Pun Ngai (2005: 163) has written how rural labour migrants or *dagonmei* transform their bodies into objects for consumption, and are forced to confront themselves as something hostile and alien. Aihwa Ong's writings present a similarly dystopian portrait, showing offshore zones in China as carceral work camps in which men and women are valued for their labour alone and are condemned in perpetuity to live the bare life of a commodity (Ong 2006).

Yet many different 'economic and moral possibilities' exist on the floor of the global factory (Graeber 2010: 1–2), and the diversity of economic transactions that take place here are not limited to commodity exchange or to the terms of the labour–capital relation. In other discussions and bodies of literature, anthropologists have consistently pointed to the blurring and overlapping of exchange categories in the modern industrial workplace (Prentice 2008; Parry, Mollona and De Neve 2009). As Mayfair Yang has shown, for example, the organization of labour in contemporary China's manufacturing and service sectors depends on *guanxi* – social ties, networks or connectedness – and mechanisms for producing relatedness through gift giving (Yang 1989). Meanwhile, Mao Mollona's ethnography of labour in contemporary Sheffield's small machine workshops reminds us how opaque the theoretical distinctions between gift and commodity economies, and alienated and non-alienated labour, actually are for the subjective, experiential and symbolic ways that manual workers conceive of and shape their relationships of production (Mollona 2009).

The ethnography of work at an outpost of large-scale export manufacturing in contemporary India that I present here makes a contribution to these debates by exploring how different acts of giving on the global shop floor shape the labour process in different ways. Examining the transactions that took place on the floor of Worldwide Diamonds, I explore how they were premised on different transactional logics, underpinned by principals of cooperation, exchange and hierarchy in ways that performed different kinds of social action. As I show, acts of giving constituted the performative and relational grounds on which people came to know themselves and sought to shape the world around them.

Cooperation (or Capital's Free Gift)

During my first few visits, Worldwide Diamonds' Preparation Department conformed to my expectations of a global sweatshop. The dusty, poorly ventilated open-plan space was divided into work sections by hardboard dividers. Rows of workers wore identical blue uniforms and stood or sat to operate machines beneath fluorescent strip lights. In each section, workers were directly overseen by a section monitor who wore a maroon coloured uniform. Off the factory floor, a department supervisor and a department manager oversaw the quality and rate of production. Wages here were paid at a piece rate, which was subject to constant adjustment as the company's management sought to extract ever greater value from their workers' labour. Work on the shift was hyper-intensive, and each work section was required to meet daily, weekly and monthly production targets. Eight-hour shifts frequently become twelve, and six-day weeks sometimes became seven as the factory struggled to meet client orders on time.

Each work section was monitored by a CCTV camera that relayed real-time images of the factory to banks of screens in a central control room. Here the factory employed a surveillance manager to keep watch for slowdowns in productivity, for attempted theft and for any sign of political action. Any sluggishness or sleepiness that was caught on camera prompted a telephone call to the shop floor. Alarms rang if a diamond got lost, and several hours of video would be reviewed to check anybody who could have palmed or secreted the missing stone. The movements of people who had been singled out as 'trouble makers' were closely tracked, and their gatherings or conversations raised immediate concern about some imminent labour action, the downing of tools or an organized 'go-slow'.

Beneath this complex surveillance apparatus, however, existed a complex economy of gifts and gift transactions. The earliest transactions that a new trainee here became party to involved the transmission of skilled knowledge, as a learned technical competency with machines, tools and raw materials was passed down to them from more experienced co-workers (Cross 2011b). Piece-rate work in a factory like this one depended upon a whole host of similar micro-interactions with other people, from those who give a novice hints and tips, offering guidance, support and initiation onto the shift to those interactions with co-workers upon whom each individual is dependent if they are to maintain minimum rates of productivity and so guarantee their wage. In the cornering, hand blocking and bruiting sections where I learned to cut and polish rough diamonds in 2005, acts of giving between co-workers frequently proceeded according to what David Graeber has called a principal of 'from each according to their abilities, to each according to their needs'; these were transactions in which individuals recognized each other's mutual interdependence and in which the taking of accounts would have been considered inappropriate, offensive or bizarre (Graeber 2011: 94–99). Cornering-workers, for example, shared the hammers that they used to adjust their spindle machines and small pieces of fabric to mop up machine oil. Meanwhile in the blocking section, where rudimentary hand tools were used to push rough diamonds backwards and forwards on a rotating scaife, workers shared pieces of torn cloth to prevent blistering. Across the department, people shared black marker pens, variously used to mark the surface of rough diamonds, to sketch cutting edges and angles on the white table surfaces, and to record production tallies on scraps of paper.

Cooperation, Marx wrote in the first volume of *Capital*, is the 'necessary concomitant of all production on a large scale' (Marx 1990: 453), and a 'free gift to capital' (ibid.: 451). Marx saw cooperation as a natural, integral part of any economic system, a social phenomenon that takes place spontaneously and naturally with the simultaneous employment of large numbers of people in one place, along with a concentrated mass of machines and tools for production. In his example, a dozen masons passing stones from the bottom to the top of a ladder might each be said to perform the same movements and actions, but taken together these separate actions form connected parts of one single operation. This kind of cooperation takes a distinct form, Marx argued, when people are brought together by capital for the purposes of waged labour. In the capitalist factory, cooperation served both to increase the productive power of the individual and also to create a kind of collective power that capitalists sought to harness, manage and control for the purposes of profitable exploitation and expansion (ibid.: 453). For Marx, this cooperation is usually hidden from view or invisible because it appears to us as the social effect of having brought people together in one place and putting them to work. For Graeber, this principal of cooperation, mutual aid and solidarity exists in many different kinds of social contexts, not just work groups, and it is one of the ironies of contemporary capitalism that the internal organization of some of today's largest corporations comes to hinge upon it (Graeber 2011: 100).

A global subcontracting company like Worldwide Diamonds could not function without the raft of transactions that took place as people involved in the common project of production collaborated by establishing certain things that could be shared or made freely available to others. As workers passed tools or materials between each other on the factory floor, and shared knowledge and skills, they established their mutuality and interdependence, offering us a reminder of how central mutual aid, assistance and cooperation are to global commodity production.

One phenomenon in particular, the redistribution of blessed or sacred food (*prasadam*, Hindi *prasada*) on the factory floor offers a particular insight into the principal of cooperation. As Arjun Appadurai has written, food in South India can be used to signal, indicate and construct social relations characterized by equality, intimacy or solidarity, as much as rank or difference (Appadurai 1981: 507); and the 'gastro-politics' of holy food as it was redistributed by factory workers returning from a pilgrimage might be said to hinge on the principal of 'from each according to their ability, to each according to their need'.

In coastal Andhra Pradesh, a pilgrimage to the state's most holy site, the temple to Lord Venkateshwara (Vishnu) at Tirupati, is considered by Hindus of all castes and ages a necessary trip. People make the pilgrimage at times of wealth as well as ill health. For some, a pilgrimage to Tirupati is considered one of the only opportunities to travel outside the district, and pilgrims invariably bring home with them large quantities of sanctified food to distribute. When one of Worldwide Diamonds' Hindu factory workers returned from a pilgrimage to Andhra's most important holy site, they invariably brought with them a large quantity of *prasadam* to distribute amongst their work colleagues.

Prasadam is a collective noun for substances – often items of food, but also water, flowers, ash and powder – that have been offered to a deity during worship, and which are subsequently distributed to priests, devotees, relatives and friends. When these substances are offered to and symbolically consumed by a deity (in its image form), they undergo a transmutation, becoming *prasada*, potent substances that are imbued with a divine power and grace and which can be absorbed into the human body (Fuller 2004: 74–75). In the ritual symbolism of everyday Hinduism, the adornment of the body with *prasada* substances like ash or flowers or the swallowing of *prasada* food marks the absorption of divine grace and power into the body, effecting a merger between deity and worshipper. But, like all Hindu rituals and substances, the distribution of *prasadam* is about relationships between people as much as between the worshiper and a deity.

Over the course of a year I watched several of the Preparation Department's workers make the pilgrimage to Tirupati. When they returned to work they brought with them carrier bags full of *prasadam*, usually a mixture of puffed rice, groundnuts, gram (pulses) and jaggery (a kind of sugar). On their first day back at work, they asked permission to walk around the department from section to section, enabling their colleagues and workmates to share the blessed food. These acts of giving took place in public and en masse, with the donor making a point to offer food to every one of the department's 150 strong workforce, including cleaners and security guards as well as co-workers, monitors, supervisors and department managers, irrespective of caste or religion. This distribution and consumption of *prasadam*, the highest form of leftovers, on the floor of Worldwide Diamonds gave real, material form to the workforce as a collective body or organic entity. It was a process of co-substantiation through which, as Marx put it, people as cooperators become members of a 'total productive organism' (Marx 1990: 448).

As I will show, however, the shop-floor relationships between workers involved other kinds of transactions, premised not upon principals of mutuality but upon principals of reciprocity and hierarchy.

Reciprocity and Recognition

Every day, people arrived at the entrance to the Preparation Department carrying small items of food that by the end of the day they would have given to somebody else. These things were carried past the security guards posted at the doors to the department under people's regulation blue uniforms, wedged into their trouser pockets, tied into the corner of their *saris*, or tucked inside their *churidars* (tightly fitting trouser pants). An incredible range of foodstuffs were smuggled onto the factory floor in this way to be passed from hand to hand, underneath a table surface or in a subtle brush of fingers, in a manner that sought not to draw attention from managers.

The things circulating in the cornering, blocking and bruiting sections included the ubiquitous single rupee boiled sweets, lozenges, éclairs and toffees that are found in the smallest of street-side trade stores across India, as well as brand-name chocolates, like five rupee bars of Cadbury Five Star or ten rupee bars of Dairy Milk. They also included seasonal fruits and nuts, lemons and gooseberries, handfuls of aniseed, sultanas, cashews, fried potato chips, Bombay mix and popcorn, even entire cobs of maize. Alongside foodstuffs were other kinds of things. Some of the most popular non-food gift items were images, playing cards or stickers with colour pictures of deities and saints or matinee film-star heroes and heroines. Alongside these were handmade things. All manner of origami paper objects circulated around the Preparation Department, including boxes, animals and flowers, tiny pieces of folded artistry that were made at home, or during lunch breaks from scraps of paper, including the computerized diamond labels or production charts, that had been picked up or lifted off the factory floor.

At first these exchanges seemed so petty that I overlooked them, seeing them as insignificant or insubstantial. They took place with such frequency as to be part of the factory's social fabric – as normal as conversation. Yet during the months I spent on the factory floor it become apparent that what appeared to be mundane or spontaneous gifts between workers could be mapped onto more complex shop-floor relationships between people with different levels of experience or different workloads, and between people whose tasks tied them into workplace relationships with each other. While the intimate knowledge of machines and materials that passed between workers appeared to be transacted according to a principal of solidarity and mutual aid, these acts of giving appeared more clearly animated by a reciprocal logic of gift exchange and equivalence. Gifts objects, things and foodstuffs were exchanged for favours, preferential treatment and even labour from co-workers as people struggled to meet their daily production targets and complete their own work tasks. These gifts were passed backwards and forwards in such a way that each gift appeared to cancel the other out, and in such a way that each party appeared to be keeping account, motivated by the ways that the exchange reflected upon and rearranged their relationship. As Graeber puts it, the principal of equivalence between the objects of exchange also implies an equivalence or parity between the parties to an exchange (Graeber 2011: 103), and these transactions marked the floor of the factory out as a particular kind of social space, one that differed in important ways from the caste landscape beyond its walls.

Cornering-section workers collected stones from the fixers, who cemented each and every rough diamond onto a cylindrical rod that could be inserted into a spindle machine. As they ground the angular corners away, rough stones invariably broke off their holdings, sometimes flicking onto the floor or falling onto the work surface. Cornering-workers were allowed to walk these diamonds over to the fixing table themselves, and if they wanted to get back to work and finish the stone they needed a fixer who would give them priority, dipping the stone in concrete over a heater while they waited. On the A-shift cornering section, workers like Appala Raju and Condom Rao went out of their way to build good relationships with the three women fixers by giving them small gifts of chocolate, handed over in the mornings to coincide with the small stainless steel beaker of milky tea that the company granted each worker.

These exchanges continued off the factory floor during the half-hour lunch break, when more substantial foodstuffs, rice and curries, were shared between co-workers out in the open, beneath a line of palm trees or beneath a corrugated shelter. Every day, people came to the factory carrying portions of home-cooked food – prepared by themselves, or by sisters or mothers – which they shared with colleagues. Many of these exchanges of boiled rice and curries took place against the grain of local caste hierarchies, with the parents and extended families of many factory workers still recognizing symbolic and social restrictions on inter-caste contact. Exchanges that took place between people from farming or landowning castes and Dalit communities, then, marked the factory as a space of transgression from widely accepted and observed social prohibitions on inter-caste exchange and commensality.

Like all of the factory's units, the Preparation Department was broadly representative of coastal Andhra Pradesh's caste demographics. Recruited into the factory as entry level workers and thrown together on the shift were the higher ranking Velamas, Gavaras and Kapus, who are the district's major landowners, as well as a cross-section of occupational castes, Mallas, Palles and Vadabalijas. In north coastal Andhra, inter-caste relationships between these communities has been tightly regulated, marked by endogamy and restrictions on contact. Yet references to each others' caste were studiously erased from everyday interactions between workers. Thrown together on the A-shift, the young men and women here chose to represent the factory as a caste-less place that marked a distinctive break from the adult social worlds they inhabited in rural villages and peri-urban neighbourhoods. Here, as in the small power plant in nearby southern Orissa where Christian Strümpell (2008) conducted fieldwork, young workers recognized the industrial workplace as a uniquely commensurable space, a space of inter-caste contact and inter-commensurability that marked a distinct break with those places where they had been born and brought up. In many sections, people who had worked closely alongside each other for several years claimed disinterest in the caste identities of their co-workers. And, over several years the factory had given rise to numerous inter-caste relationships between workers, several of which had ended in elopement and marriage. Many of the transactions that took place between workers on the factory floor fitted into this broader pattern, violating and erasing historical restrictions on inter-caste contact.

Some of these exchanges were quietly libidinal. For many workers, the factory was experienced as a space of comparative freedom from adult social mores and the relatively strict prohibitions on sexual contact that are imposed by families in provincial Andhra Pradesh. On Worldwide Diamonds' mixed-sex A-shift, petty gift exchanges could be flirtatious and suggestive. Young adolescent men could frequently be found giving small gifts to the unmarried girls and young mothers whom they worked alongside. For their part, many young women appeared to see these as strategic exchanges that enabled them to cope with the intensity of the factory's production regime. Many married women on the A-shift exchanged a little extra home-cooked food, spiced with some lascivious talk and sexual innuendo, for a little help with production from their unmarried male co-workers. And some unmarried young men, wracked with sexual desire, found themselves cutting and polishing a few extra stones to help them reach production targets or took responsibility for cutting 'problem stones', those with minor flaws, gluts and fractures, that were easier to break or over-cut.

In the preparation department's table section, for example, I spent eight weeks working alongside Rama Laxshmi, a married woman with two children who had worked there for several years, and Durga Rao, a lanky young trainee with a wispy beard and a gangly gait. As the older, married woman, Rama Laxshmi enjoyed a position of sexual authority over Durga Rao, and as the two of them pushed rough stones backwards and forwards across a rotating scaife, blocking facets into hard or delicate diamonds, they played footsie under the table or sang romantic songs to each other over the machine noise. During lunch breaks, the two of them sat together in the shade under a palm tree in the factory car park. Rama brought Durga homemade curries with egg or chicken, or portions of curd. During the shift, these exchanges were also translated into the labour process, as Rama asked Durga to help her meet production targets. She passed the biggest or most difficult stones on to him, and after he had finished them they were passed back and counted under her own name. When her young suitor began to lobby for a transfer to a different work section where he would be paid per stone, Rama tried to persuade him to stay.

These everyday, inter-personal exchanges on the factory floor were accompanied by ostentatious and very public acts of giving, as individual workers pooled money together in order to buy gifts for each other. Workers were regularly asked to make contributions to a pool or pot of money that could be used to purchase a gift for colleagues on important occasions, including birthdays, marriages, births and the occasion of a new child's *annaprasana*, celebrated when they first consume solid food. On these occasions, someone on the shift would take responsibility for collecting contributions, and a cohort of people would be deputized to buy an ornamental object from one of the many gift shops or 'fancy shops' that flourish in the towns of Annakappalle, or around the junctions of the main highway. These gifts might cost anywhere between 100 and 500 rupees, and were selected specifically for their utility as an object of household display; the options invariably included vases of plastic flowers coated in bright paints and sparkling glitter, imitation wooden clocks, glitzy lamp stands, fake silver picture frames and photo albums.

These collective acts of giving were accompanied by expectations of reciprocity, and they were accompanied by a subtle taking of account as people noted who gave what, to whom and on what occasion. Givers expected that their gifts would be met with a counter-gift at the appropriate moment, whilst recipients were concerned to give back. This taking of account was most apparent when new trainees appeared on the factory floor. Oblivious to the significance of this gift economy for the social life of the shop floor, these newcomers were frequently criticized for failing to participate in gift exchanges. 'Newcomers don't know how to give', and 'newcomers don't give money for weddings' were common complaints among the Preparation Department's more established workers.

This gift economy, based on reciprocal exchange and mutual recognition, was an integral part of the factory's social life. These transactions proved essential as workers struggled to meet their work targets and vital for maintaining social ties across the factory floor. As I will show, however, these acts of giving between workers differed in important ways from those that took place between workers and their managers, that is, between people who occupied positions of differential status, power and authority in social and workplace hierarchies.

'Soap' and the 'Gift of Labour'

Workers like Prakash, who I quoted earlier, did not have a phrase for the acts of giving that I have just described, but they took place between people who occupied broadly equivalent positions of status and power in the factory's formal hierarchy, and were distinguished by the ambiguity of their intentions. These exchanges, however, were clearly differentiated from other kinds that took place between people in unequal positions of power and authority. The exchanges that took place between workers and their shop-floor monitors, managers and supervisors were distinguished from those that took place between co-workers by the intentionality of the giver and the meanings attached to the gift. These exchanges were premised on an explicit difference in the social position of giver and recipient, and while they invoked the language of reciprocity they hinged primarily on what Graeber calls a 'logic of precedent', or a 'web of habit and custom' (Graeber 2011: 109). Gifts to managers both recognized and appealed to the recipient as a person of higher social rank and status. They were gifts that were intended to broker a pathway to patronage, protection and security, and to make a recipient feel disposed to respond or act in this way (see also Graeber 2001: 225).

In north coastal Andhra, the English word 'gift' serves as a basic translation for over thirty different Telugu words, each referring to a different exchange category, denoting different contexts of exchange, different degrees of instrumentality on the part of the giver, different relationships with a recipient and different kinds of gift. Some of the most important vernacular categories for practising Hindus describe gifts to priests and to deities that are part of everyday temple rituals. These include *kanuka*, offerings of food objects and cash that are said to be made with homage, courtesy or reverence; and *mokku*, a collective noun for offerings which are said to have been given to a God with a more explicit or directed purpose and intent, as in when people pray for divine intervention to bring about a change in fortune or health, to bring wisdom in decision making or to bring about a particularly desirable course of events, for example in matters of the heart.

In the Worldwide Diamonds factory, young Telugu workers described gifts that are given in order to have specific effects as 'soap'. This is a deliberate and witty vernacular play on the English word: 'to soap someone' is to try to smooth or lubricate your relationship in the pursuit of specific ends. But underlying the joke was a distinction between acts of giving that served to maintain social relations and acts of giving that served a more narrowly defined instrumental purpose. Jonathan Parry (2000) observed a similar distinction between the etiquette and practice associated with 'gifts', 'commissions' and 'bribes' among people seeking access to public-sector employment in the Central Indian steel town of Bhilai. In popular discourse, 'gifts' were given to maintain social relations rather than for any specific favours; 'commissions' were given in 'gratitude' for servicing contracts, while 'bribes' are given for a narrowly defined instrumental purpose.

At Worldwide Diamonds there was considerable ambiguity and ambivalence around what constituted 'soap'. Debates about real or imagined exchanges lay at the heart of many of the intrigues and squabbles that animated daily life on the factory floor. In every section of the Preparation Department, machine workers presented their monitors with small gifts that were explicitly intended to win their favourable treatment on the factory floor. Gifts that 'soaped' might range from ubiquitous items of home-cooked food, to cinema tickets for the latest Telugu films and invitations to family homes for Sunday dinner. In the cornering section, for example, senior blue-uniformed machine workers regularly brought extra portions of food which they pushed onto the plate of Laxman, their section monitor, during the lunch break. Laxman was the only labour migrant in the work section. He rented a small room in a highway township with a group of other workers from the northern coastal district of Srikakulum and, consequently, was the only male worker in the section who did not live in a domestic environment attended by mothers, daughters or sisters-in-law. The cheap rice that Laxman burnt each night over his gas stove was supplemented during the factory lunch break with homemade delicacies, curries with chicken, fish, aubergine and okra, prepared by the wives, mothers and sisters of some of his male colleagues. In turn, Laxman ensured that these workers enjoyed a favourable supply of stock on the factory floor, giving them preferential access to rough stones when the stock was low and ensuring that they had access to the larger stones with a higher piece rate when stock was full.

Every one of the factory's departments was overseen by managers who were responsible for its organization and productivity, control and discipline. While the caste background of blue-collar workers was studiously erased from everyday conversation or talk on the factory floor, the high-caste backgrounds of these managers elicited malicious anti-Brahminical comments and critique. But as individual workers struggled to secure personal advantage or promotion in the workplace, their ability to 'soap' the managers was pivotal. Over the year I spent in the Preparation Department, I watched several monitors present small gift items and objects up the factory hierarchy to their high-caste managers. The most striking of these were the handmade pieces of diamond-related art. Laxman once spent several weeks developing a portfolio of pencil sketches, showing diamonds in their various stages of production, which he eventually presented to one of the factory managers. Patnaik, the blocking-section monitor, went a step further. Patnaik had a side hobby making scale models from discarded pieces of polystyrene, and the fruits of his creative labour included cars, planes, spacecraft and a Japanese bullet train. In mid 2005, Patnaik brought his latest piece, an intricate diamond cut from a single lump of polystyrene and engraved with detailed facets, into the factory and formally presented it to the department manager who had it installed on her desk in a glass box as a 'learning tool'. Such objects were unique gifts. By materializing the skill and technical prowess of their creators, they spoke of an individual's pride in their craft. And, as visible demonstrations of an individual's practical competencies and capabilities, they made a public expression of desire for mobility in the factory's internal labour market.

Those workers who secured promotions to monitor or supervisor were regularly fingered by shop-floor gossip for having 'soaped' or 'polished' their way up the ladder with gifts. What such commentaries obliquely acknowledged was that 'soaping' required skill and etiquette, not just material things but also demonstrations of deference and subservience. 'Some people will get opportunities and promotions here', people like Appala Raju complained to me. 'Not everyone – only some people. Those kind of people who go to their department manager or their head monitor and ask about everything and say, "Yes, Sir!" or "What about this, Sir?" or "What about that?" They are the people who polish, you know. Polish. Soap. There are many people who know how to do that around here'.

In conversations in their homes outside the factory, people nourished private bitterness against co-workers who they felt had outdone them for a promotion by lathering up and soaping a superior. Hari, the Preparation Department's senior monitor, who had worked his way up from an entry-level position on the factory floor, put it bluntly:

> *If* one person gets something, someone else will look at them and shout, Soap! Or, Polish! And if it goes the other way round, the other person will say the same thing. Everyone talks about soap around here. They don't think, 'If I work harder, if I work very hard, then I might get something too'. No. Instead that person says, 'Oh! Look! That person is soaping or polishing to get something'. But things don't work like that. Well . . . maybe they work like that in 10 per cent or 15 per cent of cases, but not every time.

Many of Worldwide Diamonds' white-collar Brahmin managers sought to explicitly position themselves outside this exchange economy. Worldwide Diamonds' management trainees were aged between twenty-two and twenty-six, and had masters degrees in engineering or management from provincial English-medium colleges in South India. As they saw it, the biggest everyday challenge of modern factory management was to avoid becoming embroiled in a web of close, binding, personal relationships with the people they were employed to manage and control. They clamoured away from relationships with the factory's workforce, and often struggled to avoid or refuse these kind of gifts, afraid that any intimation of closeness, friendship or intimacy with individuals might offer them some kind of leverage in requests for a promotion, a wage increase, extra leave, extra overtime or a reduction in workload. The art pieces described above, for example, were never accepted on a personal basis. Instead, managers accepted them 'on behalf of the department' and left them on public view inside the factory. Vikram described the dilemma as he reflected on his experiences on the shop floor:

> People would invite us to their home. They'll say, 'Come, bring your wife, bring your children, you can eat with us, there is a very nice temple close by'. Or they will say, 'Come to my village for the festival'. And a few days later they'll say, 'Sir, please pass these stones', or they'll ask me about a promotion, or they'll try to get me to ask someone higher to push their salary.

In response, many young managers chose to cultivate an ethic of detachment, carefully managing and limiting their exchanges with workers (Cross 2011a). Detachment was seen as a precondition for the rational, market-oriented calculations and impartial decisions required of a modern professional, essential for achieving control and productivity. Achieving detachment meant purging oneself of sentiment, foreclosing any affective ties of obligation or reciprocity. Managers like Vikram put these problems succinctly during interviews with me on and off the factory floor: 'You can't try to build good relations with workers here. You'll never be successful like that. If you want them to meet targets and to keep the quality up then you have to be strict, you have to be disciplined. You can't go with your sentiments. You can't get production with sentiments'. Such managerial anxieties stand testament to the constant work or effort involved in successfully achieving a degree of 'distance' from workers.

The hierarchical exchanges taking place on the floor of Worldwide Diamonds exhibited considerable continuity with those documented by anthropologists in South India's agricultural economy. Here, as Filippo and Caroline Osella (1996) have written, agricultural labourers can be found constantly manoeuvring to bring reciprocity into the sphere of non-reciprocity while landowners and employers constantly struggle to deny them, or to set the terms of the exchange. The same struggles took place over the idea of labour itself.

In their struggle to build relationships with their employers, Telugu workers all sought to establish an idea of their labour as a gift that was being given between related individuals, whether friends or kin. The Telugu men and women employed in the Preparation Department appeared deeply committed to the idea that their labour was being 'given' to their company (personified in the figure of the CEO, the general manager or their department managers) rather than sold. No one spoke of their work in the same terms used locally to describe daily waged labour (*koolipani*), contract work in local public sector industries (*udyogamu*) or employment (*gujurani*). Of course, factory work was to toil or to exert oneself in a task (*kastapadu*), and Worldwide Diamonds' workers invariably referred to themselves collectively as those who push themselves (*kastapadivallu*). But the terms with which people described this transaction constantly played down or denied the commercial or commodity aspect of their relationship with the company. Instead, they emphasized the idea that their physical and mental exertions were being given rather than sold, and they invoked the personal, intimate and familial aspects of this exchange (see also Mollona 2005).

The stock expression in the Preparation Department when workers described their relationship to the company explicitly used the Telugu verb *ichchuta*, 'to give', as in, 'we're giving our hard work and they are giving money' (*manam kastapadu istunavu vallu dubulu istunadu*). Workers spoke variously of 'giving production', giving their life (*jivitamistunannu*) and, once or twice, giving their blood (*raktamistunannu*) to the company. Some spoke of work as a constant stream or continuous flow (*dharamu*), a word that also connotes acts of giving in everyday Hindu ritual practice, such as when a ceremonial gift is preceded by the pouring of water into the hand of a recipient. Some spoke of their attachment or devotion (*asangam*) to the company. Workers frequently invoked the idiom of kinship to describe their relationship, and sometimes appealed to their managers in these terms.

What emerged here is an idea of labour as an expression of commitment to a relationship. Or, as David Graeber has written, a medium of practical or creative action through which relationships can be made (Graeber 2001: 41). Labour was not a gift object but was an activity through which workers could constitute a sphere of exchange, a sphere in which long-term reciprocal ties, moral and social bonds could become important or significant relations, and within which people can expect to be reciprocated over time with forms of protection, security and patronage (Munn 1977; Graeber 2001). This conceptualization is rooted in the particularities of place and the idioms, language and moral economy of rural South India (cf. Narotzky, this volume). Despite a history of political radicalization by Maoists and Marxists, labour relationships in this northeast corner of coastal Andhra Pradesh have remained rooted in a moral economy of patronage and clientage. This is an economy in which allegiance and obedience bring rewards, in which deference reaps favour and in which service garners protection. On the floor of the Preparation Department, however, workers' also recognized the failure of this exchange relationship, and that attempts to elicit the company's patronage through hard work were met with a refusal to reciprocate appropriately. The problem, as workers often said, was simple: 'We are giving production but we're not getting anything back'.

Sweatshop Exchanges

If anthropologists have rarely explored the diversity of economic transactions that take place in the global factory, it is because, in a critical or Marxist tradition, we have been primed to see these institutions primarily as arenas of commodity exchange, spaces in which labour is alienated from the body of the worker and commoditized. For many anthropologists, the world's economic zones and offshore factories are socially and politically important because they are spaces in which the commoditization and alienation of labour reaches some kind of contemporary apotheosis. Yet such a position can blind us to other kinds of economic transactions that might take place on these factory floors, to the ways in which 'the gift' may manifest itself in global production networks, or the ways that relationships of cooperation, exchange and hierarchy between a global labour force and their employers are constituted through acts of giving.

As I have shown, the gift is integral to the operation of a low-cost global subcontracting unit like Worldwide Diamonds, and, on the shop floor, acts of giving constantly shift between different kinds of transactional logic. Workers in the global factory, like people anywhere, as Graeber (2011: 114) would argue, are constantly shifting between 'modalities' of giving, moving backwards and forwards between different kinds of moral accounting. Just as acts of giving could express and underpin relations of cooperation and equality between workers, so too they could express and underpin relations of inequality and hierarchy between workers and their managers. On the factory floor, like any other social context, these principles often became entangled, leaving it difficult for the observer to understand, as Graeber puts it, 'which predominates' (ibid.: 115).

As Marx wrote, the fusing together of many forces into a single collective force in the modern factory could give rise to cooperation, but it could also beget a fierce rivalry between individuals, a 'stimulation of the animal spirits', which factory owners could carefully manage in ways that heightened their efficiency (Marx 1990: 443). In the wake of Foucauldian social theory (Rose 1989; Miller and Rose 1995), anthropologists of work, labour and industry in the global economy have frequently chosen to focus their analytical attention on the latter, revealing the individuating technologies of the self that have emerged out of Taylorist management practices and market-oriented calculations. Yet this problematic has overshadowed how gifts and acts of giving perform relatedness and relational social action in ways that are pivotal to the organization of labour and capital in the global economy. As I have shown here, on the floor of a global sweatshop like Worldwide Diamonds, the moral logics of cooperation, reciprocity and hierarchy that underpinned transactions between workers and their managers were vital to its success as a hyper-efficient, low-cost and competitive subcontractor. They serve as a reminder that gifts and gift giving are both something more than just 'relationships in production', and yet constitute the very fabric of commodity production; the personalized, localized and contextual economic relations they articulate are key to the organization of contemporary capitalism.

Acknowledgements

The research on which the chapter is based was funded by the UK's Economic and Social Research Council. Sections of this chapter have previously appeared in *Research in Economic Anthropology*, 2012. Thanks to two anonymous reviewers and Jens Kjaerulff for questions and comments.

References

Appadurai, A. 1981. 'Gastro-politics in Hindu South Asia', *American Ethnologist* 8(3): 494–511.

Blim, M. 1992. 'Introduction', in F.A. Rothstein and M. Blim (eds), *Anthropology and the Global Factory: Studies of the New Industrialisation in the Late Twentieth Century*. New York: Bergin and Garvey.

Burawoy, M. 1982. *Manufacturing Consent: Changes in the Labor Process under Monopoly Capitalism*. Chicago: University of Chicago Press.

——— 1985. *The Politics of Production: Factory Regimes under Capitalism and Socialism*. London: Verso.

Calıskan, K., and M. Callon. 2009. 'Economization, Part 1: Shifting Attention from the Economy towards Processes of Economization', *Economy and Society* 38(3): 369–398.

Coleman, S. 2004. 'The Charismatic Gift', *Journal of the Royal Anthropological Institute* 10(2): 421–442.

Cross, J. 2010. 'Neoliberalism as Unexceptional: Economic Zones and the Everyday Precariousness of Working Life in South India', *Critique of Anthropology* 30(4): 355–373.

——— 2011a. 'Detachment as a Corporate Ethic: Materialising CSR in the Diamond Supply Chain', *Focaal* 62: 34–46.

——— 2011b. 'Technological Intimacy: Re-engaging with Gender and Technology in The Global Factory', *Ethnography* 13: 119–143.

——— 2013. 'The Coming of the Corporate Gift', *Theory, Culture and Society* 31(2–3): 121–145.

——— 2014. *Dream Zones: Anticipating Capitalism and Development in India*. London: Pluto Press.

Fuller, C.J. 2004. *The Camphor Flame: Popular Hinduism and Society in India*. Princeton: Princeton University Press.

Goffman, E. 1961. *Asylums*. Harmondsworth: Penguin.

Graeber, D. 2001. *Towards an Anthropological Theory of Value: The False Coin of Our Own Dreams*. New York: Palgrave.

——— 2010. 'On the Moral Grounds of Economic Relations: A Maussian Approach'. Working Papers Series No. 6. Online Publication, Open Anthropology Cooperative Press. Retrieved 30 September 2014 from: http://openanthcoop.net/press/2010/11/17/on-the-moral-grounds-of-economic-relations/

——— 2011. *Debt: The First 5,000 Years*. New York: Melville House.

Gregory, C.A. 1982. *Gifts and Commodities*. London: Academic Press.

——— 1997. *Savage Money: The Anthropology and Politics of Commodity Exchange*. Amsterdam: Harwood Academic.

Harvey, D. 1990. *The Condition of Postmodernity*. London: Blackwell.

——— 2005. *A Brief History of Neoliberalism*. Oxford: Oxford University Press.

Hewamanne, S. 2003. 'Performing "Dis-respectability": New Tastes, Cultural Practices, and Identity Performances by Sri Lanka's Free Trade Zone Garment-factory Workers', *Cultural Dynamics* 15(1): 71–101.

Lynch, C. 1999. 'Good Girls or Juki Girls? Learning and Identity in Garment Factories', *Anthropology of Work Review* 19(3): 18–22.

Marx, K. 1990. *Capital: A Critique of Political Economy*, Vol. 1. London: Penguin.

Mauss, M. 1966. *The Gift*, trans. I. Cunnison. London: Cohen and West.

Miller, P., and N. Rose. 1995. 'Production, Identity, and Democracy', *Theory, Culture and Society* 24(3): 427–467.

Mills, M.B. 1999. *Consuming Desires, Contested Selves: Thai Women in the Global Labour Force*. New Brunswick, NJ: Rutgers University Press.

Mollona, M. 2005. 'Gifts of Labour: Steel Production and Technological Imagination in an Area of Urban Deprivation, Sheffield, UK', *Critique of Anthropology* 25(2): 177–198.

———— 2009. *Made in Sheffield: An Ethnography of Industrial Work and Politics.* Oxford: Berghahn Books.

Munn, N.D. 1977. 'The Spatiotemporal Transformations of Gawa Canoes', *Journal de la Societe des Oceanistes* 33(54): 39–53.

Ngai, P. 2005. *Made in China: Factory Workers in a Global Workplace.* Durham, NC: Duke University Press.

Ong, A. 1987. *Spirits of Resistance and Capitalist Discipline.* New York: State University of New York Press.

———— 2006. *Neoliberalism as Exception.* Durham, NC: Duke University Press.

Osella, F., and C. Osella. 1996. 'Articulation of Physical and Social Bodies in Kerala', *Contributions to Indian Sociology* 30(1): 37–68.

Parry, J.P. 2000. 'The "Crisis of Corruption" and "the Idea of India": A Worm's Eye View', in Italo Pardo (ed.), *Morals of Legitimacy: Between Agency and the System.* Oxford: Berghahn Books, pp. 27–55.

Parry, J.P., M. Mollona, and G. De Neve (eds). 2009. *Industrial Work and Life: An Anthropological Reader.* Oxford: Berg.

Prentice, R. 2008. '"Thiefing a Chance": Moral Meanings of Theft in a Trinidadian Garment Factory', in K.E. Browne and B.L. Milgram (eds), *Economics and Morality: Anthropological Approaches.* New York: Altamira Press, pp. 123–141.

Rose, N. 1989. *Governing the Soul: The Shaping of the Private Self.* London: Free Association Press.

Ross, A. 2009. *Nice Work if You Can Get It: Life and Labor in Precarious Times.* New York: New York University Press.

Salzinger, L. 2003. *Genders in Production: Making Workers in Mexico's Global Factories.* Berkeley: University of California Press.

Strathern, M. 1991. 'Partners and Consumers: Making Relations Visible', *New Literary History* 22(3): 581–601.

Strümpell, C. 2008. '"We Work Together, We Eat Together": Conviviality and Modernity in a Company Settlement in South Orissa', *Contributions to Indian Sociology* 42(3): 351–381.

Tsing, A. 2009. 'Supply Chains and the Human Condition', *Rethinking Marxism* 21(2): 148–176.

Wolf, D. 1992. *Factory Daughters: Gender, Household Dynamics and Rural Industrialisation in Java.* Berkeley: University of California Press.

Wright, M. 2006. *Disposable Women and Other Myths of Global Capitalism.* London: Routledge.

Yang, M.M. 1989. 'The Gift Economy and State Power in China', *Comparative Studies in Society and History* 31(1): 25–54.

2

Unveiling the Work of the Gift

Neoliberalism and the Flexible Margins of the Nation-State

Tinna Grétarsdóttir

In 2000, at the Canadian Museum of Civilization, a cast of Ásmundur Sveinsson's sculpture *The First White Mother in America* was unveiled during the opening event of the Icelandic millennium celebration in North America to commemorate the discovery of America by the Vikings. A gift to Canada on behalf of the Icelandic people, the cast portrays Guðríður Þorbjarnardóttir standing in the belly of a ship, holding her son Snorri Þorfinnsson high on her left shoulder. Guðríður and Snorri are figures in the Saga of the Greenlanders and the Saga of Erik the Red, in which Guðríður sails to Vinland (claimed to be North America) and gives birth to her son. A perfect symbol for Icelandic–North American relations, a cast of the sculpture *The First White Mother in America* was shipped to North America once before, sixty years ago, where it was unveiled in New York as part of the World's Fair exhibit in 1939.

As it turned out, the gift of the cast to the Canadian nation auspiciously aligned with Snorri's one-thousandth birthday. A wide variety of guests from the Icelandic-Canadian community were invited to the special celebration at the Canadian Museum of Civilization, and politicians from both Iceland and Canada made special appearances. Icelandic-Canadian astronaut Bjarni Tryggvason even appeared in full gear at the unveiling, 'representing the new millennium's explorer' (Isfeld 2000: 3). With the help of two Canadian children, the Icelandic prime minister unveiled the sculpture and presented it to Canada's prime minister. He used the occasion to announce

Iceland's plan to open an embassy in Canada the following year, and thereby strengthen the formal ties between the two nations.

As at all proper birthday parties, the event was celebrated with a rendition of the birthday song – 350 schoolchildren were joined by Iceland's soprano soloist, Diddú, in singing 'Happy Birthday' to Snorri in Icelandic. Guests enjoyed a piece of the super-sized birthday cake, and the schoolchildren were given tee-shirts imprinted with the slogan 'Iceland Naturally', which they wore during the ceremony (see Isfeld 2000; Isfeld and Gústafsson 2000). The tee-shirts were part of a presentation that marked the formal launch of the website for the Iceland Naturally nation-branding programme, which was meant to 'build a relationship between Iceland and American and Canadian consumers interested in Iceland and its products'.[1] Discovery and exploration were key themes in strengthening the link between Iceland and North American Icelanders. At the unveiling of the cast of the sculpture, the transatlantic nature of the Icelandic-Canadian ethnic group was emphasized on medallions, which featured two engravings: on one side a representation of the sculpture honouring Iceland's past explorers, on the other a representation of Bjarni Tryggvason in his space suit. The medallions featuring these 'two great role models' were given to the audience at the ceremony (Isfeld and Gústafsson 2000: 1), and Guðríður Þorbjarnardóttir and Bjarni Tryggvason were offered as icons, representing the Icelandic entrepreneurial, daring spirit. The medallions were later presented to select members of the Icelandic-Canadian community to honour its many hard workers for their 'efforts to build connections between Iceland and Canadian Icelanders' (Cadham 2008). The ceremony continued into the evening with a reception and dinner at the Chateau Laurier, a luncheon for members of the business community and a week-long programme marketing Icelandic products by Iceland Naturally (Isfeld 2000).

In this chapter I argue that the ceremonial presentation of the gift is a site of interconnecting social spaces where the work of transnational practices, neoliberal politics and identity takes place. I explore this argument by examining ethnic networking between Icelanders and Canadians of Icelandic decent, particularly the ways in which the neoliberal economic restructuring pursued by Iceland from 1994 to 2008, including the branding and marketing of Iceland, relied on personal connections and ethnic networking.[2] Such restructuring was manifest in the implementation of programmes of privatization, the deregulation of the state and the adoption of a range of discourses and practices that were used to reform and direct individuals, not just within Iceland but also across national borders – Icelanders and

Canadians of Icelandic decent were empowered in order that they become enterprising, flexible and creative, as is appropriate to the neoliberal project (see Rose 1999).

Based on ethnographic field research conducted periodically in Canada and Iceland throughout the period between 2003 and 2008,[3] I explore the transfer of the gift from Iceland to Canada not merely as a device to create and promote Iceland and the Icelandic presence in Canada, but more significantly as a technology that allows Iceland to enter a Canadian community in order to influence identities, ethnic bodies and relations of power that operate beyond the state. The unveiling of the gift carved out a space to affect the behaviour and activities of ethnic bodies, as well as mobilize communal volunteer work and lobbying across borders. The changing needs of nation building in the course of the neoliberal restructuring in Iceland involved inclusionary practices towards Icelandic-Canadians, as well as rendering the margins of the Icelandic nation-state more flexible (see Das and Poole 2004). The gift-giving ceremony is, thus, entangled with transnational politics and reformed political and economic conditions in Iceland, conditions that hold hands with reimagined, nationalized accounts of Icelandic identity, as reflected in the discourse of *útrás* (conquest) and the stretching of the margins of the nation-state. The cast of Sveinsson's sculpture produces transnational obligations intended to create and foster a set of ethnic relations and subjectivities, which may be converted into other resources. The gift, therefore, amounts to investment with a desired rate of return, within what Garsten (this volume) refers to as 'an economy of connection'.

Gift exchange and the pursuit of flexible capitalism are thus analysed in the multifarious context of neoliberal politics and market expansion, ethnic networking and voluntary work, all of which is entangled with opportunism and emotions. Like other chapters in this volume (e.g. Cross, Garsten), the chapter reveals how gift exchange and economic relations are intertwined. It shows how the Icelandic neoliberal project in Canada is aided by the 'work' of gift exchange embedded in a specific cultural and historical context, and intended to set in motion an interplay of actors, connections, symbols, claims and intentions that shift among local, national and transnational spheres (cf. Knox, this volume).

In order to develop this interpretation, I draw on anthropological literature on exchange, particularly as it extends from Nancy Munn's ethnography of Gawan participation in the ceremonial gift exchange of the *kula* ring in the Massim region (Munn 1986). I propose that the presentation of the gift of *The First White Mother in America*

resembles certain aspects of Gawan *kula* exchange, in which participants sought to 'act upon the mind[s] . . . of the other[s]' (Munn 1986:
56), 'draw others into their own intentionalities', 'spread fame, [and]
extend their networks' (Thomas 2001: 9). In Munn's study, exchanges
are central to value transformation and community viability. Gift
exchanges connect people into spatiotemporal relationships and can
bring participants reputation and influence (Munn 1986: 56, 115;
Miller 2001; Thomas 2001). Thus, exchanges can be seen to create a
social network or a social infrastructure (Miller 2001: 151–52; Thomas
2001: 9; Munn 1986). Moreover, while the gift itself can signify the
agency of another, it also constitutes, in and of itself, a social actor
(Miller 2001: 151). Following such leads, I argue that the Icelandic
gift of *The First White Mother in America* serves as a kind of 'trap',
intended to 'entrap the will of others' into a set of social relationships and exchanges (ibid.:151–52). A political and social function of
the gift of *The First White Mother in America* which this perspective
allows us to appreciate is the distinctive form of affective action that
this gift sets in motion within a particular 'social-relational matrix'
(Gell 1998: 7; Miller 2001: 151–52; see also Thomas 2001). It captures
the Icelandic-Canadian community's imagination, and incites various
types of action, organization and recognition tying in with Iceland's
neoliberal agenda.

Stretching the Margins of the Icelandic Nation-State

Tracking the management, the expectations and the anticipated results
of the ceremonial presentation of the sculpture in Canada necessi-
tates linking the gift – its transaction and movement across space –
to state power and neoliberal capitalism in Iceland. I will begin by
discussing the political changes in Iceland since the early 1990s,
which occurred with the aggressive intervention of market logic
and new modes of governing and social engineering (Ásmundsson,
Lárusson and Grétarsdóttir 2011: 3; see also Rose 1999). Over nearly
two decades, neoliberal ambitions transformed the country's socio-
economic structures until those structures finally experienced a
severe and abrupt collapse in 2008. As one professor at the London
School of Economics put it, 'No western country in peacetime has
crashed so quickly and so badly' (Sanger 2008). In 1994, Iceland
became a member of the EEA (European Economic Area) and, after
that, decentralization, privatization, entrepreneurial and performance
management were noticeable parts of governmental reform policies.

Freedom and the well-being of the people would be guaranteed by the competitive global marketplace rather than the state (Árnason, Hafsteinsson and Grétarsdóttir 2007).

This restructuring manifested itself in privatization programmes (the fishing industry, telecommunications, banks, education) and state deregulation according to neoliberal doctrines. The legal spheres of the market and tax system were transformed in order to create a more favourable business climate. Corporation tax, for example, was reduced to one of the lowest in Europe. Greater class division also emerged during this time, forming a new, 'super rich' elite that was listed for a number of years on the Forbes list of the richest people in the world. The stock market developed rapidly, and Icelandic investment abroad sharply increased. Foreign investment in the country was mainly based on heavy industry, such as aluminium production.

Iceland, with its approximately 315,000 inhabitants, intended to make itself visible on an international scale by participating in the global market. The aim was to reconstruct the country into a 'global financial centre' (Ásgrímsson 2005) as promoted by political leaders and business entrepreneurs. Icelanders were urged to be 'both creative Icelander[s] and efficacious cosmopolitan[s]' (Grímsson 2006). Government officials consistently stressed that Icelanders had to conform to the new global economy, gain ground in the neoliberal global community and 'exploit the opportunities that lay ahead of them – or otherwise be left behind' (Ásmundsson, Lárusson and Grétarsdóttir 2011: 5; see also Ásgrímsson 2004). Iceland was struggling for global visibility – in other words, it was in the midst of 'entering the world map', or *komast á kortið* as the Icelandic phrase goes.

The course of creating new economic opportunities and relations across national borders led to expansion of the Icelandic Ministry of Foreign Affairs. In addition to opening numerous new embassies, Iceland competed for a seat on the UN Security Council for 2009/10. Moreover, increasing funds were put into nation branding, as the country was promoted as a destination for businesses and mass tourism. The expectations of governmental goals, in terms of entering the global scene, were high, as can be seen in its attempt to secure a seat on the UN Security Council. Iceland was 'ready to take on an active role for international peace and security'.[4] However, Iceland lost its bid and was defeated in the elections.

In the 1990s, building and strengthening relations with Canada became a priority. In 1998, the Canada/Iceland EFTA, a free trade agreement, was already in the pipeline.[5] The Icelandic foreign ministry opened a consulate general office in Winnipeg in 1999 and an embassy in Ottawa in 2001. Beyond tangible and concrete efforts to increase ties with Canada, Iceland urgently hoped to 'wake the giant', as one official at the Icelandic Ministry of Foreign Affairs told me in an interview – wake the old Icelandic-Canadian community in order to tune them toward Icelandic culture, and to use them to further boost the Icelandic economy.

Icelandic North Americans were viewed as a ready-made market, and as a canal by which Iceland could enter the North American market as a whole. The 'major task' as stated by the Icelandic president in New York in 1996, was to: 'motivat[e] this large community . . . [I]t has been rightly pointed out that we can learn a great deal from the way that people of Irish and Italian descent here in the USA have taken advantage of their connections with their mother countries in order to boost trade, strengthen interests and weave a versatile cultural and social tapestry' (Grímsson 1996).

Comparing Icelandic-Canadians with the Italians or the Irish, however, is tricky. Unlike the Italians, the Icelandic community in Canada has not been replenished with new immigrant generations from Iceland. The community is composed mainly of third-, fourth- and fifth-generation descendants of Icelandic immigrants, and has a limited history of renewal of its Icelandic connection through the fresh perspective of new Icelandic immigrants to Canada. Thus, many in the community oppose any direct comparison with other groups, such as the Italians in Canada, who 'were here in great numbers prior to the Second World War, and have arrived in huge numbers since the 1950s', as one of my respondents stated. He went on, 'We are an old, old community, from way back'.

Canadians of Icelandic decent are 'well assimilated', and their relationship with the old homeland can be characterized as nostalgic and sentimental. Icelandic identity in Canada is tied to family roots and routes in Canada through historical landscapes, migrant trauma, kinship, family narratives and literature, to name a few (see Brydon 1991; Neijmann 1997; Eyford 2003; Bertram 2010, 2011). Narratives and images of Iceland, as well as notions of Icelandicness, are often rooted in nineteenth- to early twentieth-century Iceland. Those who have participated in Icelandic organizations and things Icelandic in the community have traditionally been people who are in their fifties or older. One of the main concerns of the Icelandic-Canadian community is to get younger generations interested in their heritage and involved in the community's activities. But getting young people interested in Iceland has also appealed to the Icelandic state in recent years. In a letter of recommendation for the Iceland registry project, an Icelandic official at the Ministry of Foreign Affairs makes this clear:

> Although it is not possible to presume that all those who are registered will become eagerly Iceland-inclined in every matter, such a 'conscious' group is indisputably a great support and could certainly become a source for investments and the flow of capital to the country. It should be underlined that the awareness of young Western Icelander's [a term frequently used for North Americans of Icelandic descent in Iceland] origins is fading, and what might take place with this registry is to reach out to the last generation before these people simply disappear into a North America sea of nations.[6]

People of the younger generation describe themselves as having three, four or even five different ethnic backgrounds to choose from – or, as Sara Loftson stated, 'I am quintessential Canadian, a cultural fruit salad with an ounce of Ukrainian, a pinch of Polish, a little bit of Lebanese and inch of Icelandic' (Loftson 2007: 32). Thus, revitalizing the Icelandic community, renewing transnational relations, 'updating' and modernizing Icelandic-Canadian identity for the sake of contemporary, commercial and corporate Iceland has been an ongoing agenda of the Icelandic government since the late 1990s. The hope is to highlight that 'inch' of Icelandicness and make it particularly relevant to Canadians with a degree of Icelandic heritage. Various programmes have been initiated and funds granted by the Icelandic government to map and reach the Icelandic-Canadian community and revitalize their Icelandic identity. The ceremonial presentation of the sculpture *The First White Mother in America* is one outcome of this work.

Útrás: Narratives of Conquest

At a press conference in 1999, within the thematic framework of 'Reunion', the Icelandic government announced that the moment of the millennium would be used to, first, promote Iceland and celebrate the common history of Iceland and North America by commemorating Leifur Eiríksson's discovery of America; and, second, strengthen relations between Icelanders and people of Icelandic descent in North America (PMO 2000). As a result of this planning and preparation, the Leifur Eiríksson Millennium Commission of Iceland was created and named after the ninth-century Norse explorer of the

Icelandic Sagas. The Leifur Eiríksson millennium celebrations in North America and the launching of the Iceland Naturally marketing programme were together the most extensive promotional ventures ever carried out by the Icelandic government in North America.

The period from the early 1990s until the collapse of Iceland's economy in late 2008 will be referred to in Iceland's future history books as the time of the 'Icelandic conquest' or, in Icelandic, the era of *útrás* (see Helgason 2006). During this period, expressions such as 'incursion', 'go viking' and 'gaining ground on foreign shores' were 'used in governmental and public discourses in relation to various activities of the Icelandic state, business entrepreneurs, and other cosmopolitans participating in the new global economy' (Ásmundsson, Lárusson and Grétarsdóttir 2011: 6). The Icelandic media was imbued with 'success stories' of the international enterprises of Icelanders, especially in business and banking (ibid.). Further, Icelandic activities on foreign shores were presented as 'conquests'. The 'conquistadors' were 'often referred to as a new generation of "modern Vikings"' (ibid.: 6; Helgason 2006: 6–7). These modern Vikings became visible in Canada in business sectors and, as one CEO remarked at the opening of an office of the bank Landsbanki in Winnipeg in 2007, 'One might say that we are offering Western Icelanders a chance to take advantage of our international financial experience and expertise, and at the same time to be part of the positive development of Icelandic enterprises and the Icelandic economy'.[7] The bank built close connections with the Icelandic-Canadian community, funded several community events and recruited some community members who aided the bank in lining up potential clients.

The rising rhetoric of *útrás* in Iceland was used to portray the nation's global enterprises and the spirit of entrepreneurialism, which had been elevated to the level of a cultural characteristic of Icelandic society (Ásmundsson, Lárusson and Grétarsdóttir 2011). The term *útrás* became associated with discourses on 'heroic' Vikings and expeditions during the Icelandic settlement period. Such expeditions are associated with an image of the nation's ancestors as essentially independent, innovative, resourceful and global (see PMO 2008). In other words, the notion of *útrás* referred to modern Icelanders who were, like their ancestors, risk-takers bursting with creative enterprise (see Grímsson 2006). Reinventing national narratives was one key feature in the process of managing the nation, reimagining and representing national identity while shaping a globalized, neoliberal nation-state. *Útrás* was used to refer to everything from Icelandic corporations opening factories in China, Bulgaria and elsewhere to

Icelandic musicians performing concerts abroad. *Útrás*, however, was not as widely used in the context of foreign-born immigrants in Iceland, or of the flow of migrant workers to the country during the period. These populations were mainly excluded from the discourse of *útrás*, and were not included in the image of flexible, risk-taking, modern-day Vikings seeking new shores. Of course, the racial implications are obvious: immigrants to Iceland cannot be included in the narrative of contemporary Viking conquest. Thus, while the discourse of *útrás* excluded immigrant populations residing in Iceland, it nevertheless did include populations outside its borders, namely Canadian people of Icelandic descent.

This new meaning of *útrás* – connected to entrepreneurial success abroad appearing extensively in newspaper headlines and book titles in the late 1990s early 2000s – did not appear in Icelandic dictionaries until in 2002.[8] Recent dictionaries (see also Helgason 2006) give examples such as 'Icelandic businesses in *útrás*'[9] and '*útrás* of enterprise'.[10] But in older dictionaries, the meaning of the term is 'mouth (of a river)' (*ós (vatnsfalls)*), 'runoff' (*afrennsli*) and 'bolt' (*útstreymi*).[11] Other definitions of *útrás* in Icelandic dictionaries are 'rushing out of a fortress' (*framrás úr vígi*), 'canal' (*farvegur*) and 'onrush/outburst' (*framrás*).[12] Where *útrás* meant 'rushing out of a fortress', it often referred to those who are on the defensive rather than those on the attack, but also to those who strike as part of a defence mechanism (Helgason 2006: 6–7). Thus, the discourse of *útrás* generally depicted Iceland's new global economy and the country's domestic reconfigurations as defensive strikes when there were no alternatives in order to handle the globalizing pressures that 'hit' the country. This definition can be spotted in the statement by the Minister of Foreign Affairs: 'It is a fact that globalization has just begun and we need to learn quickly how to proceed down that path into the future. We have no choice. We are back to our historic beginnings of Icelandic conquests – we go Viking again but use modern methods' (Ásgrímsson 2004; Helgason 2006).

The millennium celebration in Canada played an important role in pulling together constellations of ethnic, economic and political networking in line with these new narratives of conquest and the national profile. The distinctive characteristics of the *útrás* rhetoric tapped into the ethnic pride of people of Icelandic descent in North America. Icelandic-Canadians and their descendants, who often used to be shunned for leaving Iceland, were now presented, at home and abroad, as part of the nation's extended family in public discourse. Instead of characterizing North Americans of Icelandic heritage as 'deserters', they were rebranded as entrepreneurial and daring – in line with the rhetoric of *útrás* (conquest). The government promotional booklet, 'Discovery: Iceland's Amazing Adventure' (GoI 2002), which was published in the wake of the millennium celebrations, included not just Icelanders but more importantly the Icelandic diaspora in North America as people of *útrás*. In the booklet, Canadians of Icelandic decent are presented as people who, in an unfavourable climate of natural catastrophes and economic hardship, were driven by 'ever-restless Viking spirit . . . to become explorers of new lands' (ibid.: 10).

The notions of independence and entrepreneurship that lay at the core of the *útrás* discourse in Iceland resembled long-established Icelandic-Canadian narratives, from early twentieth-century historical accounts that created the Icelandic-Canadian identity in the New World (see Neijmann 1997; Wolf 2001). References to ancestral Viking heritage were used by immigrants and their successors to enhance racial and symbolic capital in the wider Canadian sociopolitical landscape dominated by Anglo-Saxon culture (Ward 2000; Bertram 2010). Narratives of Icelandic-Canadians display them as people who, like their mythic ancestors, are people of independence, freedom, liberty and enterprise (Neijmann 1997: 77; see also Beck 1943; Lindal 1944; Walters 1953). In the same 'spirit of independence and progress' (Beck 1943: 10) as their ancestors – the original settlers of Iceland – they too, with 'Viking blood in [their] veins', were people who could 'seek new horizons' (Salverson 1942: 2).

Interestingly, contemporary Icelandic historians seldom refer to the Nordic settlers of Iceland as Vikings. In fact, more often than not, historians describe Iceland's settlers as farmers. The Icelandic meaning of the term refers to Norse sea voyagers who pursued mercantilism, raids and pillaging.[13] Some scholars have pointed out that one reason to reject the idea that Vikings settled in Iceland is that that there were no valuable resources to pillage there (see Björnsson 2005).

It seems that modern Icelanders, however, accept the idea of being the Vikings' successors, as is reflected in the increasing use of the term in headlines in the Icelandic newspaper *Morgunblaðið*: 'Incursion of Modern Vikings in UK', 'Invasion of Icelandic Bands into New York', 'Icelandic Compositions go Viking'.[14] Young artists organized art events overseas with the theme 'Berlin Invasion' and, when foreign media covered the 'Next-generation Viking Invasion' on Icelandic business activities overseas,[15] it hit the news in Iceland as a sign of success. After the collapse of the Icelandic economy, the Icelandic use of the term 'Viking' as raiders becomes even more salient, both globally and locally.

It seems, then, that we are witnessing what Berlant refers to as the 'hack[ing] away at the hyphen between the nation and the state', which 'require[s] the development of new technologies of patriotism that keep the nation at the center of the public's identification' (Berlant 1998: 174; see also Árnason, Hafsteinsson and Grétarsdóttir 2007). These technologies emerged in official and unofficial idioms where the entrepreneurial and international affairs of Icelanders were referred to metaphorically as 'conquests', 'going Viking' and 'gaining ground on foreign shores'. The subjective techniques of the neoliberal turn were put forth not as breaks from tradition (as in Asian nations; see Ong 2006), but in consonance with Icelandic historical and cultural heritage (see Grétarsdóttir, Ásmundsson and Lárusson 2014). Thus, Icelanders reimagined themselves and were reimagined into being, not so much by rediscovering their golden past and their historical cultural heritage, but by creating it as the necessary ground for their neoliberal project. The discourse of *útrás* served as an important part of the new order: a new technology of patriotism that simultaneously provided a 'powerful obstacle to the formation of a counter-hegemonic cultural politics' (McKay 1994: 306). *Útrás*, with creative performance and entrepreneurship at its core, appeared as a central narrative that was needed to orient the people toward the idea of a new global and performance-driven economy. Whereas the market logic penetrated politics and other social sectors in Iceland, *útrás* was the idiom that configured public rhetoric and established 'a political and social "commonsense," based on a commandeering of history and identity' that prevented a critical dialogue with the past as well as a realistic understanding of the present (ibid.: 295).

Given the normalization and wide utilization of the term, as well as the depoliticized connotation it acquired, the rhetoric of *útrás* can be seen as instrumental in advocating neoliberal policies, in particular those that lacked support. Those who did not harmonize with *útrás* were pressured to believe that neoliberal restructuring granted them prosperity, regardless of whether it clashed with their ethical and moral values, duties and obligations, rights and justice. 'Corporate nationalism' (Mackey 2002: 123), and the reinvention and celebration of the Icelandic heritage 'of discovery and enterprise', were not just in play at home but also abroad in Canada, carving out new subjects that were not within the conventional national space. The reimaginings of the nation, which rested on inherited qualities, were also used abroad in the process of (re)shaping and (re)constructing a sense of diasporic identity and commonalities between Icelanders and people of Icelandic descent in Canada.

Sculpting Transnational Practices

While renewing the relationship with the Icelandic-Canadian community and mobilizing it to collaborate in commemorating the one-thousandth anniversary of the discovery of North America, Icelandic representatives and officials stressed the indestructible nature of kinship ties, history and common heritage. For instance, the Icelandic president stated at the Icelandic festival in Gimli in 1997:

> I have used the concept 'the Icelandic community' to indicate the broad association of all people of Icelandic descent . . . Our common sense of belonging to one community is indeed stronger than any formalities that determine where we pay taxes or how we go through passport control at international airports. To strengthen the sense of family among all people of Icelandic descent is indeed a part of my mandate, to offer the service of the Icelandic Presidency to you all. (Grímsson 1997)

The Icelandic president repeatedly stressed these kinship ties in speeches he gave while visiting communities across North America in 1997 and 1999. But, as the quotation above indicates, borders and foreign citizenship of third-, fourth- and fifth-generation Icelandic-Canadians are portrayed as simple and pale formalities in comparison with the timeless and borderless communal ties between Icelanders. Moreover, on several occasions, the president reminded the Icelandic-Canadian community of the kindred spirits of the nation, stating, 'Both our societies were created by people who crossed the ocean to settle in a new land. The spirit of discovery, the energy of the pioneers, became the bulwarks of our civilization' (Grímsson 1999).

While preparing for the millennium celebration, governmental representatives and members of the Leifur Eiríksson Millennium Commission of Iceland called for meetings with leaders in Icelandic North American communities in order to mobilize people and establish a formal forum for a working relationship between their organizations. 'It all started in the year 1997 when the president of Iceland, Ólafur Ragnar Grímsson visited New Iceland, Canada, and asked us how we could strengthen the relationship between the countries and how we wanted to celebrate the millennium', said one

of the community leaders explaining the sudden presence and interest of the Icelandic governmental agents in revitalizing links between
the communities. 'The president asked us to get a group together of
movers and shakers and do something significant in the year 2000',
said another community leader, commenting on the community's
meeting with the Icelandic president and government officials.

The Icelandic government planned various events for the millennium celebration, including a re-enactment of the Viking expedi-
tion of Leifur Eiríksson to numerous harbours in North America;
a two-year touring Viking exhibition; a touring Icelandic Saga manuscript exhibit; a touring theoretical performance titled *The Saga
of Guðríður*; and the presentation of Sveinsson's sculpture as a gift
from Iceland to the Canadian people. Manitoban farmer David
Gislason originally proposed the idea of the gift to Icelandic authorities. Gislason was one of the 'movers and shakers' in the community, recruited by the Icelandic government to cooperate in planning,
funding and executing the Icelandic millennium project in Canada.
He stated in the community's paper that the millennium, for most
of us, 'was as yet only a far distant calendar date which we had not
given serious thought to, beyond the consideration that our computers might crash on 1 January, 2000. That all changed' (Gislason
1999: 1). Gislason became the chairman of the Icelandic-Canadian
Millennium-125 Commission, which was formed in the course of the
mobilization by the Icelandic authorities to recruit the community to
collaborate with them and the Icelandic Leifur Eiríksson Millennium
Commission in executing the celebration. Thus, the Millennium-125
Commission, piloted by leaders of the Icelandic-Canadian community, was established as a reaction to Icelandic governmental plans
in Canada. While the Millennium-125 Commission was a product
of the Icelandic state's mobilization, it created and advocated its
own mission by using the opportunity to simultaneously celebrate
125 years of Icelandic settlement in Manitoba.

The Millennium-125 Commission worked closely with Icelandic
government officials in Canada, the United States and Iceland,
and operated as an intermediary between the Icelandic state, on the
one hand, and the Icelandic-Canadian community on the other. The
commission, which was granted charitable status under the Income
Tax Act in Canada, acted as an extension of the Icelandic consulate in
Winnipeg. It played a crucial role as it formally performed and represented the Icelandic millennium proposal to the Canadian government
when an occasion required that the presence of the Icelandic government be downplayed. It played a crucial role in applying for funds to

the Millennium Bureau of Canada, as the Canadian government only funded Canadian projects. The celebration associated with the unveiling of *The First White Mother in America* was one of the Millennium-125 projects to which the Millennium Bureau of Canada allocated grants.

Gislason's idea to erect a cast of Sveinsson's sculpture as part of the Millennium celebration can be traced to his visit to Iceland in 1994, when he attended the convention of the Icelandic National League of Iceland. During his visit, Gislason attended a ceremony in Skagafjörður, north Iceland, when the president of Iceland, Vigdís Finnbogadóttir, unveiled a cast of *The First White Mother in America* at Glaumbær, where, according to the Saga, Guðríður and her family lived after returning from their travels.

The locals in the region of Skagafjörður had appealed to people of Icelandic descent in North America to help contribute financially to the erection of a cast of the sculpture in commemoration of the fiftieth anniversary of the Icelandic republic in 1994. Icelandic Sagas and Saga characters are today increasingly staged as part of the cultural tourist landscape in Iceland. Guðríður and her family have indeed become heroes of the region Skagafjörður, attracting tourists to the museum at Glaumbær, not least among whom are North Americans of Icelandic descent.

In an interview, Gislason told me that he had been emotionally moved by the presentation of the sculpture in Skagafjörður and, at the same time, he became fascinated with Guðríður's story, which he (re)introduced to the Icelandic-Canadian community under the heading, 'The Spell of Guðríður' (see Gislason 2002: 8). His reactions to the sculpture have been reported in newspaper interviews both in Canada and in Iceland:

> Her story is so powerful and ties us well together, . . . [the story reflects] a strong thread in the destiny of the Icelandic people. Guðríður lived with her husband for 3 years in Canada . . . There she gave birth to Snorri, who we, Western Icelanders, relate to. He is the first Icelander born in Canada. Later they move to Iceland, and Þorfinnur [her husband] buys Glaumbær.
>
> The statue at the church of Glaumbær is a gift from Western Icelanders to the Icelandic nation . . . [Another] statue will go to Ottawa and be presented as a gift from the Icelandic nation to people of Icelandic descent in North America. So tell me if you don't find it a strange destiny. (Sæberg 1999)

According to Gislason, the sculpture was not only symbolic because it represented transnational ties 'that bind us as a people from Iceland

Fig. 2.1 *Reproduction of* The First White Mother in America *by Ásmundur Sveinsson in the cemetery at Glaumbær, Iceland. Photograph courtesy of the Skagafjörður Heritage Museum/Hjörtur H.*

to Canada' but because people of Icelandic descent in North America were involved in presenting and placing a cast of the sculpture in Glaumbær (Gislason 2002: 8).

As the planning of the millennium celebration began to unfold, Gislason, who is fluent in Icelandic, an ambitious translator and a passionate reader, introduced and translated the story of Guðríður in the community newspaper *Lögberg-Heimskringla*. The sculpture, according to Gislason, links Iceland to Canada and attests to 'the reality of the Vinland adventurers of a thousand years ago. These were not only the fierce Viking warriors that we all visualize . . . [but] also women . . . [who bore] children [here]' (Gislason 1999: 6).

As Bertram (2011) has argued, migrant/child-centred narratives inhabit an essential place in Icelandic-Canadian oral narratives of the settlement years. Thus, the female-focused narrative of Guðríður and her child, which is indeed an account of a migrant experience, although an ancient one, fit with more recent narratives focusing on the pioneers and the settlement years. As stated above, it was the more humanitarian aspects of 'ancient settlement', depicted in the notion of woman and child as opposed to the image of fierce Vikings that Gislason wanted to highlight. Such an emphasis on humanitarianism is in line with portrayals of migration and settlement accounts of the Canadian West, as characterized by the heritage campaigns since the implementation of Canada's multiculturalism policy (Bertram 2010; 2011). Thus, the story of Guðríður, represented by the sculpture, fits nicely into today's models of national heritage recollections and narratives of pioneering.

The revival of the characters Guðríður and Snorri, in Canada as well as in Iceland, was also a strategic decision because of the contested nationality (Icelandic or Norwegian) of Leifur Eiríksson, who is generally recognized to have discovered the New World. This has been a serious concern for the Icelandic community in Canada as well as in Iceland, and, as a matter of fact, has entered parliamentary proposed resolutions in Iceland.[16] As already mentioned, Icelandic-Canadians, as well as other people of Nordic descent in North America, have historically promoted their role in the colonization of the Americas through Vikings and Leifur Eiríksson. While the Viking subject has been celebrated in North American popular culture, the Norse legacy in the history of the New World was relatively unnoticed until the archaeological discovery of the finds at L'Anse aux Meadows in the 1960s (Fitzhugh and Ward 2000: 353).

Thus, for many in the Icelandic-Canadian community, Guðríður's story has a significant resonance as it offers a realistic option to promote the discovery of Canada and the 'Norse legacy' in the wider public Canadian space since Norse settlement has now been acknowledged in museum exhibitions, publications and tourism. While the nationality of Leifur Eiríksson remained controversial, Guðríður became an ancestral mother to both Icelanders and Icelandic-Canadians. 'Everyone knows about Leif the Lucky; children are still named after him here, now we also have Guðríður and Snorri. They will also become a symbol for many Canadians', said one of my respondents. Some even argued that Guðríður and Snorri have replaced Leifur Eiríksson. One person described his experience when the sculpture was unveiled: 'Guðriður became our hero. Norwegians could not steal her, she was an Icelander. We owned her'. Thus, the sculpture of *The First White Mother in America* contributed to the Norse legacy in Canada by carving out new footsteps of North American Viking figures with a clear nationality.

The sculpture not only added another dimension to the Viking legacy in North America by providing additional characters, it also represented contemporary ties – especially though the figure of Snorri. The significance of the sculpture was thus not just a reminder of the Vinland voyages, but also a symbol of the modern ties that exist between the two countries. The sculpture was seen to symbolically join Icelanders and Icelandic-Canadians together. As Gislason (who referred to the event as 'Snorri day in Canada') contended, Icelandic-Canadians thought of Snorri in particular as 'being the first-born Icelander' in Canada. In recent years many Icelandic clubs in North America have their Snorri's – people who have visited Iceland through the Snorri visiting programme. It is common to hear, 'I am a Snorri' or 'We have [a number of] Snorris in our club'. One of my respondents who had travelled from Edmonton to be present at the unveiling of the sculpture at the Canadian Museum of Civilization told me, 'people know as much about Guðríður now as they do about Leifur Eiríksson, and then the Snorri programme makes people more aware of her and the story as well'. She also proudly informed me that her granddaughter was going over to Iceland as a Snorri, and that her son was going to meet her over there to tour the country. At the end she stated, 'I am really excited that my family has started to get interested in Iceland'.

While the sculpture played a central role in revitalizing the figures of Guðríður and Snorri and linking the communities across the Atlantic, it was also a significant means of recognition and acknowledgement for the Icelandic-Canadian community in the wider Canadian context. According to many people with whom I spoke, the sculpture was a symbolic mixture of Icelandic and Icelandic-Canadian achievements. Interestingly, many had an opinion about the sculpture, even though many of them had only read about its unveiling in the community newspaper and newsletters or had been introduced to the story of Guðríður through the travelling theatre performance that was also part of the millennium programme. Whereas the sculpture played a central role in revitalizing the figures of Guðríður and Snorri and linking the communities across the Atlantic, it was also a significant means of recognition and acknowledgement for the Icelandic-Canadian community in the wider Canadian context.

My respondents emphasized that the sculpture paid tribute to the presence of the Icelandic-Canadian community as it memorialized their place in Canada and their 'long history in Canada going back a thousand years'. The desire to be recognized by the wider community was cited by many as a very important part of the presentation, especially because Icelandic-Canadians are a small ethnic group. As Irene Thorvaldson, from Gimli, Manitoba, explained to me:

> It is very important for us, or it is important for me, that the wider community recognizes the Icelandic-Canadian community. . . Icelanders are a very small population. And here, amongst the many ethnic groups, there are only few of us . . . In this context, it is important. I can't explain why this is important for me. It is a feeling and it is very difficult to put it into words . . . The sailing of Leifur Eiríksson's replica was also a big event in Canada . . . There were several people from here who went all the way to the coast to see the replica.

The significance of the sculpture was heightened by then Canadian Prime Minister Jean Chrétien, who received and unveiled the sculpture on behalf of the Canadian nation. The experience of the event, its value and meaning, were evidently amplified by Chrétien's presence. As Cole Johnson, who attended the event, stated to me: 'Of all the events carried out the millennium year, I guess that the revealing of the statue of Guðríður . . . was the one that stood out. It was such a national recognition. Our Prime Minister Jean Chrétien was there, the *only event* where the Canadian Prime Minister was present'.

The Magic of the Gift

The sculpture obviously symbolically mediated the identities, history and place of the communities across the Atlantic. Yet, I realized that in order to fully understand the value of the sculpture and its relationship to the process of 'self creation' or community revitalization, I could not ignore contexts that added to the layers of significance which were not tied to its iconic or symbolic dimensions but had more to do with the efficacy of the sculpture or its mode of action. Thus, it is important to add yet another layer to the analysis – namely, the 'gifting' itself. The act of gifting generates further meaning for the sculpture, meaning that is more directly related to the magic of the gift, the obligation of receiving and reciprocating (Mauss 1990). While the giving of the gift was, to some extent, a collaborative project, the Canadian community did not only propose the gift, it was the recipient of the gift, and thus the onus was on them to co-produce its ceremonial reception – an obligation that involved communal work, personal and mutual efforts and consolidation within the Icelandic-Canadian community.

Many of the people I interviewed told me that the presentation of the gift was a 'magic spark' for the community, as it generated volunteer work by people of Icelandic descent, which contributed to the recreation and revival of the community. The gift extended the capacity of people to act as a community and retain the group's social relations and efficacy. As one respondent explained, the magic of the event was that Icelandic-Canadians were surfacing 'all over the place' and volunteering to act on behalf of the community. In the wake of organizing the celebrations, Gerry Einarson took the initiative and rallied people of Icelandic descent to work on things Icelandic, particularly the planning of the celebration. One method used to locate people of Icelandic descent was to pick out Icelandic names from the phone directory and call them! The group of people that was formed in the process of organizing the sculpture's unveiling later established the club Friends of Iceland, which became an official chapter of the Icelandic National League of North America. Along with the preparations of the 'return of Guðríður', as one respondent stated, was the making of related historic materials for twelve elementary school classes in the Ottawa area.

In a community newspaper article with the emblematic headline 'Snorri Þorfinnsson was the Inspiration', Einarson refers to the celebration and to the reinforcement of the community with these words: 'Snorri was a great kick off and we go from there' (Guðbjartsson 2004: 9). In another newspaper article, Kathy Arnason, who was involved in planning the celebrations, states that the community efforts, support and travel of the dispersed Icelandic-Canadian community was central to the event which left a legacy of 'education, friendship, support, and co-operation' (Arnason 2000: 5). Another organizer, Mary Gordon, reminded me that the unveiling of the sculpture was quite different from the rest of the events initiated by the Icelandic government that took place during the millennium celebration. She stated, 'It was our event and it was national'.

Importantly, for some it marked the idea that Icelandic-Canadians were able to contribute significantly and have power over the millennium celebration when it easily could had been entirely Icelandic. Icelandic-Canadians were thereby able to reframe the celebration and adapt it towards their local aspirations. The community insisted that their local history be integrated with the Icelandic millennium festival and receive acknowledgment from the wider national community. Gordon told me that 'it was not an easy task, but we hung on to it', then added, 'Of course we acknowledged the fact that Iceland was more or less paying for this [but] they also had to appreciate that there are many persons putting hours into this on a voluntarily basis and some even their money'. The unveiling of Sveinsson's sculpture in the Canadian Museum of Civilization was thus indicative of the Icelandic-Canadian community's agency in responding creatively to the actions of the Icelandic authorities, and their plans in the business of networking as well as their branding campaign. Moreover, proliferation of new clubs, especially in places where none previously existed, was indeed on the agenda of the Icelandic state as reflected in these words of the Icelandic consul: 'We need at least one chapter (club) in each Canadian province. We also need chapters (clubs) in all the larger cities … We need a chapter in Newfoundland, in Nova Scotia, New Brunswick and Prince Edward Island … [and] in Ottawa … Re-organization is … important, not only for your sake but also for the sake of Iceland' (Gestsson 2000a: 3).

The sculpture thus mobilizes what anthropologist Alfred Gell, drawing in part on Munn's work, conceives of as a wider 'network of intentionalities' (Gell 1992: 43). The sculpture 'is not simply a "product" or endpoint of action' (Thomas 2001: 5); as a gift it becomes a vehicle or index for different agencies, and it can be seen to have an active role in the transnational network. The giving of the gift not only mediates the actions of the exchange practitioners, captivates the attention of participants and spreads 'fame' and reputation (cf. Munn 1986; Gell 1998; Miller 2001). The 'gifting' – the action of the gift – must also be regarded in its own right as a form of agency, a capacity to 'entrap the will of others' (Miller 2001: 152). The sculpture, in the form of a gift, thus plays an important role in constructing 'governable subjects' (Rose 1999) who are compelled – through the process of receiving the gift – to act and organize themselves in ways that contribute to (trans)nationalist emotions, heritage and kinship. Such a contribution inevitably strengthens the interests of the gift's givers – in this case, the neoliberal interests of the Icelandic state.

Strengthening the relationship between Canada and Iceland by revitalizing Icelandic-Canadian identity directly and indirectly served the promotional agenda of the Icelandic government. As stated in the campaign outline by Fleishman Hillard, a global marketing and communication consultant to the Icelandic government in 1999, people of Icelandic origin in North America are one of the core targets of Iceland Naturally.[17] The Iceland Naturally programme worked closely with the millennium committee to arrange and execute events in Canada during the millennium year. Since then, Iceland Naturally has continued to promote Iceland in Canada.

One of the main concerns of the Icelandic authorities was a return on their investment in the millennium celebrations. This productivity is measured in terms of strengthening and creating new Icelandic-Canadian chapters where none previously existed, opening trade and investment between the countries, tracking the number of Canadian tourists visiting Iceland, evaluating the media coverage of Iceland in the course of the celebrations and improving governmental relationships between Iceland and Canada. For instance, one of my respondents within the Icelandic Foreign Service indicated that the Canadian government's decision to open an embassy in Iceland in 2002, ten years before it was initially planned, is considered a successful outcome of this process. Finally, according to a millennium report compiled for the prime minister of Iceland, the outcome of the millennium celebration in Canada was productive: '. . . Iceland obtained much greater promotion for less money than ever before due to voluntary work wrought by the Icelandic-Canadians who restore great valuables to Iceland. The Icelandic-Canadians are namely a treasure of Iceland, we touched it slightly this year, there is much more left' (Gestsson 2000b: 15).

Conclusion

In the Icelandic-Canadian community, Icelandic heritage is seldom celebrated in everyday contexts, but is increasingly a part of cultural institutions and emphasized in exhibits, spectacles, presentations, performances and collections. The invention and presentation of collective symbols, such as Guðríður and Snorri (embodied in Sveinsson's sculpture), plays an important role in cultural reproduction.

According to Arjun Appadurai, in such instances 'culture becomes less what Pierre Bourdieu would have called habitus (a tacit realm of reproducible practices and dispositions) and more an arena for conscious choice, justification, and representation' (Appadurai 1996: 44). While the sculpture symbolically represents people of Icelandic heritage as well as their place in, and their contribution to, Canadian history, its placement and significance are indeed part of the practices of people in the community. It is through actions such as organizing, funding and recruiting people in planning the unveiling of the sculpture that Icelandic-Canadian identity and community is practised and (re)made.

Within the walls of the Canadian Museum of Civilization, the sculpture becomes an extension of the community as well as of people's capacity to bring the community into 'being' through the practices of organizing, planning and executing the unveiling of the sculpture.[18] Moreover, the presentation of the gift is an example of a joint venture where giving and receiving cannot be divided. This blurring is analogous to the merging of producers/consumers and leisure/work increasingly manifested in flexible capitalism and its extraction of free labour (cf. Narotzky, this volume).

The collaboration of Icelandic-Canadians in planning and presenting the sculpture reflect the subtle methods of neoliberal modes of government across nation-states. The endeavours considered underline the active role that gift exchange and gift relations play in facilitating the new global economy. They also highlight the nation-state's flexible margins, as well as the technologies that shape subjectivities within and across national and transnational spheres. In an attempt to follow Saskia Sassen's inquiry – 'to decode what [the] national means today' (2001: 276) – this chapter has shed light on a function of the national and nationalized accounts in neoliberal reformations that emerged in Iceland in the 1990s. Moreover, as Eva Mackey argues, the legitimation of the Canadian politics of pluralism has shifted since the late 1980s as a result of the rise of global capitalism. It has a new emphasis. Canada's multicultural heritage has increasingly been considered a 'resource' that makes 'good business sense' (Mackey 2002: 68).

Examining the circumstances of the presentation of the sculpture unveils the neoliberal endeavour to constitute and mobilize subjects to be creative and productive towards (re)crafting an Icelandic presence within the wider Canadian social and business milieu through ethnic networking. In practical terms, the circumstances of the presentation of the sculpture bear a resemblance to aspects of gift exchange familiar from Melanesia. In this case, the Icelandic state and the Icelandic Canadian community 'sought to spread fame' and 'draw others into their intentionalities' (Thomas 2001: 9). In other words, the gift of *The First White Mother in America* was used, in different ways, to distribute Icelandic interests within and across boundaries.

In terms of the revitalization of the figure of Guðríður, it was so successful that people literally believed in her existence. Since the year 2000, travellers from North America have come on pilgrimages to Glaumbær. According to the director of the Skagafjörður Heritage Museum travellers ask to see her place of burial and become somewhat puzzled when they realize that no such place exists.

Acknowledgements

This chapter is a revised version of an essay published in the Icelandic journal *Ritið* in 2010. Part of the research was published in *Þjóðarspegill Conference Proceedings*, University of Iceland in 2009 and 2010. I would like to thank Edda – Center of Excellence, University of Iceland, for supporting the writing of the chapter.

Notes

1 Quoted from the Iceland Naturally website. Retrieved 1 October 2003 from: www.icelandnaturally.com.
2 I will use the terms 'Canadians of Icelandic decent' and 'Icelandic-Canadians' interchangeably. The term 'Western Icelanders' also appears in the text. The term is frequently used in Iceland for North Americans of Icelandic descent. Names of my respondents are pseudonym.
3 Informal and formal interviews were conducted with members of the Icelandic-Canadian community. Interviews were also conducted with Icelandic diplomats, ambassadors and directors. The research for this chapter also draws on archival materials, particularly from the Icelandic Ministry of Foreign Affairs, and a large body of written and visual materials, such as television programmes, newspaper articles and formal speeches.
4 Quoted from 'When Three Become Two: Austria More Equal than Others', *IceNews*, 10 May 2008. Retrieved 3 April 2009 from: icenews.is/index.php/information/security-council/.
5 The free-trade agreement between Iceland/EFTA was not signed until January 2008.

6 E. Benediktsson, Letter to Minister of Foreign Affairs, 29 October 1993. Committee for Promotion of Relations between Iceland and Persons of Iceland Descent in North America. Reykjavik: Ministry of Foreign Affairs, 67.F.1a, 1 June 1993 to 12 February 1994.
7 Quoted from the Iceland Guest website. Retrieved 1 October 2008 from: www.icelandguest.com/in-focus/nr/899/.
8 See *Íslensk Orðabók* [Icelandic dictionary], 3rd edn., ed. M. Árnason (Reykjavík: Edda, 2002), p.1676. See also Helgason (2006).
9 *Íslensk Orðabók*, 3rd edn. (2002), p.1676.
10 *Stóra orðabókin – um íslenska málnotkun* [Icelandic dictionary], ed. J.H. Jónsson (Reykjavík: JPV, 2005), p.1473.
11 *Íslensk Orðabók* [Icelandic dictionary], 2nd edn., ed. Á. Böðvarsson (Reykjavík: Mál og Menning, 1996), p.1103
12 *Íslensk Orðabók*, 3rd edn. (2002), p.1676.
13 *Íslensk Orðabók*, 2nd edn. (1996), p.1154.
14 *Morgunblaðið*, 27 March 2004, 11 September 2005 and 10 June 2006 respectively.
15 *Guardian*, 16 June 2005.
16 See Althingi 113 Legislative Session, 1991. Proposed Parliamentary Resolution 476. Retrieved 20 October 2014 from http://www.althingi.is/altext/113/s/1042.html. In the parliamentary resolution, Snorri is introduced as the first specifically white child in America.
17 Fleishman Hillard, 'Icelandic Leifur Eiríksson Millennium Commission of Iceland', 1999. Reykjavik: National Archives of Iceland, PR fyrirtæki A/16 1 1998–2001. 3.I.2.
18 The cast of the *First White Mother in America* was later moved from the Canadian Museum of Civilization to be displayed at the National Library and Archives.

References

Appadurai, A. 1996. *Modernity at Large: Cultural Dimension of Globalization*. Minnesota: University of Minnesota Press.
Árnason, A., S.B. Hafsteinsson and T. Grétarsdóttir. 2007. 'Acceleration Nation: An Investigation into the Violence of Speed and the Uses of Accidents in Iceland', *Culture, Theory and Critique* 48(2): 199–217.
Arnason, K. 2000. 'Honouring the "Friends of Iceland": Exemplary Volunteers in the Year of National Volunteers', *Lögberg Heimskringla*, 5 May.
Ásgrímsson, H. 2004. 'Hátíðarræða Halldórs Ásgrímssonar, utanríkisráðherra, á ársfundi Viðskipta og hagfræðideildar Háskóla Íslands 27 janúar 2004' [Speech by the Icelandic Minister of Foreign Affairs, Halldór Ásgrímsson at the Department of Business and

Economics, University of Iceland, 27 January 2004]. Retrieved 5 January 2006 from: www.utanrikisraduneyti.is/frettaefni/raedurHA/nr/2122.

——— 2005. 'Ræða Halldórs Ásgrímssonar, *forsætisráðherra, á Viðskiptaþingi Verslunarráðs*, February 8, 2005' [Speech by Prime Minister Halldór Ásgrímsson. Annual Meeting of the Chamber of Commerce, February 8, 2005]. Retrieved 5 January 2006 from: http://eng.forsaetisraduneyti.is/minister/Speeches_HA/nr/1709.

Ásmundsson, Á., H. Lárusson and T. Grétarsdóttir. 2011. *Koddu* [Catalogue]. Reykjavik: Living Art Museum.

Beck, R. 1943. 'Leif Ericsson and his Discovery of America', *Icelandic Canadian* 1(3): 6–10.

Berlant, L. 1998. 'Live Sex Acts [Parental Advisory: Explicit Material]', in N.B. Dirks (ed.), *Near Ruins: Cultural Theory at the End of the Century*. Minneapolis: University of Minnesota Press, pp.173–198.

Bertram, L. 2010. 'Public Spectacles, Private Narratives: Canadian Heritage Campaigns, Maternal Trauma, and the Rise of the Koffort (Trunk) in Icelandic-Canadian Popular Memory', *Material Culture Review* 71: 39–53.

——— 2011. 'Resurfacing Landscape of Trauma: Multiculturalism, Cemeteries, and the Migrant Body, 1875 Onwards', in M. Chazan, L. Helps, A. Stanley and S. Thakkar (eds), *Home and Native Land: Unsettling Multiculturalism in Canada*. Toronto: Between the Lines Press, pp.157–174.

Björnsson, Á. 2005. 'Fri os fra vikingerne' [Free us from the Vikings], in A. Mortensen (ed.), *Fólkaleikur: Heiðursrit til Jóan Paula Joensen*. Tórshavn: Föroya Fróðskaparfelag,, pp.53–61.

Brydon, A. 1991. 'Celebrating Ethnicity: The Icelanders of Manitoba', *Scandinavian-Canadian Studies* 4: 1–14.

Cadham, J. 2008. 'Cadham's Homepage'. Retrieved 25 October 2008 from: www.joan-eyolfson-cadham.ca/honours.htm#info.

Das, V. and D. Poole. 2004. 'State and Its Margins: Comparative Ethnographies', in V. Das and D. Poole (eds), *Anthropology in the Margins of the State*. Santa Fe: SAR Press, pp.3–33.

Eyford, R. 2003. 'Icelandic Migration to Canada, 1872–1875: New Perspective on the "Myth of Beginnings"', MA diss. Ottawa: Carleton University.

Fitzhugh, W.W., and E.I. Ward. 2000. 'Celebrating the Viking Past: A Viking Millennium in America', in W.W. Fitzhugh and E.I. Ward (eds), *Vikings: The North Atlantic Saga*. Washington: Smithsonian Institution Press, pp.351–353.

Gell, A. 1992. 'The Enchantment of Technology and the Technology of Enchantment', in J. Coote and A. Shelton (eds), *Anthropology, Art and Aesthetics*. Oxford: Oxford University Press, pp.40–63.

——— 1998. *Art and Agency: An Anthropological Theory*. Oxford: Clarendon Press.

Gestsson, S. 2000a. 'Celebration Only Begun', *Lögberg Heimskringla*, 12 May.

———— 2000b. 'Starfsskýrsla um hátíðarhöldin í Kanada árið 2000: Endurfundir Íslendinga með íbúum Norður Ameríku. Skýrsla landafundanefndar til forsætisráðherra' [Reunion of Icelanders and inhabitants of North America: The Millennium Commission Report to the Prime Minister's Office]. Reykjavík: Prime Minister's Office.

Gislason, D. 1999. 'A Millennium to Celebrate', *Lögberg Heimskringla*, 22 January.

———— 2002. 'The Spell of Gudridur', *Lögberg Heimskringla*, 20 December.

GoI. 2002. 'Discovery: Iceland's Amazing Adventure'. Reykjavik: Government of Iceland.

Grétarsdóttir, T. Ásmundsson Á and Lárusson H. 2014. 'Creativity and Crisis', in E. P. Durrenberger and G. Palsson (eds), *Gambling Debt, Iceland's Rise and Fall in the Global Economy*. Boulder: University Press of Colorado, pp. 93–105.

Grímsson, Ó.R. 1996. 'Address by his Excellency Ólafur Ragnar Grímsson, President of Iceland, at the Icelandic American Chamber of Commerce, New York, 5 December 1996'. Retrieved 7 March 2004 from: http:// forseti.is/media/files/96.12.05.Isl-am.verslrad.NY.enska.pdf.

———— 1997. 'Address by Ólafur Ragnar Grímsson, President of Iceland, on Íslendingadagur í Gimli, 4 August 1997'. Retrieved 3 April 2007 from: www.forseti.is/media/files/97.08.04.GIMLI.pdf.

———— 1999. 'Speech by Ólafur Ragnar Grímsson, President of Iceland, at a Dinner in Regina, Canada, 28 July 1999'. Retrieved 7 March 2004 from: http://forseti.is/media/files/99.07.28.Kanada.Regina.dinner.pdf.

———— 2006. 'Fyrirlestur forseta Íslands Ólafs Ragnar Grímssonar í fyrirlestraröð Sagnfræðingafélagsins 10 Januar 2006' [Lecture by Ólafur Ragnar Grímsson, President of Iceland, at the Association of Icelandic Historians]. Retrieved 3 April 2007 from: http://forseti.is/media/files/06.01.10.Sagnfrfel.pdf.

Guðbjartsson, S. 2004. 'Snorri Þorfinnsson was the Inspiration', *Lögberg Heimskringla*, 27 August.

Helgason, J.K. 2006. 'Víkingar efnisins' [Material Vikings], *Morgunblaðið, Lesbók*, 11 November.

Isfeld, H. 2000. 'Who's Coming to Ottawa? Iceland, Naturally! Iceland Launches Millennium Celebrations April 6', *Lögberg Heimskringla*, 10 March.

Isfeld, H., and J. Gústafsson. 2000. 'Iceland in Canada', *Lögberg Heimskringla* (special issue), 14 April.

Lindal, W.J. 1944. 'The Spirit of Iceland', *Icelandic Canadian* 2(4): 4–5.

Loftson, S. 2007. 'Snorri Reflection', *Icelandic Canadian* 61(1): 32.

Mackey, E. 2002. *The House of Difference: Cultural Politics and National Identity in Canada*. Toronto: University of Toronto.

McKay, I. 1994. *The Quest of the Folk: Antimodernism and Cultural Selection in Twentieth Century Nova Scotia*. Montreal: McGill-Queen's University Press.

Mauss, M. 1990 [1925]. *The Gift: The Form and Reason for Exchange in Archaic Societes*, trans. W.D. Halls. London: Routledge.

Miller, D. 2001. 'The Fame of Trinis: Websites as Traps', in C. Pinney and N. Thomas (eds), *Beyond Aesthetics: Art and the Technologies of Enchantment*. Oxford: Berg, pp. 137–165.

Munn, N.D. 1986. *The Fame of Gawa: A Symbolic Study of Value Transformation in a Massim (Papua New Guinea) Society*. Durham, NC: Duke University Press.

Neijmann, D.L. 1997. *The Icelandic Voice in Canadian Letters: The Contribution of Icelandic Canadian Writers to Canadian Literature*. Ottawa: Carleton Press.

Ong, A. 2006. *Neoliberalism as Exception*. Durham, NC: Duke University Press.

PMO. 2000. 'Endurfundir Íslendinga með íbúum Norður Ameríku. Skýrsla landafundanefndar til forsætirsráðherra' [Reunion of Icelanders and inhabitants of North America: The Millennium Commission Report to the Prime Minister's Office]. Reykjavík: Prime Minister's Office.

——— 2008. 'Ímynd Íslands, Styrkur staða og stefna. Skýrsla nefndar' [Image of Iceland, strength, position and direction]. Reykjavik: Prime Minister's Office.

Rose, N. 1999. *Powers of Freedom: Reframing Political Thought*. Cambridge: Cambridge University Press.

Salverson, L.G. 1942. 'Editorial', *Icelandic Canadian* 1(1): 1–2.

Sanger, T. 2008. 'Milton and the Meltdown in Iceland', *Progressive Economics Forum*, 14 October 2008. Retrieved 21 December 2011 from: www.progressive-economics.ca/2008/10/14/milton-and-the-meltdown-in-iceland/.

Sassen, S. 2001. 'Spatialities and Temporalities of the Global: Elements for a Theorization', in A. Appadurai (ed) *Globalization*. Durham: Duke University Press, pp. 260–278.

Sæberg, Á. 1999. 'Ísland þúsund ár á aldamótaári í Vesturheimi' [Iceland Thousand Year at the Millennium], *Morgunblaðið*, 3 January 1999. Retrieved 6 January 2002 from: http://mbl.is/mm/gagnasafn/grein. html?grein_id=440732.

Thomas, N. 2001. 'Introduction', in C. Pinney and N. Thomas (eds), *Beyond Aesthetics: Art and the Technologies of Enchantment*. Oxford: Berg, pp. 1–12.

Walters, T. 1953. *Modern Sagas: The Story of Icelanders in North America*. Fargo: North Dakota Institute for Regional Studies.

Ward, E.I. 2000. 'Reflections on an Icon: Vikings in American Culture', in W.W. Fitzhugh and E.I. Ward (eds), *Vikings: The North Atlantic Saga*. Washington: Smithsonian Institution Press, pp. 365–373.

Wolf, K. 2001. 'The Recovery of Vínland in Western Icelandic Literature', in A. Wawn and Þ. Sigurðardóttir (eds), *Approaches to Vínland*. Reykjavík: Sigurður Nordal Institute, pp. 207–219.

3

Flexibility Frictions

Economies of Connection in Contemporary Forms of Work

Christina Garsten

Flex Fads at Work

Organizational life is torn with frictions, contradictions and strains. It is within organizations that we find others with similar interests, agendas or passions, and that we are able to collectively pursue them. But it is also here that we get caught in debates, battles and political wars, where energies are consumed and projects stalled. It is in organizations that we experience the elation of having accomplished something grand. However, it is also in organizations that we experience the drudgery of routines, rules and boredom. Organizations constrain us, impose rigidities and shape our subjectivities. But they are likewise arenas for personal development, learning and empowerment. On the whole, organizations are conflictual social worlds.

Contemporary versions of the 'organization man' (Whyte 2002) are intrinsically linked with notions of flexibility. With the advent of 'flexible capitalism', we are seeing a proliferation of images of work and organization, as well as subjectivities, in continuous change and radical transformation. As with capitalism itself – universalizing and globalizing in its ambitions, yet highly fractured and ambiguous (Mitchell 2002; Yanagisako 2002; Tsing 2005) – such images are not altogether coherent but messy, uneven and subject to resistance. What remains certain is that, as local economies become more tied into global financial flows, as organizational structures are transformed in line with new flexible templates and labour markets are re-regulated, our relations to work and our subjectivities change as well (Miller and Rose 1995: 428).

At this point in time, flexibility is no longer the neologism is used to be. Long gone is the time at which we talked and wrote about flexibility as the new, emerging order of things. We are now attuned to such notions as flexible production, flexible working hours, flexible employment, flexible technologies, flexible bodies and flexible minds. This is not to say that these notions have everywhere filtered into our daily lives. By no means. Production processes in many industries are still relatively inflexible; some employees face strict timely regulation at work; the desired form of employment is for many still the full-time contract; technical gadgets still require a lot of adjustment on the part of humans and, perhaps most importantly, bodies and minds are hard to change overnight. Nevertheless, much *is* flex these days, or expected to be so. These expectations and aspirations infuse contemporary working lives. We have even reached a point at which the ability of an organization, a working group or an individual to be flexible, in order to be 'employable', has become a key stratification mechanism, promoting those who are able to be so before those who are not, or who are not willing to be (Garsten and Jacobsson 2004, 2013). Moreover, this stratification process works for the benefit of those who are in a position to decide upon what and who needs to adjust to what, so that having the resources and the influence needed to decide on these matters means that flexibility can be imposed on the conditions of those more deeply rooted, as it were.

Throughout a large part of my life as a researcher into the social worlds of organizations, I have come across prescriptions of flexibility in one way or other. During my fieldwork at Apple Computer, the mission of flexibility was a key component of the corporate culture that was being nurtured. Not always explicitly framed in terms of 'flexibility', but in synonyms or related terms, such as 'versatility', 'adaptability' and most commonly 'change', the corporate culture of Apple Computer recognized and encouraged the value of being able to change and bend. This was a capacity expected and explicitly fostered among employees, in the organizational structure and in the range of technologies it produced (Garsten 1994). At Olsten Staffing Services, a global staffing agency, the fostering of flexibility is part and parcel of the very business vision. The company offers flexible staffing solutions and a 'just-in-time' workforce, and the 'consultants' working for Olsten are explicitly taught about the need of being flexible: in attitude, in working hours, in assignments and in the range of tasks they should be ready to take on (Garsten 2008). In my ongoing research on policy think tanks, among them the Center for Global Development, flexibility is yet again present, but in a different fashion. Flexibility among 'think-tankers' is first and foremost a matter of flexing between roles and target groups, between different organizations and institutions. The driven think-tanker knows how to work the different roles of public intellectual, policy advocate and university professor, all the while moving between and amongst foundations, multilateral institutions, national government agencies, corporate boards and the media (Garsten 2013, 2014).

Other scholars have made similar observations and arguments. For example, Krause-Jensen (2010) describes with rich ethnographic detail the making of the 'flexible firm', by maximizing 'lightness' through stimulating flexible forms of production at the high-tech company Bang and Olufsen. Henson (1996) provides a convincing description of working as a 'temp', as part of the 'flexible workforce'. And Janine Wedel (2009) has revealed the workings of 'flexians', the elite groups of people in US policy making. In all of these accounts, flexibility figures prominently.

Flexibility, as we see, comes in a myriad of guises. The concept is at least as agile as that which it signifies. In this sense, it may appear a hollow notion. But it is a notion with performative powers. However, as indicated above, we should not be led to think that the ideology of flexibility translates easily into practice. Often, the very practice of flexibility relies on ingrained and inert structures and anticipations. It may appear that flexibility is thus a misnomer. This, however, would be throwing the baby out with the bathwater, as it were. As I will show, flexibility is relational in that it depends for its articulation on rigidity, inertia and standardization – those 'others' that are to be resisted and combated. It is as a mirror image of these connotations that flexibility in the workplace gains its appeal and leverage. Moreover, and despite the variability of its realization in practice, it is not a misnomer in the sense that it triggers expectations and imaginaries among people, and mobilizes action in a certain direction. Flexibility has performative power in that it articulates a given point of direction as the desired goal. The notion of flexibility is essentially a powerful governance tool in that it may be filled with a range of different meanings, and thus used to various ends (cf. Martin 1994; Garsten 2008).

Whilst notions and expressions of flexibility at work are different, they also share some key features, and point to some important trends in the worlds of work in 'disorganized' capitalism.[1] What is perhaps most interesting, to my mind, is the way in which

the flexibilization of work contracts encourages a flexible orientation to work itself. As the contractual arrangements and employee–
employer relation change, so do our relations to work. When work
becomes contingent, this fosters a more transactional way of relating to work and to the employer, as seen in the temporary-staffing
industry. When change becomes an everyday constant, as at Apple
Computer, you either invest your emotions in the community of
work, or opt out. Similarly, when influence and authority cannot
be taken for granted and leaned against with the ease of privilege,
working the network flexibly and flexing between roles becomes an
important part of the job. We can thus identify a number of flexible
orientations to work.

From a critical neo-Marxist point of view, work has been seen to
involve elements of exchange, in which workers provide their capacities and skills in return for monetary compensation and certain rights
and benefits (see e.g. Braverman 1974; Burawoy 1979; Willis 1977).
The view of work as a form of exchange has been criticized by scholars as a dehumanizing and disempowering position, arguing instead
in favour of enhanced opportunities for learning, skill-enhancement
and empowerment (see e.g. Kanter 1983; Pink 2001). In the world
of practice, the notion of work as exchange has been fought against
by management, emphasizing loyalty and commitment as opposed
to laying bare the naked transactional aspects of the contract. While
I tend to view a consistent commodity perspective on work as too
one-dimensional, since work is tangled with sociality, emotions and
aspirations, it does, however, serve to highlight key aspects of work
relations. A distinctive feature of capitalist labour markets is the subordination of work to the discipline of market regulation. As Peck
eloquently puts it, relying on Polanyi, '[t]he clash between market
discipline and the social foundations of labor renders the capitalist
labor market a "satanic mill"' (Peck 1996: 25). I will here, somewhat
eclectically, build on this clash and make use of certain aspects of the
notions of 'commodity exchange' and 'gift exchange' to highlight on
the one hand a short-term and instrumental relation to work, and
on the other a more long-term, socially invested kind of relation
(Parry and Bloch 1989). Both of these are at work in capitalist practice more generally, but are found in particular ways in the context of
the flexibility doctrine. As Kjaerulff posits in the introduction to this
volume, in contemporary flexible capitalist work, 'gift-like' moralities and social relations proliferate in, and even sustain, the kind of
accentuated commodity exchange that more widely has been touted
as tearing social relations apart.

The tangling of gift and commodity forms of exchange accentuates the market-infused sociality of work-life as sustained by an 'economy of connections' (Garsten 2013). This is an 'economy' in the sense that social connections and referrals are provided as 'gifts' between trusted parties. The connection may provide access to yet other, valuable resources, like information, attention or a job opportunity, and hence to money. This gift economy intertwines itself into the organizational structures of society, erecting pillars of social capital, in Bourdieu's sense, that attach to key positions in organizational hierarchies. The social capital that derives from resources linked to a durable network of relationships of mutual recognition provides the members with the backing of 'credentials' which, in Bourdieu's words, 'entitles them to credit, in the various sense of the word' (Bourdieu 1986: 51). The 'economy of connections' is thus an economy in the double sense of the term, as a system of exchange of valuables (connections and their translation into other resources), and as involving investment and interest in the cultivating of certain relationships.[2] In organizational life, we may thus see how flexibility is also articulated at the level of the forms of exchange that are implied, the nature of transactions involved, as well as the types of investments that come into play. We are thus dealing here with two notions of flexibility: one which centres on the organizational form and on the nature of the work contract, and one that focuses on the practice of social relationships.

Flexible forms of organization are by nature ambiguous. They encompass both stable forms of work organization and more volatile 'network' environments. They are spaces of insecurity and risk at the same time as they are spaces for creativity and opportunity. They nurture short-term, opportunistic relations, whilst depending on long-term social investment and relations of trust. Flexible forms of work organization come with a set of ambiguities. How are we to make sense of these double-edged characteristics?

Threshold Positions: Liminality as Premise

The different orientations to work that arise with flexibilization may be understood as related to the interstitial positions of many groups of professionals. The work organizations in which I have done research all embrace change in one way or another. The continuous presence of change, contingency and upheaval means that employees have to navigate in changing organizational landscapes, and to find their ways among points of reference that have a tendency to escape from vision. This sense of indeterminacy is a structural trait of many work organizations today, underscored by managerial rhetoric. Moreover, the networked high-flexibility character of emergent organizational forms combines with the ideological displacement of the symbolic boundary between work and non-work in fostering subjectivities that are at once responsive to changing organizational needs, and that find new ways of resisting organizational impositions (see e.g. Fleming 2009). In this organizational indeterminacy, liminality is more a premise than an exception.

The concept of liminality is attributed to Arnold van Gennep (2004) and Victor Turner (1967, 1969). At its core, liminality refers to 'in-between situations and conditions' brought about by the dislocation of established structures. This idea was developed further in a concise definition of liminality that would inform Turner's future writings: 'Liminality may perhaps be regarded as the Nay to all positive structural assertions, but as in some sense the source of them all, and, more than that, as a realm of pure possibility whence novel configurations of ideas and relations may arise' (Turner 1967: 97). Through the lens of Turner's notion of liminality – that particular kind of being 'betwixt and between' social structures characteristic of artists, shamans and entrepreneurs alike – we may get a clearer sense of how flexibility plays out.

In the case of temporary employees, the liminal position is poignant. As I have elaborated in greater detail elsewhere (Garsten 1999), flexible forms of work are in some sense liminal in relation to established structures of work arrangements. Temporary-staffing work challenges established work arrangements. The position of the 'temp' evokes indeed 'the Nay to all positive structural assertions', in that it is in many ways 'a job-not' (ibid.). Firstly, temps are not prototypical workers who tread the same paths every morning to their given location. They change workplaces as they change assignments and clients. Being ready to move to a different location is a taken-for-granted frame of mind. Secondly, temping is by definition temporary. Temporary employees often lack the contractual bond created by a regular employment position. In the USA, they are hired by assignment and only appear on the agency's payroll during the course of an assignment. In between assignments, they constitute the pool of resources from which the agency and clients can choose according to need. Even so, they are drawn into extended circles of loyalty to the corporation and to their clients. Being a temp is also a transitory position, with a moving target. It may turn out to be a road to permanent employment, an exploratory phase in the sphere of work and organization or a passage to a shift in career. It may likewise prove to be a dead-end street, with an increased sense of marginality in relation to organizational resources and to the labour market. Furthermore, the status of being a temp is often an ambiguous one, fraught with tension. On the one hand, it suggests novel ways of organizing and relating to work, a free-agent kind of work-life and empowered individuals. On the other hand, it bears connotations of occupying the lowest rung on the status ladder, having to do the boring and repetitious tasks no one else will take on and, not least, being substitutable. Characteristic of temping is a 'manufactured uncertainty' (Giddens 1994: 184). Many aspects of working life, such as if and when there will be a next assignment and where one will go for the next one, are undecided until shortly before the current assignment is terminated. The continuity of work is organized only in terms of 'scenario thinking', in the way of an as-if construction of possible future outcomes (ibid.). The temporal and spatial fragmentation on which temping depends – being on-call for short-term assignments and ready to move around to different client organizations – reasserts liminality in relation to organizational structures (Garsten 1999).

Temping provides an institutional pocket that challenges the way we view work, organization and subjectivity. While innovation may take place in established social structures, it is at the interfaces and gaps that innovation most frequently occurs. It is also here that the ambiguities of flexibility are more clearly manifested. As a consequence of being betwixt and between more regular positions, reflexivity is enhanced, turning control and monitoring onto the self (Garsten and Haunschild 2014). Being a temp implies dealing in a versatile way with the organizational tensions involved; the rhetoric of organizational change, competition and contingency, and the agentic power of the free agent. The mobile and transient position of temporary employees furthermore undermines the development of community in the workplace. Community becomes inherently fragile and episodic. This fosters a short-term and instrumental way of relating to work, as a form of commodity exchange, resembling the instrumental means–ends rationality described by Weber (1978). On the other hand, it nurtures as well a sense of individual responsibility for one's career, along with which comes a heightened awareness of the need to cultivate key relational bonds and to establish relations of trust with people who may have an influence on one's career trajectory, an enforced 'responsibilization' (cf. Clarke 2005; Fogde 2011). In the case of temporary employees, this means most frequently nurturing ties to one's assignment coordinator at the staffing agency, and to the client organization, which may be a potential future employer.

The ambiguities of flexibility also manifest themselves in various versions in other forms of work. Some of these features are as well recognizable in the hacker-slacker high-tech industry, as at Apple Computer, and in the polished policy world, as among the think tanks I have studied, albeit in different ways. With the constant reorganizing and reshuffling of organizational structures and positions at Apple Computer, employees are encouraged to 'network, network, network!' The social network of team mates, colleagues, managers and business acquaintances, and of friends both inside and outside the organization, is not just a way to secure the distribution of corporate values, but provides the closest to a safety-net that one can get. In the case of a major reorganization, your next position may depend entirely on knowing the right people in the right places. Indeterminacy and liminality are built into the very organizational structure by a continuous reshuffling of these, so that ruptures appear in unforeseen places at unexpected times. As an employee, you are much better off well networked and connected than left without ties to safeguard you. Thus, cultivating long-term social connections with others is a major and necessary investment in a flexible environment, and it also ensures a flexible adaptation to change. Such connections may prove vital in putting one's name on the new organizational chart, and when a new team is being put together.

The employees of Apple Computer did not content themselves with being alert to organizational reorganization, however. Well aware of the liquid character of organizations in high-wired Silicon Valley, they cultivated bonds outside Apple. College friends, subcontractors, business partners, as well as competitors, were drawn upon to extend the reach of their social nets. These nets were cast widely and strategically, as well as long term. There was thus a simultaneous cultivation of community and identification with the company, and a constant gazing outwards for new career opportunities.

'Think-tankers', more precisely people employed at or affiliated with think tanks, experience flexibility in yet other ways. The fellows, directors, researchers and presidents of think tanks are highly educated, well-positioned experts in their fields. Ideally, they have high-level academic degrees, experience of working in a government body or in some multilateral organization, and have acquired expertise in their particular area of interest. These experiences provide them with a relatively strong professional and relational platform from which to drawn upon. Washington DC is a densely tangled 'netscape', in which connections are vital. Ties from college, from working together at the World Bank, in the US government or in a non-governmental organization are maintained and cultivated. 'Inside the Beltway', as it were, think-tankers all know each other, or are at least aware of who is who. Key in this context is not just cultivating connections, but knowing who to call and when, and making flexible use of one's network (Garsten 2013). Flexibly managing one's network of connections is perhaps the most valuable skill of all. 'These ties persist', as one of my informants put it.

The liminality of think-tankers emerge from their professional position as experts, public intellectuals, academics and/or government officials on leave – or any combination of these. They juggle with different hats and affiliations, which bestows upon them a powerful liminal evocation. As 'flexians', in Wedel's (2009) rendering, they are strategic in manoeuvring their roles and repertoires in pursuit of knowledge and influence. They 'operate at the interstices of official and private power' (ibid.: 61), carefully watching out for information and for relevant contacts.

Yet another important liminal feature resides in the position of think tanks in the wider organizational landscape. Think tanks are hard to locate in the established and conventional categorization of organizational types. They are neither this nor that. To place them in the civil society sector, among non-governmental organizations or non-state actors only succeeds to a limited extent in defining them. Think tanks are to be found along the vast stretch of research institutes dealing mainly with the 'thinking of thoughts' on the one hand, and 'do tanks', working to implement ideas as policy on the other (see e.g. McGann 2007; Weidenbaum 2008). Another central liminal feature relates to the fact that while they wish to make an impact in policy making, they may only do so indirectly, based on their knowledge. Their legal status means that think tanks are not supposed to engage in lobbying, instead educating and providing rigorous analysis, before policy as it were.[3] The funding structure is another significant aspect. Many think tanks strive to assure a broad range of different sponsors, in order not to be too strongly attached to a particular foundation, government body, corporation or individual. A broad portfolio of donors grants them a degree of organizational independence. It is precisely this liminal position, 'betwixt and between' the established and conventional organizational structures of state, market and civil society, that makes for power, authority and influence in the world of policy making. And as with other liminal groups, not only does the threshold position provide power and capacity, but it comes with connotations of ambiguity and ambivalence. From the outside, think-tankers are met simultaneously with awe, admiration, suspicion and mistrust. Hence, rigorous analysis and evidence-based knowledge are emphasized as key resources to establish credibility and legitimacy.

Flexible Performers: The Crafting of Individual Actors

A central feature of late capitalism, as experienced in the Western hemisphere, is that it relies to a large extent on the promotion of the individual as the central unit of agency. The individual actor is celebrated and nurtured as the originator and driver of creativity, innovation and change. Only in terms of work communities or teams are social groups encouraged and nurtured in organizational life. Late capitalism premises the individual as the agentic entity on which both risk and opportunities, duties and responsibilities, are to be bestowed. The need to adapt to these conditions calls, in Beck's words, 'upon the individual kindly to constitute herself or himself as an individual, to plan, understand, design and act – or to suffer the consequences which have been self-inflicted in case of failure' (Beck 1992: 16). It is when, in between jobs, between organizations and between positions – in a state of liminality – that we experience most clearly the pressure to constitute ourselves and to display our professional identity and skills as resources. In the flux of organizational worlds, things may not always proceed according to plan, but the very idea of being able to plan, to construct one's work-life and career in the face of flux, delineates the realm of individual agency and power. There is today a whole machinery of services set up to cater to the needs of individuals: coaching professionals, mentoring professionals, how-to and self-help literature on virtually every aspect of working life, and so on. The reinventing of employees as able actors is a prominent theme in contemporary 'make-over culture' (cf. McGee 2005).

Meyer and Jepperson argue that 'the modern (European, now global) cultural system constructs the modern actor as an *authorized agent* for various interests via an ongoing relocation into society of agency originally located in transcendental authority or in natural forces environing the social system' (Meyer and Jepperson 2000: 110, original emphasis). In their view, this authorized agentic capability is as an essential feature of what modern theory and culture call an 'actor', and helps explain a number of otherwise anomalous or little analysed features of modern individuals, organizations and states, including isomorphism and standardization, decoupling and the capacity for prolific collective action. Much social theory about contemporary work and labour markets takes for granted 'the core conceit of modern culture: that modern actors – individuals, organizations, nation-states – are autochthonous and natural entities, no longer really embedded in culture', as Meyer and Jepperson (ibid.: 100) have it. Their argument has informed organizational theory in relating notions of the agentic individual to organizational forms and their standardization. It is also a highly seductive notion, which works by invoking freedom, individuality, responsibility and development, and which is dressed up as benevolent and empowering (Foucault 1991).

The discourse of flexibility points to a tension between individual control of the work situation and the self on the one hand, and the framework provided by the work organization on the other. Whilst flexibilization would at first glance appear to strike a contrast with rigidity, structure, standardization and the like, the case is not as simple as that. The individualization of risk in the labour market goes hand in hand with the casting of individual agents. What is basically a structural and ideological matter of organizing work and employment is in flexible capitalism portrayed as a problem for individuals to solve. 'Risks and contradictions are being socially produced; it is just the duty and necessity of coping with them which is being individualized', as Bauman (2001: 47) puts it.

This notion of the agentic individual becomes ever more potent when seen in light of Fleming's suggestive analysis of the quest for 'authenticity' in present-day workplaces (Fleming 2009). Managerial discourse and an overall ideological, liberalist rhetoric celebrate personal authenticity at work, involving expressions of difference and uniqueness. 'Especially salient', he writes, 'are the notions of difference, diversity, dissent, and the invocation of non-work themes within the conventional boundaries of the firm' (ibid.: viii). The invocation of the non-work sphere of life in the workplace plays a significant role in the making up of employees. The 'just-be-yourself' imperative combines here with allusions to organizational change and flexibly emerging organizational forms to impose a new form of managerial control in which individuals are to construct themselves authentically in response to 'what now seems like an eternal and edgeless universe with no end' (ibid.: viii).

The composition of capitalist employment thus favours players with high potency and agentic capacity, 'flexible performers', who ideally reveal their authentic selves in agile balancing acts responsive to an endlessly changing organizational landscape. The discursive façade of work as infused with endless opportunities is played out against a capitalist logic that not only encourages but demands flexibility on the part of its workers. Elsewhere, I have presented the idea that the notion of the flexible employee is closely related to present-day images of the market (Garsten 2002). The market is now a mobilizing metaphor in the 'making up' of individuals in the labour market (cf. Hacking 1986). Analogous to the notion of 'economic man' in neo-classical economics, late capitalism has fostered the appearance of 'market man' (*Homo mercans*) as a model for thought and action. The employee of the market economy has to learn how to adapt flexibly to the needs of clients, customers and stakeholders, and to make him- or herself an attractive prospect for employment.

Market man (or woman) is orientated towards market transactions, and has learnt to value him- or herself as a product in the market and take on the idea of 'enterprise' as a mode of action (Miller and Rose 1995). He or she is embedded in a discourse that places prime value on the marketability of goods and services as well as skills, competences, manners and attitudes. Market man is flexible, autonomous, self-reliant and disciplined (Garsten 2002). Generally, in present-day discourse, there is the assumption that the sort of person contained in the market model is the true or valid person, the standard against which other notions of the self are measured, and usually found wanting (Carrier 1997: 27).

The agentic and market-oriented capacity is also detectable in performance evaluation procedures. In the temporary-staffing industry, temporary employees are evaluated on criteria reflecting their capacity to adapt to the needs of the client, on their attitude and their service orientation. Reflexivity is encouraged as a way to apprehend one's strengths and weaknesses, isolating those aspects of oneself that one can improve. As Fleming notes, the cultural logic of late capitalism encourages almost crippling levels of reflexivity: 'Reflexivity is now a sited activity that folds the individual back on himself or herself' (Fleming 2009: 6). This compulsive emphasis on the individual, on self-reflexivity and continuous improvement, shapes individual action in the direction of what is desired in the market.

Flexible capitalism, by way of rituals of evaluation, recognition and sanction, not only shapes the mindsets and actions of people – it inscribes itself onto our bodies. Thus the notions of 'flexible bodies' (Martin 1994) and 'make-over culture' (McGee 2005) are not separate from flexible work, but deeply entwined with it. What de Certeau has written on 'the scriptural economy' has a bearing here:

> There is no law that is not inscribed on bodies. Every law has a hold on the body. The very idea of an individual that can be isolated from the group was established along with the necessity, in penal justice, of having a body that could be marked by punishment, and in matrimonial law, of having a body that could be marked with a price in transactions among collectivities. From birth to mourning after death, law 'takes hold of' bodies in order to make them its text. Through all sorts of initiations (in rituals, at school, etc.), it transforms them into tables of the law, into living tableaux of rules and customs, into actors in the drama organized by a social order. (de Certeau 1988: 139)

Even though he speaks of law and justice, we may by analogy recognize how new forms of control, soft or hard, build on the notion of a separate individual, and inscribe themselves on our minds as well as our bodies.

All About Ties: An Economy of Connections

If the market enters as a central organizing model in the labour market, how then is this articulated in flexible forms of work? We will need to take a closer look at how different forms of exchange infuse social relations, or are modelled upon them. In doing so, I aim not to provide a strictly economistic portrayal of social relations and exchange elements, but to evoke and discuss some of the exchange aspects of work relations. We will see how flexible work models accentuate the market elements of work, and how gift and commodity exchange aspects are interweaved in what may be called 'an economy of connections' (Garsten 2013; cf. Steege 2007).

In a general sense, anthropologists understand gifts to differ from commodities in that the former involve some element of inter-personal dependence: the giver of a gift remains an element of the good or service and does not alienate him- or herself from it. A gift implies an intention to develop or maintain a social relationship between parties to the exchange. In contrast, the exchange of commodities is often seen not to carry any implied residual obligations or relationships between the people involved (Gregory 1982; Bell 1991). Forms of economic relations built on gift exchange, whilst giving rise to important analyses of mostly tribal economies (Lévi-Strauss 1969; Sahlins 1972; Mauss 1974), have not received much attention in economics, with some notable exceptions (e.g. Becker 1974; Akerlof 1982).

Duran Bell challenges the neo-classical conception of exchange theory by suggesting that commodity exchange is a special case of gift exchange. Contrary to what is often argued, alienation is not the essential distinction between the two. 'Both gift and commodity exchange are manifestations of reciprocal allocations between two parties', he argues, 'and it is often the case that elements of gift-exchange relations display functional relationships of the form common in commodity relations' (Bell 1991: 157). This approach appears promising in attempting to understand how both commodity exchange and gift exchange are encouraged in the flexible labour market. What I take from Bell's argument is the contention that they both rely on reciprocal allocations, and are thus grounded in social relations. Moreover, they are not easily confined to different social groups and structures, but often appear tangled with one another. A similar point has been made by Carrier, who states that 'people, objects, and social relations form a whole that is created and recreated in different ways when people transact with each other in gift and commodity relations' (Carrier 1991: 119).

Aspects of commodity exchange appear most discernibly in the temporary-staffing sector. The market for flexible staffing essentially builds on workers being employed and allocated in response to market signals. Moreover, workers are broken loose from long-term contractual bonds with clients and agencies in order to operate in the market according to demand. Relative to the established norm of the regular full-time employment contract, the temporary-staffing sector constitutes a radical form of human association, in that it builds on the loosening of organizational and contractual ties – and, we may add, collegial ties – in favour of free-moving human capital. Furthermore, the organizational logic of temping is one that evacuates the uniqueness of a person from labour. It builds on the core principle that any individual in an organization is substitutable (Selznick 1948: 25; Ahrne 1994: 18). If one position is vacant, it may be filled by someone else with adequate qualifications. Hence the manufactured uncertainty and competitiveness that arises out of knowing you are replaceable, and the continuous emphasis on learning in order to stay on the books and to be employable, to build one's personal brand. Any attempt to construct a sort of uniqueness inside a system that continuously attempts to evacuate it would appear, we have to admit, futile (cf. Fleming 2009). The flexible-staffing industry, despite its many and varied forms, fosters depersonalization and disenchantment, and opens the gate to alienation.

Temporary employees, for their part, organize their social allocations accordingly. Developing shared experiences and interests with other temps is generally of little interest to them, since these are first and foremost competitors and not colleagues. The social aspect of work is undermined by continuous movement across client organizations, as well as by the fact that assignments are by nature temporary. Temporary employees experience a lack of collegial community. Concepts such as 'colleague', 'competitor' and 'client' are often vague and interchangeable (Garsten 2003, 2008). To begin with, interest in getting to know one's fellow colleagues is scant, since temps will rarely end up working within the same client organization anyway. Interest in participating in social events organized by staffing agencies is low, since they hardly know anyone who might attend. At the client's workplace, most temps prefer to keep a distance from their workmates, since they prefer to focus on the task at hand and not to get too involved socially. Moreover, they are recommended by the staffing agency not to take part in gossiping or back talking (Garsten 2008). Professional and single-stranded relations are encouraged, which strips them off much of the potentially rich sociality of the work group. Commodity exchange elements are clearly visible here. A just-in-time logic of demand and supply distributes temps accordingly. An immediate return in the form a wage, based on hours of assignment and clear pricing mechanisms, is expected from the agency. And temps compete amongst themselves for the attractive assignments.

If the commodity exchange aspects are a poignant part of the flexible-staffing industry, other aspects figure as well. If the assignment is a long-term one, the temp may invest socially in getting to know workmates at the client organization. Also, alongside immediate returns, lingers the potential of an employment offer from a client, or a more interesting assignment offer from the assignment coordinator at the staffing agency. Temporary employees may thus invest considerable social energy in relations with a client organization they are interested in for permanent employment, just as they may direct their attention to cultivating relations with their assignment coordinator.

Bell declares that:

> If gift exchange is recognized to be an ongoing personal relationship between parties, where gifts may come in the form of goods and services, fervent expressions of appreciation, respects and love, then each person has an apparently firm basis for knowing the amount of utility experienced by the other. The value of a gift to the receiver is indicated by the value of the reciprocal response. (Bell 1991: 159)

The type of relation that may develop between a temporary employee and his or her client, or between a temporary employee and an assignment coordinator, may display aspects of gift exchange in that the temporary employee invests in the provision of services and in the relation beyond what is recognized in wage compensation, with the expectation that it will pay off one day in the future. The 'value' of services rendered and the social energy invested is often recognized by the client and the agency, evidence of which becomes apparent in evaluations and awards. In a number of cases, informants have told me how this investment has contributed to them getting a job offer from a client, or advancing in the hierarchy of consultants at the agency.

We can relate the commodity exchange relation that arises from the contingent position of temps in the labour market to that of regular employees in the high-tech industry. What informed employees' relation to work at Apple Computer was less of a short-term transactional view and more of long-term social commitment. Work, and the flexibility that is imbued in it, is part of a lifestyle. You invest in work, identify with the company and its products and become, to varying degrees, an 'evangelist' for the company and its products. 'We live and breathe Apple', as one of my informants succinctly put it. And just as you invest in the company, you also nurture long-term connections outside, ties that may come in handy in the case of a major reorganization. In an environment in constant turmoil, information about when and where changes are likely to occur become 'hard currency' (Garsten 1994). Getting close to someone who might harbour relevant information is an investment in social ties. In turn, people who are in command of such information were oftentimes seen to act much like Melanesian 'Big Men', distributing information – itself a kind of valuable – at strategic points in time and to well-chosen people (ibid.).

In general, both management and employees at Apple resisted the notion of work as labour, and embraced a gift exchange relation with the corporation. Most employees invested a good portion of their energy, loyalty and commitment in their job, in the team and in the company at large, with the expectation of getting in return not only a fat pay check, perks and bonuses, but also promotion opportunities, recognition and the experience of being part of a highly successful, select group of people. What undermined and challenged a personalized and emotionally endowed relation to work, colleagues and management were the intermittent reorganizations and upheavals that shook the ground, much like recurring earthquakes. These not only served the managerial purpose of keeping employees on their toes, but also worked to remind them of the commoditized elements of work: that relations with the corporation were fickle and dependent upon their performance as well as on managerial schemes and whims; and relations with colleagues were highly competitive and subject to political games and manoeuvring.

At think tanks, what is perhaps most striking in terms of the employees' orientation to work is the degree to which the gift element of exchange is elaborated on in a highly competitive and politicized area. Introductions and referrals to high-ranking, influential people are given as 'gifts', in the sense that they are tokens of a relationship that is seen valuable enough to invest in and where there may be an anticipation of return. In return, the recipient of the gift is expected to recognize the value in the act of the giver, to provide information back to the giver about the unfolding of the contact and, most importantly, to be ready to help out with a useful connection at some point in the future. Ideally, recurrent giving serves to circulate and redistribute valuables, in the form of connections, within the community of professionals. Over time, this contributes to the building up of what is essentially a dense network of connections around particular policy areas.

Such 'gifts' differ with regards to their value. The gift of a connection from someone with good credentials is more valuable than one from someone with lesser credentials, or who carries less of a brand name. My first experience of doing fieldwork in Washington DC was indeed related to being an outsider regarding the 'economy of connections', as it were. My academic credentials from Sweden counted for little in this community, and to squeeze into the exchange circle as an outsider and a 'nobody' took effort, perseverance and strategizing. Once I got the hang of it, and had something to offer in return, connecting became an easier game. Melissa Fisher (2012) also experienced similar challenges to access in her fieldwork among female Wall Street investors, where her way into the field was to a large extent dependent upon getting the right connections from the right person.

The type of reciprocity involved here can be seen as a form of 'balanced reciprocity' (Sahlins 1972), in that it relies on informal connections and that the expectation of a return is not connected to a specific point in time. Whilst there is an element of 'economy' in the exchange of referrals and information among professionals, we should be careful not to overemphasize these aspects. A note of caution is in place here. Gouldner (1960) made an important analytic distinction between reciprocity as a pattern of social exchange and reciprocity as a general moral belief. The moral norm of reciprocity constitutes, in Gouldner's view, an important 'causal force' in social life. It ensures that a person does not end up gaining at the expense of another's beneficial acts towards him or her (see also Uehara 1995). It balances and structures relations and acts of exchange. The moral aspect is highly present among groups of think-tankers. Connections depend on trust, and introductions are made not on a whim but after weighing the costs and benefits. If trusted with a favour, you are expected to recognize the mutuality it entails. And this expectation of mutuality is, most often, implicit. Reciprocity can thus be seen to underlie the principles of trust, respect and the sense of what is appropriate and what is not in professional relations.

Hence, we see that in flexible capitalism, modes of relating to work vary greatly, and the quality of relation between professionals takes on different characteristics. In flexible employment, flexibility entails adapting to the changing demands and needs of the market, of clients and of agencies. This agile expectation fosters in turn a predominantly opportunistic orientation to work and to employers, clients and colleagues on the part of temps. The job is contingent, and to 'stay on the books' temporary employees develop an instrumental and transaction-orientated mindset. More long-term orientation and reciprocal gift-type relations are fostered with clients with whom one would like a full-time employment offer, and to the assignment coordinator, who is in charge of placements.

The type of market rationality that is prevalent in late capitalism centres primarily on the individual and the flexible exchange of services and skills in the workplace or across organizations. The transactional approach rests on the assumption of autonomous individuals who are, at once, their own masters and who can bend flexibly to market needs. The rhetoric of organizational change that underpins these assumptions contributes by positioning individuals in the liminal spaces, at the thresholds, of shifting organizational boundaries. The sociality of long-term investment on the other hand signifies a non-commoditized relation that is continuously endangered when utilized to advance one's position or get access to valuable resources in a competitive labour market.

Concluding Notes: Flexibility, Liminality and the Bottom-line Value of Social Ties

Flexibility is an evocative sign of our times. It signifies at once agile bodies and mindsets, adjustable organizational templates and production processes, contingent employment contracts and versatile roles and repertoires. It signals a point of direction with open-ended solutions, and a great degree of variation. By its very nature, anything flexible escapes rigid definition. However, flexibility is closely linked to the intensification of capitalist market-based solutions. Flexibility emerges as a compass in a labour market that is increasingly responsive to market signals, supply and demand, and in which individuals are encouraged to bend accordingly. As Kjaerulff states in the introduction to this volume, this development obscures 'a more entangled and ambiguous mix of "gift and commodity" exchange, in which relationships not only decline, but simultaneously proliferate'. Flexible capitalism thus shapes and influences social relations and subjectivities in certain ways.

Flexible capitalism feeds on, and in turn nurtures, a variety of flexibilities. In this nexus, the recasting of organizational boundaries, of work and non-work spheres, and of contractual arrangements, opens up liminal spheres in which conventional understandings of work, labour and subjectivity are tried out, and where the ambiguous dimensions of gift and commodity relations are at play. Flexible organizations and positions foster a degree of liminality in the practice of social relations. Flexibility embraces a repertoire of capacities and skills, and defies a definite list of acceptable features. It thrives on ambiguity, and is plastic enough as a term to cover whatever attitudes, skills and behaviours are necessary for market adaptation.

The discourse and practices of 'flexibility' are individualizing in their consequences, positioning the individual as the primary source of responsible agency. This may imply developing a short-term, commodity-type exchange relation with both employers and work, as seen most clearly in the case of temporary staffing. It may also mean that employees develop a more long-term and gift-type relation with their employer, colleagues and work, as evinced primarily among high-tech employees and policy professionals. In each type of position, however, these types of exchange relations are tangled with each other and not easily distilled from one another. Each type of relation reveals the tensions of the logic of the market on one hand, and the social foundations of work on the other. This assemblage of commodity and gift exchange elements infuses work with a certain friction, or discord. In flexible capitalism, with continuously changing organizational boundaries and positions, an 'economy of connections' takes shape, in which market logics and sociality are at once emphasized. The existence of networks of connections within and among organizations is not a natural or a social given, but the product of investment strategies aimed at establishing or maintaining social relationships that are usable in the short or long term, and that imply durable obligations (Bourdieu 1986: 52). As a policy intellectual at one of the DC5 think tanks put it: 'Networking is all we do. Without networks you are no one. Being at this institution offers a wealth of networking opportunities'.

Notes

1 The notion of 'disorganized capitalism' as outlined by Lash and Urry (1988, 1994) comes close to the situation of diversity and friction described above. Lash and Urry emphasize the enhancement of flows of capital, labour, images, information and commodities across space and time; the importance of networks and information technology; of processes of individualization and reflexivity; and the reliance on signs in communicative processes, processes that are relevant for the amplification of 'flexibility'.
2 See Steege (2007) for an interesting account of how the 'economy of connections' became a way to secure one's survival in postwar Berlin.
3 Many think tanks in the USA are non-profit organizations, which provides them with a tax-exempt status. Organizations classified as 501(c)(3) are prohibited from conducting political campaign activities to intervene in elections to public office, but may conduct a limited amount of lobbying to influence legislation.

References

Ahrne, G. 1994. *Social Organizations: Interaction Inside, Outside and Between Organizations*. London: Sage.
Akerlof, G.A. 1982. 'Labor Contracts as Partial Gift Exchange', *Quarterly Journal of Economics* 97: 547–569.
Bauman, Z. 2001. *The Individualized Society*. Cambridge: Polity Press.
Beck, U. 1992. *Risk Society: Towards a New Modernity*. London: Sage.
Becker, G.S. 1974. 'A Theory of Social Interactions', *Journal of Political Economy* 82: 1063–1093.
Bell, D. 1991. 'Modes of Exchange: Gift and Commodity', *Journal of Socio-Economics* 20(2): 155–167.
Bourdieu, P. 1986. 'Forms of Capital', in J.E. Richardson (ed.), *Handbook of Theory of Research for the Sociology of Education*. New York: Greenwood Press, pp. 241–258.

Braverman, H. 1974. *Labour and Monopoly Capital: The Degradation of Work in the Twentieth Century*. New York: Monthly Review Press.

Burawoy, M. 1979. *Manufacturing Consent: Changes in the Labor Process under Monopoly Capitalism*. Chicago: University of Chicago Press.

Carrier, J.G. 1991. 'Gift, Commodities, and Social Relations: A Maussian View of Exchange', *Sociological Forum* 6(19): 199–136.

——— 1997. 'Introduction', in J.G. Carrier (ed.), *Meanings of the Market*. Oxford: Berg, pp. 1–67.

Clarke, J. 2005. 'New Labour's Citizens: Activated, Empowered, Responsibilized, Abandoned?' *Critical Social Policy* 25(4): 447–463.

de Certeau, M. 1988 [1984]. *The Practice of Everyday Life*, trans. S. Rendall. Berkeley: University of California Press.

Fisher, M. 2012. *Wall Street Women*. Durham, NC: Duke University Press.

Fleming, P. 2009. *Authenticity and the Cultural Politics of Work: New Forms of Informal Control*. Oxford: Oxford University Press.

Fogde, M. 2011. 'Governing through Career Coaching: Negotiations of Self-Marketing', *Organization* 18(1): 65–82.

Foucault, M. 1991. *Discipline and Punish: The Birth of the Prison*. Harmondsworth: Penguin.

Garsten, C. 1994. *Apple World: Core and Periphery in a Transnational Organizational Culture*, Stockholm Studies in Social Anthropology, 33. Stockholm: Almqvist and Wiksell International.

——— 1999. 'Betwixt and Between: Temporary Employees as Liminal Subjects in Flexible Organizations', *Organization Studies* 20(4): 601–617.

——— 2002. 'Flex Fads: New Economy, New Employees', in I. Holmberg, M. Salzer-Mörling and L. Strannegård (eds), *Stuck in the Future: Tracing the 'New Economy'*. Stockholm: Book House Publishing, pp. 241–265.

——— 2003. 'Colleague, Competitor, or Client: Social Boundaries in Flexible Work Arrangements', in N. Paulsen and T Hernes (eds), *Managing Boundaries in Organizations: Multiple Perspectives*. Basingstoke: Palgrave Macmillan, pp. 244–261.

——— 2008. *Workplace Vagabonds: Career and Community in Changing Worlds of Work*. Basingstoke: Palgrave Macmillan.

——— 2013. 'All About Ties: Think Tanks and the Economy of Connections', in C. Garsten and A. Nyqvist (eds), *Organisational Anthropology: Doing Ethnography in and among Complex Organisations*. London: Pluto Press, pp. 139–154.

——— 2014. 'Global Swirl at Dupont Circle: Think Tanks, Connectivity, and the Making of "the Global"', in: T.H. Eriksen, C. Garsten and S. Randeria (eds), *Anthropology Now and Next*. Oxford: Berghahn, pp. 70–90.

Garsten, C., and A. Haunschild. 2014. 'Transient and Flexible Work Lives: Liminal Organizations and the Reflexive Habitus', in B. Koene, C. Garsten and N. Galais (eds), *Management and Organization of Temporary Agency Work*. London: Routledge, pp. 23–37.

Garsten, C., and K. Jacobsson (eds). 2004. *Learning to be Employable: New Agendas on Work, Employability and Learning in a Globalizing World*. Basingstoke: Palgrave Macmillan.

——— 2013. 'Sorting People In and Out: The Plasticity of the Categories of Employability, Work Capacity and Disability as Technologies of Government', *Ephemera* 13(4): 825–850.

Giddens, A. 1994. 'Living in a Post-Traditional Society', in U. Beck, A. Giddens and S. Lash (eds), *Reflexive Modernization: Politics, Tradition and Aesthetics in the Modern Social Order*. Cambridge: Polity.

Gouldner, A.W. 1960. 'The Norm of Reciprocity: A Preliminary Statement', *American Sociological Review* 25: 161–178.

Gregory, C. 1982. *Gifts and Commodities*. London: Academic Press.

Hacking, I. 1986. 'Making Up People', in T. Heller et al. (eds), *Reconstructing Individualism*. Stanford: Stanford University Press, pp. 222–236.

Henson, K.D. 1996. *Just a Temp*. Philadelphia: Temple University Press.

Kanter, R.M. 1983. *The Change Masters*. New York: Simon and Schuster.

Krause-Jensen, J. 2010. *Flexible Firm: The Design of Culture at Bang & Olufsen*. New York: Berghahn Books.

Lash, S., and J. Urry. 1988. *The End of Organized Capitalism*. Gerrards Cross: Polity Press.

——— 1994. *Economies of Signs and Space*. London: Sage.

Lévi-Strauss, C. 1969. *The Elementary Structures of Kinship*. London: Eyre and Spotttiswoode.

McGann, J.G. 2007. *Think Tanks and Policy Advice in the United States: Academics, Advisors and Advocates*. New York: Routledge.

McGee, M. 2005. *Self-Help, Inc.: Makeover Culture in American Life*. Oxford: Oxford University Press.

Martin, E. 1994. *Flexible Bodies: Tracking Immunity in American Culture – From the Days of Polio to the Age of AIDS*. Boston: Beacon Press.

Mauss, M. 1974. *The Gift*, trans. I. Cunnison. London: Routledge and Kegan Paul.

Meyer, J.W., and R.L. Jepperson. 2000. 'The "Actors" of Modern Society: The Cultural Construction of Social Agency', *Sociological Theory* 18(1): 100–120.

Miller, P., and N. Rose. 1995. 'Production, Identity, and Democracy', *Theory and Society* 24: 427–467.

Mitchell, T. 2002. *Rule of Experts: Egypt, Techno-politics, Modernity*. Berkeley: University of California Press.

Parry, J., and M. Bloch (eds). 1989. *Money and the Morality of Exchange*. Cambridge: Cambridge University Press.

Peck, J. 1996. *Work-Place: The Social Regulation of Labor Markets*. New York: Guilford Press.

Pink, D.H. 2001. *Free Agent Nation: How American's New Independent Workers Are Transforming the Way We Live*. New York: Warner Books.

Polanyi, K. 1944. *The Great Transformation*. New York: Farrar and Rinehart.

Sahlins, M. 1972. *Stone Age Economics*. New York: Aldine de Gruyter.

Selznick, P. 1948. 'Foundations of the Theory of Organizations', *Sociological Review* 13(1): 25–35.

Sennett, R. 1998. *The Corrosion of Character: The Personal Consequences of Work in the New Capitalism*. New York: Norton.

Steege, P. 2007. *Black Market, Cold War: Everyday Life in Berlin, 1946–1949*. Cambridge: Cambridge University Press.

Tsing, A.L. 2005. *Friction: An Ethnography of Global Connection*. Princeton: Princeton University Press.

Turner, V.W. 1967. 'Betwixt and Between: The Liminal Period in Rites de Passage', in *The Forest of Symbols*. Ithaca, NY: Cornell University Press, pp. 93–111.

————— 1969. *The Ritual Process: Structure and Anti-Structure*. Chicago: Aldine.

Uehara, E.S. 1995. 'Reciprocity Reconsidered: Gouldner's "Moral Norm of Reciprocity" and Social Support', *Journal of Social and Personal Relationships* 12(4): 483–502.

Van Gennep, A. 2004 [1909]. *The Rites of Passage*. London. Routledge.

Weber, M. 1978 [1921]. *Economy and Society*. Berkeley: University of California Press.

Wedel, J.R. 2009. *Shadow Elite: How the World's New Power Brokers Undermine Democracy, Government, and the Free Market*. New York: Basic Books.

Weidenbaum, M. 2008. *The Competition of Ideas: The World of Washington Think Tanks*. New Brunswick, NJ: Transaction Press.

Whyte, W.H. 2002 [1956]. *The Organization Man*. Philadelphia: University of Pennsylvania Press.

Willis, P. 1977. *Learning to Labor: How Working Class Kids Get Working Class Jobs*. New York: Columbia University Press.

Yanagisako, S. 2002. *Producing Culture and Capital: Family Firms in Italy*. Princeton: Princeton University Press.

4

Taking Over the Gift

The Circulation and Exchange of Options, Labour and 'Lucky Money' in Alberta's Oil and Gas Industry

Caura Wood

> Make no mistake. This is a takeover. We're not about to share power. They'll do it our way.
> —CEO speaking to employees about their publicly announced takeover of another junior producer

> You're not a victim but a participant in this process.
> —Gas company president

Anthropology has turned to the study of finance in recent years, pointing to the centrality of finance in contemporary flexible capitalism. Ethnographic work in this subfield now includes the study of stock exchanges (Hertz 1998; Zaloom 2006), the frames, methods and culture of traders (Zaloom 2006, 2009; Preda 2009; Appadurai 2011; Lépinay 2011), the practices of Wall Street bankers, their cultures of smartness and the shareholder paradigm (Ho 2009), the study of money (Bloch and Parry 1989; Maurer 2006), alternative forms of banking and new forms of payment (Maurer 2005, 2012). Some studies return to questions from economic anthropology and exchange theory, particularly with respect to the location of the social in finance and the gift in commodity exchange (Appadurai 2011; Miyazaki 2013). With respect to the specific intersection of work, finance and flexible capitalism, ethnographic studies have tended to focus on technical expertise and back-office workers (Riles 2004, 2011), the methods and forms of calculative reason employed by derivatives traders, and the often anonymous market spaces where trades of equities, derivatives, short selling and arbitraging are transacted by financial professionals (Zaloom 2006; Miyazaki 2013). Much less attention has been given to the financialization of work in corporate offices, and the increasingly routine application of market logics to everyday corporate life (for exceptions see Cefkin 2009; Garsten, Knox, this volume; Ho 2009; Welker et al. 2011).

In this chapter I am interested in derivatives at work, meaning the routine use of company stock options issued to employees as part of their compensation package. My particular interest is with the work that options perform as a site of contested value.[1] The study of derivatives at work (as opposed to a study of the work of trading derivatives) brings these seemingly abstract financial objects into the visible and immediate space of everyday practical purpose. In these spaces, options have a social life that exceeds the legalities of the stock option as a document that sets the terms of ownership and exchange. Options have use value (cf. Introduction, this volume): they attract, hold and retain employees; they produce sociality and connection and appear as an inalienable possession, a gift. They are also a potential site of capital return and reward that can only be realized through exchange and circulation. In this uneasy and ambiguous merger of the spirit of the gift with the spirit of capital and commodity exchange, workers are unevenly constituted as market participants. Tracing the social life of options at work thus provides a fruitful path for exploring work in flexible capitalism as an ambiguous practice of exchange (see Introduction, this volume).[2] Indeed, this exploration illuminates a more unexpected element of my fieldwork among junior energy corporations in Alberta, Canada. Even in sites shaped by speculative finance capital – sites that epitomize flexible capitalism – I found elements of the gift.

In order to illuminate this paradox, I will describe the acceleration of mergers and acquisitions ('M and A' or 'takeovers') among two junior oil and gas firms during the recent energy boom in the province of Alberta, the heart of Canada's oil and gas economy. During the years between 2000 and 2006, Alberta's energy industry experienced an intense period of M and A activity. In the midst of such transactions, corporate energy workers frequently circulate as objects of exchange; workers are reduced to a commodity status much like the barrels of oil that they work to produce and sell. Workers are 'acquired' or 'dispositioned' when one firm takes over or merges with another. However, these junior firms also tend to financialize

workers, offering stock options to all employees of the firm that tie
a portion of a worker's compensation to the uncertain vicissitudes of
the market. When options are 'in the money', they extend a portion
of surplus value to employees and become a powerful technique
of flexible capitalism that can entice employees to rally around the
common goal of 'value creation' understood as corporate capital
accumulation and shareholder value.[3] Workers are thus caught within
overlapping and contradictory regimes of exchange: the exchange of
alienable labour time for wages; the exchange of alienable labourers as commodities or 'knowledge assets' for cash and/or retention
bonuses; the exchange of labour time for inalienable optioned equity
(capital), the receipt of which is often considered by workers and
employers alike in terms of a gift. This chapter therefore explores
the frequent expression of ambivalence over the risky business of
work where the potential rewards of options are contingent upon
a corporation's collective performance, and on the (un)luckiness of
the market. This risky business is set against, and indeed exchanged
for, a transient, temporary and uncertain working future. Success in
this context hinges on liquidation and circulation. As a result, I will
suggest these circulating workers are situated ambiguously between
a Marxist story about commoditization, objectification, alienation
and the extraction of surplus value, and a Maussian story where the
option as earned equity or as gifted gain produces relations of obligation, sociality and, indeed, flexibilities, which reduce the frictions
of circulation.

In what follows, I first briefly describe the characteristics of
Alberta's junior energy industry, particularly the organization of
capital into a portfolio of sites for oil-based accumulation. I then
describe the flexible form of labouring for capital that is produced
by the requirements of finance, after which a detailed ethnography of
two takeover events will serve as my point of departure for developing the general argument.

Junior Energy Firms and Merger Mania in Alberta

Contrary to popular understanding, oil and gas in Alberta is not
strictly dominated by major, multinational corporations, or so-
called Big Oil. At various points in time, opportunities for smaller
companies, termed 'juniors' or 'start-ups', have emerged either
due to the availability of capital or to the availability of properties.
Much like junior start-ups in other sectors such as mining or IT,

junior oil and gas corporations are established for the purpose of short-term value creation for shareholders. They are often assembled by a small group of founders that cobble together some initial seed capital, and are then 'shopped' by investment bankers that seek to connect expert entrepreneurial teams with global finance capital. The expert teams offer global capital investors access to local knowledge of Alberta's energy industry, and to the geological contours of the Western Canadian Sedimentary Basin (WCSB), the five kilometre deep, hydrocarbon-rich layers of sedimentation that underlie most of Alberta and some regions of the neighbouring Provinces to the east and west. Investors find higher risk and reward opportunities in the energy sector by identifying these smaller-scale investment sites through which to concentrate their capital, and intensify potential returns. Access to the WCSB through these junior firms opens Alberta's hydrocarbons to a multiplicity of sites of connection between global capital and local labour (cf. Tsing 2005).[4] During the recent boom years of 2000 to 2006, global capital flooded Alberta's energy industry, chasing rising commodity prices. At any given time, there were hundreds of junior corporations operating in Alberta, with billions in aggregate market capital, all competing for properties, rigs, labour, future capital and infrastructure. This was a time of experimentation with capital, labour and value creation.

At the time, junior corporations were filling a market niche. These specialized teams were doing the work of exploration and development 'through the drill bit' in order to produce 'flowing barrels' (barrels of oil equivalent per day [boepd]) or 'on-stream' production.[5] Their objective was to grow to a sellable size, often defined as somewhere between 5,000 and 10,000 boepd, and then seek an exit (a liquidity event) by selling to an oil and gas income trust or larger energy firm. The trusts were also filling a market niche. By buying flowing barrels from junior producers, trusts left the discovery work (and the capital risks of discovery) to the juniors, and instead purchased their results in order to provide streams of 'lower risk' reliable income to their shareholders. The trusts were a popular product held by mutual funds and pension funds, particularly for their capacity to pay out income on a regular basis to a growing population of retirees across Canada and others seeking stable income streams. The relationship, and indeed division of labour, between junior firms and income trusts had thus become symbiotic, feeding the diverse demands of capital markets.

Mergers and acquisitions became the industry's answer to the problem of growth and the problem of investor demand for products that could offer reliable income streams and higher rates of return. In the oil and gas industry, the contradictions of capital so well outlined by Marx (1990) do not manifest in the search for new consumers in new markets (there has been no net shrinkage of demand in a world 'addicted' to oil). Instead, oil-based accumulation as currently practiced in Alberta is constrained by available inventory, capital, discovery and extraction technique, pipeline capacities, and regulatory frameworks.[6] For juniors, then, the problem of growth is understood as one that requires finding and converting land prospects into flowing production, which is structured as a race against time and a race against other juniors amidst these forces of constraint. It is a race against time because the moment a well is flowing and 'on-stream', it begins to decline. Another well must be added to replace the declining production and so on, until the company either runs out of capital or out of prospects. It is a race against other juniors because those that show the highest rates of return are typically rewarded with capital investment and 'market value'.

During the boom years, prospects were scarce but capital was plentiful, attracted to rapidly rising commodity prices. As a result, juniors began to buy one another to solve their problems of growth in order to sell to a trust and meet their obligations to capital investors for accelerated and higher rates of return.[7] In other words, junior companies were both drilling wells and absorbing one another in an effort to reach a scale attractive to energy trusts. In turn, the trusts were rapidly absorbing juniors in order to continuously renew the declining inventories of hydrocarbons that would supply income streams to their shareholders. The system appeared cannibalistic. In their attempt to satisfy capital markets, juniors were buying each other, and trusts or larger companies were buying juniors. Shareholders of these varying corporations, along with the state (through rents and royalties), were absorbing the exchange value of Alberta's hydrocarbons. Once liquidated, CEOs of junior firms would often restart with a new name and a fresh round of capital investment from the same or new connections with global capital. The end result was an intense period of merger mania that would continue up to 2007.[8]

Labouring for Capital

In this market milieu, labour became as flexible as capital. These were not only Emily Martin's 'flexible bodies' (Martin 1994), adapting to changes in technology, but also, and more importantly, they were 'circulating bodies', moving through circuits of exchange, subjected to risk and adapting to new organizational environments every couple of years or less (cf. Lee and LiPuma 2002). A job with a junior energy company was unlikely to last for more than two to three years, and workers were jostled from one company to the next in a series of primarily lateral moves (same job, new place, some new people, new boss, for example). Employees of such corporations know from the outset that employment with such a firm will be temporary: start-ups incorporate with an exit strategy already in mind. Therefore, on the one hand, start-up firms must attract capital, and on the other, they must attract skilled industry labour that will knowingly and inevitably be severed either due to failure (that is, failure to create value, resulting in liquidation) or due to success (successful value creation resulting in a divestiture of assets; liquidation). Positioned to the market as short-term investment vehicles, such firms make no promise of long-term employment or of a pension; instead, they attract labour by promising the opportunity to earn capital through the vehicle of the stock option or other similar financial instruments (a performance warrant, and/or performance bonus, or retention bonus, for example). 'Incentivized' by options and other compensation instruments such as performance bonuses or warrants, each transaction constitutes not only the loss of a job, but also a liquidity event that can trigger a possible payout.

As such, employee compensation schemes tend to be generous but are tied to performance and outcomes, not strictly to wage time. Such schemes are purportedly devised to create 'buy-in' to a firm, and thereby rally employees together around the very uneven yet shared goal of capital accumulation. These compensation schemes support a market sensibility, and are intended to align the interests of employees with that of management and shareholders. Workers are refigured as 'market man' (to borrow from Garsten, this volume). Insofar as workers have the opportunity to own some of the capital stock of the firm, through a direct share purchase (or employee share-purchase plan) or through stock options, such firms rewrite the terms of labour. In other words, workers are shareholders and labour is reconstituted as a form of capital. Labouring for wages becomes a form of unevenly *labouring for capital*. Through options, management (in concert with lead shareholders and boards of directors) seek to incentivize labour to serve capital, working not only so that others can extract the surplus value produced through it, but also to ensure that a portion of the surplus returns to them, presumably by working to 'create value with every dollar spent'. Employees are often encouraged to think of themselves as 'agile capital', as 'opportunity driven', able to identify and adapt quickly to market changes and trends. From this perspective, short-term employment is positioned as an entrepreneurial opportunity that can produce capital gains that are experienced as uneven and periodic windfalls. The temporality of work is thus restructured from labour time exchanged for wages to one wherein the daily exchange of labour time for wages becomes a meantime between moments of capital gain (or loss) from options that are in the money.

This phenomenon is captured in the ethnographic example to which I now turn, that traces two takeovers in Calgary's juniors market during those boom years. In the first example, one of my field sites, a public oil and gas company, Antler Exploration Ltd, made a takeover bid on a smaller public company named Globe Energy Ltd.[9] In this case, the bodies and assets of Globe were exchanged for stock and cash from Antler. Here, Globe employees were circulated and subjected to Antler's growth strategy, acquired through uneven relations of power, wealth and authority. In the second example, the corporation that formerly did the taking over was itself taken over. However, in this example the takeover was the realization of the seller's goals, wherein desire and attraction (rather than strictly subjection) were fully visible in the social relations of exchange. In this latter case, Antler assets were tendered for cash, and bodies migrated to the acquiring company to gain additional 'lucky money' under circumstances that were more of their choosing. As I will show, regimes of commodity and gift exchange overlap and are entangled in these transactions, producing significant ambivalence over the (un)luckiness of work within a market-oriented flexible capitalism.

Taking Bodies, Taking Stock

I had been working as an 'investor relations consultant' for Antler Exploration Ltd, a junior public company, as a means of doing research on oil and gas value creation. During my stay, takeover fever entered the corridors of my field site. One morning, an important e-mail broadcast arrived in my inbox from the president and CEO, named Max. We were all to meet in the main boardroom for an important announcement. Of course we already knew what the meeting was about. The press release was already out and most of us had read the morning headlines: 'Antler Announces Takeover of Globe'. The office was spilling over with takeover chatter before the first cups of morning coffee were even brewed. The fact that I did not know of the news in advance of the press release was a measure of my overall unimportance in the hierarchical scheme of things. My phone rang: 'Have you heard the news? We're taking over Globe'. Then a barrage of e-mails either giving instructions or looking for information: 'Get ready, your phone will be ringing off the hook today with shareholder calls'. And, 'Hey, do you know any of those Globe people? Are they coming here?' 'How long will the stock be halted?'

I grabbed my notebook and my now cold coffee and headed for the conference room. As usual there were barely enough chairs to accommodate the existing staff of forty people. The company had grown so much that employees were literally spilling into the hallways. Extra chairs were being rolled in and people were jokingly sitting on each other's laps. Then Max began to speak:

> As I'm sure you've already heard, we are taking over Globe. This is a friendly takeover offer and they are onside with it. If you haven't done so already, you will read in the press release that Antler made a bid of cash and shares for each share of their company, and now the offer will be circulated to their shareholders and that should take about thirty days. If the shareholders vote in favour and tender their shares, which we expect they will, there will be a lot of activity around here in the next few months . . . We want to grow our production base to 8,000 BOE per day and we just can't get there fast enough through the drill bit. This is a timely acquisition, and there is a lot of synergy between the two companies. It will add a new core area to our portfolio, and it will raise the bar for us, for sure.

One of the vice-presidents interjected: 'This is a great deal for Antler; this acquisition will increase our reserve base and will add a lot of undeveloped land. This deal will take us to the moon!' (He raised his fists towards the ceiling in triumph).

If the employees looked a little unsure about how to interpret the takeover, management gave them their answers: they were about to enter the big leagues; you simply were not anybody until you could take somebody over. It was a sign of both prosperity and power, measured by acceleration. They looked proud, as though they had in fact just conquered something. It was the first time that these executives had run a public company. They had something to prove and they wanted to win.

The questions from staff began to pour in: 'Will we be taking their employees too or just the assets?' 'Do we have enough space?' 'Where are these new people going to sit?' 'Will we be using our same systems or theirs?' 'Will they get to have a say in how we're going to do things?' 'How will we fit the two companies together?' To the last question, Max's answer was very clear: 'Make no mistake, this is not a democracy. We are not about to share power. This is a takeover and they will do it *our* way'.

That afternoon, I accompanied the management team to Globe Energy's offices. Their executives and staff were all assembled in their company boardroom, waiting to meet the group that had just made a bid for their company. Max introduced himself and each of the officers. He then explained my presence: 'This is my investor relations person, she's also doing research on this takeover stuff and she may want to ask you questions at some point if you're open to that'. The people listened to Max describe Antler, the company's strategy and style:

> We are very proud of what we have built at Antler. We have always maintained that if you put a good group of people together and work hard you can reach the top quartile without having to be geniuses. We started out in 1998 with just a couple of us and now we are at the 5,000 boepd mark with about forty or so people on the payroll. Our goal is to grow to over 10,000 boepd, and we think this acquisition is a great move for us. Along the way we have built a great company, we have set a lot of precedents in the way we work with our partners and with aboriginal groups, and we always try to be principled . . . Many of you will probably be joining us. I know you probably have a lot of questions for us, but I assure you, we will get to that just as soon as we can.

Next, the chief financial officer (CFO), named John, described the company's financial position, cash flow, debt, share prices, the availability of stock options for employees and so on. When he finished, Max opened the floor to questions. Globe employees asked: 'Will you be making offers to any of us?' 'What kind of bonus structures do you offer your employees?' 'Will there be any options?' 'Will there be any retention bonuses?' 'What will happen to our existing shares and options?' 'What will the severance packages look like for those that aren't offered a job?' 'How long will this take?' 'Who do we report to now?' 'Should we continue to work on our current projects?' The CFO promised that he would meet with each of them in the near future, and reassured them that most of them would be offered a job.

At this point, we took our leave. As we walked back to the office, the executives began contemplating the enormity of what they had just done, and the enormity of what was ahead. Max was worried about how the integration would go, and whether the Globe people would fit in at Antler. However, a bigger source of concern for him and for all of the other executives was whether or not the market would like the deal, or whether or not the market would think they had over paid for Globe's assets. The market was a constant source of concern.

I later asked the CFO how the deal surfaced. He explained that it was an idea driven by investment bankers to secure value for Globe shareholders:

> the takeover wasn't invited and Globe's management team wasn't particularly happy about it. The deal was driven mainly by the market and by low share prices. Their chairman said, 'We've got to do something to get things going', and they hired an investment banker. The banker brought Antler to the table. It's a very aggressive situation with these bankers. They give you a limited time offer, and that gives the target company the upper hand on price, but it will bring us to 8,000 BOEs per day so I expect it will be a good move for the company.

The Globe story was quite different from Antler. They had been in operation for over seven years, and during that time they had seen reasonably steady growth. Their CEO explained to me that over the two previous years their production had flat-lined, and their stock had fallen as a result. While management had weathered the ups and downs of the market without any layoffs, growth had become a problem. As one of their senior vice-presidents explained, their stock had been trading at a low cash-flow multiple, and some 'unfriendly' companies had been looking at their assets.[10] Their big question was how to continue to survive in a rising market with a sagging share price relative to their peers. Their answer was to try and survive by getting bigger, or failing that to sell out.

For many executives I spoke with, the worst-case scenario would be 'to go out on their knees' – to be taken out in an undesirable way, especially in a hostile situation.[11] Such an event would signal failure. For Globe, the deal was friendly. They were in a good bargaining position to negotiate a desirable price as they had good assets. Commodity prices had been rising, and there were lots of buyers on the market willing to pay inflated prices for assets. But, given their lack of growth and low share price, 'it was a case of sell or be sold', said Globe's president. Antler needed to show growth to keep their promises to the market. Investment bankers appeared to have preyed on Antler's need for an acquisition and had them as first in a line-up of bidders. 'If Antler wanted the assets', said the CFO, they would have to 'step up and pay'. The executives later rumbled, 'Yes it was expensive. But was it too expensive? Time will tell'. And, 'We really had to pay up for it but it's a case of pay and hold your nose', said one vice-president, 'you've got to do the deal because if you don't, someone else will'. Max's perspective was similar: 'No one has a crystal ball ... You just don't know in advance, but you've got to trust your instincts'. In other words, they exchanged cash and some of Antler's equity for accelerated growth.

When the deal closed in mid-July, the two companies needed to integrate. All of the Globe executives were severed. They did not appear to be concerned. After all, they had just made a 'big score' and wanted the summer off to regroup before starting another junior company. From their point of view, they had looked after their employees with stock options and a stock purchase plan and each employee would get some cash and some Antler shares in exchange for those options. In the event that some Globe employees were not offered jobs, they would get a severance package. 'It's a good time to be on the street', said one of Globe's vice-presidents, 'There are jobs and opportunity out there right now. Some management is going over and that will help those that do go. But overall, Globe people will have to blend in with Antler management and their company'.

The terms of transfer for non-management Globe employees were written into the deal. It would be three months before options would payout, followed either by job offers or severance. Those offered a comparable job had to take it or seek employment elsewhere without severance. Hinging option payouts to employee migration ensured employees would remain in place long enough to presumably transfer the needed knowledge. Even those who did not get a job offer managed to wait out the short-term contract in order to vest and exercise their options and take their gain. Most of Globe's non-executive employees were offered some kind of employment, either full time or on a three-month contract. Options that are 'in the money' hold people in place, smoothing organizational transfers. Time is exchanged for labour as capital. Yet, there is no guarantee that the value of the options will increase over that same period of time. Options can quickly become out of the money, which did indeed happen, albeit for a short period of time. In such moments, options can fail to produce the effect of retention.

Circulating Bodies

Most of these employees were not new to the takeover process, and the shuffle of bodies was repeatedly described to me. They had become accustomed to the fairly rapid circulations that characterize fast and flexible capitalism. Some described it as a matter-of-fact inevitability. Others expressed a sense of short-term distress and abandonment anxiety, or financial vulnerability; some expressed an intense ambivalence, or 'wait and see' (hands in the air, shrugged shoulders), while others pursued it as a transformative opportunity.

For example, Leslie, an operations technician explained: 'The first time it happened I cried my eyes out. I loved that company and I thought I would retire there. I was literally devastated by that takeover. Now it's no big deal. I've been through three since, and I'm sure there will be more'. Another administrator, Lisa, had just started with Globe two weeks prior. As she put it: 'It's a little upsetting. I just got here and now all of a sudden I'm changing companies again. I just have to accept it as a fact of this industry'. Her employment history had been anything but predictable. She described how she had started her career as a secretary in the oil patch six years earlier. Her first job with an intermediate producer lasted just under two years. A hostile takeover bid was made for her company, and yet another company emerged as a 'white knight'. As she explained:

> I just didn't want to work for a big company, and out of the blue I got this call from a junior. I didn't know anyone there but I took the job . . . About a year and a half later, my former manager called and offered me a job with PetroGeo Corp. I worked there for almost two years, and then they were taken over. I was severed because they brought in their own drilling group (that company had since done two more takeovers). After a couple weeks of panic, I got a job at Globe. I met my current boss at Globe through an engineer I worked for at my first job. I had the interview and got hired right away. Then, wouldn't you know it, two weeks later the Antler-Globe deal was announced. At first I was really sceptical about it. I had a lot of feelings of doubt, you know this is something that happens to you; it's not something you choose, at least not at first.

Another accountant, Jennifer, also described how she was 'shuffled' from one organization to the next. Like Lisa, she had also become accustomed to changing jobs every couple of years. During her fifteen-year career as an accountant and then production accountant, she changed jobs ten times. Most of the moves were lateral ones, meaning she did not change her role but performed the same role at new locations. Of those moves, six were involuntary (due to mergers and takeovers) while four were voluntary (she applied for the job on her own initiative). She described the situation as a fait accompli: 'You know, it's inevitable'.

Other employees, by contrast, looked at circulations in terms of transformative potential. One employee, a mid-career production accountant, described to me how he approached his job in more of an entrepreneurial way. He tried to pre-plan for two to three year employment stints where options were central to his employment decisions. As part of his plan, he would look for companies that were early in their start-up phase or which had an undervalued stock price with a good growth plan in place. As he explained it: 'There is a lot of upside potential in options if you can get in at the right time and with a company likely to attract a good buyer. I'm not really here for the salary. If I plan things well, with a bit of luck, I can walk away with a good score from options every couple of years'. Like many employees, he considered himself to be reasonably market savvy. Labour, in his view, was a 'meantime' between capital gains.

The market savvy employees were easy to spot. The stock ticker could always be seen at their computer screens. In one gaze, they could observe both the stock price volatility and that of their own net worth. For these employees, value creation was both a job and a spectator sport, where the outcome of their performance was refracted back to them in the form of a moving average. Yet, potential gains from options are not determined on the grounds of 'fairness' or some sense of 'merit' but rather by timing. Option prices are set at the market price on the date they are issued (usually the date an employee is hired). Therefore, market timing rather than strictly labour time (during which options vest) or personal performance determines the spread of the gain (the difference between the exercise price and the sell price). For employees that signed on with the company during a 'dip' in the stock price, gains could be greater than for those who joined at a much earlier point in the corporation's history but at a high stock price, for example. Growth in stock price is rarely chronologically continuous and is often volatile. Good or bad market timing (that is, luck) produces disparity in gains from options, and considerable contestation. For example: 'He got his options at $1.80. Mine were priced at $3. How is that fair?'[12]

To be sure, takeovers create intense social upheavals and uncertainties. Calculations of bodies exchanged as commodities assume a certain equivalency: one production accountant carries more or less the same exchange value as another. However, subjects are not equivalent to objects, and such calculations fail to include employee sociality. After making the initial transfer from Globe to Antler, many employees were quick to highlight the differences between 'corporate cultures'. As an emic term, 'corporate culture' is used to refer to general ways of doing things, the 'structure of feeling' of a place, to borrow from Raymond Williams (1976), and the way that working subjects identify with one another as a social group. Globe employees described their organization as 'top down', 'more muted and conservative' and 'hard working', whereas Antler employees described their company as 'fun', 'hard working', 'young', 'athletic', 'value driven and cost conscious'. As groups combine, organizational identity becomes increasingly articulated. While the organization taken over is actively being dis-membered, that organization as an identity category is regularly cited to demarcate new and old boundaries and relations of power. 'They are Globe people'; '*They* have to learn how *we* do things'. It is a negative construct and one that is categorically different from being hired independently on voluntary terms.

Market Shocks, Arrested Flows

If the executives were worried about how the market perceived the deal, the market in turn gave them something to worry about a few months after the deal closed. Much of the production that Antler had paid full price for was considered 'flush production' which had suddenly 'backed right off', meaning that the production rates of the wells came on strong due to initial high pressures but then stabilized at rates that were lower than expected. Construction delays for pipeline connection also slowed other new well production from reaching the market. As a result, production targets had not been met and the deal appeared to have failed to produce the promised growth, at least in the short term. The 'market' responded by 'clobbering' the stock, 'hammering it' from that year's high of $5.50 or so down to a low of approximately $3. The team was distressed. Employees and management were so intimately tied to the stock's market value that the volatile stock chart could well have been their own ECG chart. The stress had become visible, indeed palpable – the sense of an impending heart attack. In a move that betrayed a climate of fear, some insiders even sold off their shares, which did not help 'market confidence'.[13] The CFO explained to me: 'This is not a good position to be in. Our share price is down and we are vulnerable. We have got to turn this around. Nobody wants to exit in a position of weakness'. Max began to worry about employee retention and morale: 'Right now, the stock price is lower than the price at which many employees' options were set. Somehow we've got to keep them motivated and keep them believing in this company'. Indeed, some of the employees were echoing those concerns: 'My options are worthless right now. I mean, that's why we take the lower salaries, because we get options that are supposed to make up for it. Right now my options mean nothing. Things had better turn around soon'.

At the same time, the market was also busy constituting the corporation. The 'strong buy' ratings were swapped for 'holds'. My phone was busy with investor calls, 'What's going on over there?' 'What's wrong with the stock?' 'Why is the share price down?' 'What are you guys doing over there?' On the Bullboards people debated Antler's performance: 'They overpaid for that acquisition. The production is too low. The stock is being punished because they are not meeting production targets'.[14] Occasionally a contrarian Bullboard participant would point to the positive: 'The stock is on sale! Buy now!' Each day Max was focused on which brokerage houses were buying and selling Antler stock. He gave many presentations and told investors that the company was 'a really good deal at these prices'.

In the meantime, Max worked to assure employees that things would be fine. He did his daily rounds, talking to staff in the hallways and in their offices, and he tried to interpret and explain the issues in a general meeting:

> Look, the interest in oil and gas is minimal right now. The market doesn't believe that commodity prices will hold, but we've had great earnings and cash flow. All the energy stocks are trading at a low multiple right now. We've got the USA elections going on and investors are taking their money out of the markets. We had a weak summer for the stock, and then we did the Globe deal. The summer was also really wet, and we couldn't get our drilling on-stream fast enough. We didn't make the numbers, and as a result we had some more slide in the stock. However, we press released today. Our fundamentals are strong. We've had 100 per cent growth in production this year to date, cash flow is up 200 per cent and we're in a better position than ever. The corporation is healthy, we'll keep our debt at one times cash flow, and we're considering a stock buy-back to help things along.

Later I spoke with many employees about their perspective on the stock price and the options. Some didn't seem too worried and accepted the volatility of the market as a fact of the business. Others were quite upset and felt they were getting 'screwed'. One employee who took a keen interest in investing and financial planning explained her position on the matter:

> For some of the employees here, this is the only savings they have. They're living pay cheque to pay cheque, and without these options they'll have nothing. I don't believe they totally understand the risk they're taking . . . If you take a job with a junior or intermediate, you are signing up to take risk, and I'm sure some people around here are feeling that right about now.

By early spring, management explained that commodity prices had remained strong, and a good drilling season had more or less turned things around for Antler. The takeover trend had not settled down, and deal after deal was still being announced. The company's stock had started to rebound, indexing to management that investors were more confident that the company had sorted out its value-creation projects. By late May, Antler's stock volumes began to surge, as did rumours, on the speculation that Antler may be the next takeover target.

One morning, Max called us all into the conference room for an update as he was having a hard time squelching the rumours.

> Acquisition activity is at a fever pitch in exploration and production. Many of our peers were taken out in Q1 [the first fiscal quarter]. Each time it's a larger company and now capital is focused on fewer and fewer companies. Volumes pick up every time there's a takeover transaction. Some suggest Antler is in the line for takeover. We see that as a flattering complement to our asset base, and it's certainly better than the other way around [that is, better than being forced to sell].

Max's speech, however, did not have the desired effect. Speculation as to who might take over the corporation, when and at what price, merely increased. With the stock on a run, employees also began looking for signs of an impending change of control. Their own experience told them that a takeover was probably inevitable, even though most of them were not privy to the corporation's confidential exit strategy. Over the next thirty days or so, perceptions heightened as employees observed, tracked and debated both management and market behaviour. Changes to the CEO's normal routine, the frequent appearance of suits with ties, increases in the number of management meetings in and out of house, increases to the stock's trading volume and actual rumours – all indexed an immanent liquidity event.

Another Disposition

All of those employees who had deduced through observation and speculation that 'something was going on' at Antler had their hunches confirmed just as summer approached. I arrived in the office one Monday to find the stock halted – someone, it seemed, had leaked news about Antler's impending takeover and share prices were on a crazy run. Max immediately called the Toronto Stock Exchange to have the stock halted pending an announcement. By 11.30 AM everyone was asked to assemble in the main boardroom. It had been exactly one year since the Globe takeover, and Antler employees were preparing for another asset disposition; indeed, their own disposition or exchange. While they waited for Max to arrive, jokes started circulating about the best rumours everyone had heard. Employees made bets over possible sell dates and prices.

Shortly thereafter, Max entered the room and quietly uttered something to his legal counsel. He then welcomed everyone to the meeting and said: 'I'm going to start by reading you these press releases verbatim. So here it is'. First he read Antler's press release, then that of Houston Oil and Gas Company (HOGC). Both releases announced that Antler was being taken over by a large American corporation. Then he began to explain the meaning of the transaction:

> This is a huge day for Antler [tears well up in his eyes and he pauses for a moment]. It's extremely significant that a company like HOGC with over $20 billion in assets and three different business arms would look at us. It's a big deal that they would look at Antler's asset base. I'm proud . . . That kind of recognition is a real validation. This business is so tough. We all know the issues with the stock market, the well issues and so on. We were always different . . . We were really part of something here. You know, we went from zero to $400 million in four years. This is a logical transition for Antler's assets and all of us. Going forward, as managers and directors of public companies, we must look after shareholders and then look after staff . . . When you're a small company, it's very hard to perform well when you have to manage all the analysts and market demands. Big companies can do it better. It's good all around . . . HOGC likes our assets because they specialize in deep tight wells. They get in these deep wells and frack the shit out of it. Basically, they drill and frack their brains out.[15]

His formal presentation broke down into a casual group discussion. An exit price of over $8 per share was more than anyone could have imagined just a few months prior. Nobody seemed to overly mind that this event meant that Antler employees (especially those that had arrived from Globe) would be shuffled, yet again, to a new location with a new identity. All the shares would be tendered for cash. Options would vest and be tendered for cash. People were about to realize the 'reward side' of the 'risk equation', and many were already busy mentally calculating their new net worth. The acquiring company was willing to pay a premium price for Antler, and they needed bodies in order to succeed in Canada. By all measures it appeared that Antler's employees would be in the bargaining seat.

Jokes and memories started to fill the room. Employees interjected with some of the morning's highlights: 'It's just incredible. Antler went from being noticed by a community newspaper in the small town of Hobbema, Alberta, to getting coverage on CNN in four years' time'. 'Have you been watching the trades? Yesterday, Antler traded 19 million shares and closed at an all-time high of $8 per share!' And another: 'Holy shit! We got $55,000 per flowing barrel. That's among the highest price paid for a flowing barrel in Calgary this year'. Then Max continued: 'Houston's papers wanted to cover the story. There's even a rumour circulating in Houston that HOGC bought Calgary!'

Takers Overtaken

Many people were late for work the next day, but they put their hangovers aside in order to attend a mid-morning meeting to be hosted by HOGC in a conference room in the downtown Sheraton Hotel. Everyone was eager to meet the representatives of the acquiring company who were shortly to be their new 'bosses'. We were greeted at the hotel and given a ball cap sporting their company logo and a little desk clock sporting the same before being seated to hear the presentation.

Max approached the podium and made the introductions. Present from Houston were Earl Rentin, president of HOGC's exploration and production division, and his appointee, Morgan Rader, for heading up the Canadian arm of the operations, their legal counsel and the head of their human relations department (all men). He then thanked the delegates:

> Thanks for coming and I'll try not to cry today! [laughter from the crowd]. Earl runs US$20 billion of assets so it means a lot to us that he

took the time to be here today. I know you've got over fifty rigs going, so again thanks again for coming here today. You had left a message on my cell [phone] mentioning how happy you were to tell the HOGC story. I let people listen to the voicemail because excitement cascades down.

Exchanging places with Max, Earl took the floor – a symbolized transfer of power from one body to another, one corporation and site of capital to another, one nationality to another. Earl explained the history of the Houston Oil and Gas Company. Their corporation had started seven years previously, under a different name, at about Antler's current size and capitalization. He described how in the early years of operations the business lost money. To turn things around, they grew through acquisition, consolidated some assets and installed a new vision and management team. Earl spoke of the factors behind their recent success: regional leadership, technological advantage and specialization. Houston Oil and Gas had set out to be the 'deep tight rock kings', said Earl, 'We want to be the 900 pound silverback in our areas'. To prove it, 67 per cent of their wells were deeper than 10,000 feet, and 33 per cent of their wells were bought to get the deep rights. As Earl continued with his slides, he reported that the corporation had a 94 per cent success rate this year on wells drilled. Their completions were tubing-less and they deployed 'massive hydraulic fracturing' (what Max referred to as drilling and 'fracking their brains out'). 'The trick', explained Earl, 'is to get out the gas in really tight rock in an economical way', and their completion method of massive fracturing made some fields more economic by their method of calculation.

They aimed to stay on the front lines of the technological learning curve to achieve maximum reserve recovery. To that end, they had a whole training department designed to keep their employees at the top levels of technological competence. They modelled the corporation's learning curve and the economics of that curve and showed it to the group on their PowerPoint presentation. Their goal was to understand and predict their organization's learning curves, and then to 'drive the curve down' (by increasing turnover times, reducing unit costs, accelerating profit). However, their method of calculation appeared to be limited. Their learning curve and production rates had been slowed recently, he reported, due to environmental issues in some areas, which were not originally included as part of the model. He further described their pattern of growth: 'We find potential, buy up the acreage, buy out the partners ... We're chasing basin-centred gas plays and we find them in the minds of the team, it's not just luck'. By all appearances, Antler's assets and employees would be in the hands of another fast capitalist growth machine.

The liminal staff of Antler showed some unease with the American firm's bravado and modelling of capital. For my part, there was certainly one part culture shock and one part fascination with how the self-proclaimed silverbacks modelled themselves as competing subjects, and how they modelled their own progress using the criteria of a flexible capitalist market place. It was an aggressive masculine model of territorial take-and-dominate; a high-speed, high-intensity version of a familiar colonial theme. For HOGC, the world was understood as the surface of generalizable sites of deep tight gas (excepting the occasional 'environmental issue') where their expansionist model and methods could be applied at an increasing pace. That Alberta's WCSB might be unique, requiring a locally specific method and an experienced labouring team, such as Antler's, was not discussed, nor was Alberta's particular social and environmental conditions.

Earl turned to discuss the Antler acquisition. He described how three to four years ago the corporation entered Canada and had been growing through the drill bit. Six months prior to this takeover, they had begun to look for companies with growth potential that they could leverage to build an 'impact' presence in Canada. 'First we looked at companies that were already for sale, but then we decided to look for companies that are a good fit. Antler came clearly above both for management style and core areas, so it was the right fit'. Earl then opened the floor to Antler employees. They asked many questions about budgets and plans, timing, how employees would be organized and what their corporate culture was like. Only brief answers were given with promises of further information to follow.

After the meeting ended, Antler's management and a consortium of employees headed out for lunch and another few rounds of beer to discuss their impressions of HOGC. Nobody went back to work that day either. They had just entered a space of liminality. Oddly, I rarely heard mention of Globe at this time, unless it was with reference to an historical accomplishment. All employees had seemed to solidify around the Antler identity – a unified 'we' being taken out by a collective 'them'.

Lucky Money and the Politics of Circulation

Over the next few weeks, normal working routines were interrupted by a series of meetings that constituted the spaces and means

of 'organizational change'. A few days after being first introduced
to the new bosses, employees assembled once again, in another off-
site location to hear what the new president of the Canadian arm of
HOGC, Morgan Rader (Earl's right-hand man in Canada), had to
say to Antler employees. With him was a 'change manager' named
Bruce – an external hire whose expertise was all about merging 'corporate cultures'. He would head the integration of the two companies
– assets and staff, management and budgets. He would make sure that
everything was in alignment with HOGC's goals. He set the stage
of the meeting by explaining to the room: 'We know that nobody
likes change, we all resist change. But we're going to get through this
as efficiently and as quickly as possible. To do this, we are going to
take the genetic code of the merging corporations and remap them'.[16]
This would be a 'participatory effort', said Morgan, emphasizing that
employees were not 'victims but participants in the process'. Unlike
the first meeting, which was characterized by an interested eagerness,
here Antler staff seemed hesitant, exhibiting an ambivalent despon-
dence that was already being interpreted by the new managers as a
sign of the 'resistance' that comes with 'change'. Everyone listened
quietly while Morgan continued to explain to them how things
would be.

Morgan stressed the sense of urgency around the transition.
HOGC wanted to get 'right to it': 'This integration will be done
in world-record time'. They were, after all, a learning corporation. Where it usually takes six to twelve months for an integration
to occur, this one would be done in one month. As he continued:
'Our goal is not just to accomplish a successful and quick integration. We also want to double production within the first year. It is a
very aggressive model; it is a huge hockey stick and I'm prepared to
push down the blame'. He and a few others chuckled in a knowing
familiarity with the 'blame game'. Morgan and the 'change manager',
Bruce, explained that they had designated a group of 'sculptors' to
build the organization chart, which would stand for the new 'tran-
sitional governance structure'. These 'sculptors' were represented
more or less by the current management teams of both companies.
Employees were to provide their feedback and work goals to their
managers-cum-sculptors to help them 'shape' the new company by
assigning people, jobs and skills to the most appropriate places –
history repeating itself differently.

Antler staff had shifted from their perceived idea of a meritocratic
organization where peers were friends and growth was in part inter-
nally generated through a neoliberal entrepreneurial spirit that was

constituted as fit, hard-working, sacrificing and creative. They were now the subjects of an artistic genome project. Their genetic codes would be remapped; their bio-matter moulded by pseudo-scientific artist-sculptors. It was a confusing merger of art and science metaphors, and it was an aggressive model of change. There would be 'no time for resistance'.

Morgan opened the floor to questions, and central among them was the issue of compensation, especially as to whether there would be options or a retention bonus. Antler people had reason to believe there would be a retention bonus as talk of one had been circulating around the office. Answering the question, Morgan responded: 'You've had plenty of lucky money already. We don't want people to be here just for lucky money. If there are retention bonuses, they will be determined as this process gets underway'.

Many non-management employees congregated in the lobby to debrief after the meeting. Morgan's reference to 'lucky money' had put them off. One employee stated: 'He obviously doesn't understand that options are part of our compensation. It's not luck. We worked for those and that's why we take the lower salaries'. Another explained: 'I won't be getting too excited until I see the retention bonus. They've already turned me off by referring to our options as lucky money. They certainly have a different way of thinking than we do. That's because they're a big company. They're not used to the entrepreneurial spirit we have'.

While I have no way of knowing whether Morgan intended the remark as a slight or whether it reflected his own sense that HOGC had paid a high premium for the Antler assets (as in: they were lucky we paid so much), or merely as a reference to an (unearned) windfall, it was nonetheless perceived negatively by Antler employees. The problem with the remark was that it reframed the meaning of options from one of entitlement through entrepreneurship, earned through labour time and risk, secured by a rational employment contract, to one of luck that had no necessary connection with the value of labour and the contributions of labour to the value creation project, and no necessary connection to rational calculation. In the view of Antler staff, Morgan had misrecognized their capital returns earned through value creation as a matter of chance – akin to winning the lottery. That the situation could equally have been unlucky was never stated. Now that these employees had learned to labour for capital, any signs of reobjectification of the employee strictly within the parameters of commoditized wage labour with no additional 'upside' appeared to deny their sense of earned entitlement to a portion of surplus value. They no longer wanted to exchange labour time strictly for wages.

Employees' concerns also extended beyond matters of compensation to the geographies of knowledge and authority. One of the engineers remarked: 'They want to double the production base in one year. That's an outlandish goal when you consider the decline rates of some of these properties'. Another employee from the operations team added: 'These guys are Houston-based so we'll have to call Houston for approval every time we want to get something done here'. While members of Antler's technical team viewed themselves as having intimate knowledge of local geology and landscape, they worried that HOGC had a map of the world as Texas writ large. 'Did they understand the WCSB?' asked one. 'Did they understand the local environmental and social issues as well as the local regulations?' asked another. One basin is not the same as the next, worried some Antler staff, and the WCSB could not necessarily be generalized. The Canadians wanted specificity and nuance; the Americans wanted market dominance. A couple of others broke the tension and began to make light of the new voices of authority. They made jokes about how silverback gorillas were not 900 pounds, and how HOGC must not know that gorillas have 'small dicks'. Some had no objections: 'I don't really care what job they give me, I'll take it. Right now, I just want my cheque'.

In the end, most of the employees transferred to HOGC. Their options had already vested and could not be used as a capturing device. Instead, after considerable negotiation, employees were offered a three-month retention bonus after a six-month period of work. Most of those who transferred stayed for the six months; at least half of them resigned thereafter. Something about HOGC failed to captivate its newest employees. Then, just over two years later, HOGC was taken over under less favourable terms by another producer.

On my final day of work with the Antler team, I wished my fellow employees good luck as they underwent the transition to HOGC. As I headed toward the door, my boss handed me an envelope containing an unexpected payment. Consultants of the firm were not entitled to options or severance pay, so I was not expecting any 'lucky money'. 'It's your performance bonus', said my boss, 'thanks for the hard work'. I knew it was a form of compensation, but it felt like a gift.

Conclusion: Options and the Gift of Uncertainty

As has been shown above, flexible workers are both subjects that exchange and objects that are exchanged during corporate mergers and acquisitions. Takeovers are not neutral financial events but complex social ones that occur through unequal access to knowledge, power and capital. Some employees have more power than others to effect organizational change. Some bodies are more freely circulating while others are circulated as products of calculation, exchanged as assets in a sale of assets.

As has been shown, the option entangles gift and commodity exchange. First, the option is a form of compensation that may result in a cash sum, or may not. Thus the initial receipt of an option is symbolic and resembles a gift, but it is given in terms of a rational contract without any misrecognition of economic calculation: its stated purpose, its use value, is to incentivize and retain. The option is intended to reward the entrepreneur by offering a chance to share in capital gain. The option does not 'wound' the recipient as in Mauss's gift, for it does not create a debt (see Mauss 1990). Instead, options create a contractual obligation to give in order to get, which is structured as a function of time and performance: labour time becomes the collateral required for access to equity 'upside'.[17] The requirement of time as an exchange for the option sets up the option as a technique of capture. Second, the option-as-gift, and indeed, as future hope (Miyazaki 2007), is coupled with the option as entrepreneurial reward. But the option also represents financial risk – the reward for which is only possible if the corporation achieves growth and profitability. Overall, options and other incentives perform part of the micro-linkages between labour and capital, assembling (albeit contingently) labour to corporations to markets. As shareholders and employees alike are focused on their present and imagined future net worth, a corporation's trading symbol becomes the site of a visual spectacle where value (and luck) is publicly displayed, routinely checked, discussed, debated and, indeed, circulated.

While everyday working life in this environment falls significantly short of Mauss's notion of a 'total social phenomenon' (Mauss 1990: 3), there are nonetheless elements of gift exchange at work. Most employers in the junior market sector assume at least some ethic of care and responsibility for employees. While this ethic is often unevenly deployed, there is a definite sense of responsibility and of sociality that exceeds the wage-labour relationship or legal obligation.

In turn, as the above examples illustrate, where employees often expressed ambivalence over risk and circulation, they also expressed a positive identification with capital. Having learned to labour for capital, Antler employees did not want to 'get screwed' by a return to a strictly wage-labour model at HOGC. In this case, similarities can be seen between gift and capital with respect to techniques of circulation and return. Mauss recognized this affinity when he remarked on the circulation of Trobriand bracelets and necklaces, and the coppers of the American north-west: 'One might really say that the Trobriand or Tsimshian, although far removed from him, proceeds like the capitalist who knows how to dispose of his ready cash at the right time, in order to reconstitute at a later date this mobile form of capital' (ibid.: 74). When capital is in play, in circulation, it is marked by a pledge that binds, connects and even embeds. However, unlike the gift, once capital returns, it can disembed (through liquidity). During takeover transactions, the calculable exchangeability and presumed equivalency between labourers, their circulation as commodities and the alienability of labour from capital (the severance that comes with liquidity), undermines the spirit of return, creating ambivalence and a sense of reduction.

Mauss observed that gift exchange is not wholly disinterested, nor without calculation. A debt is created as is an obligatory return. Likewise, while commodity exchange is predominately self-interested, it is not without morality and sociality. With respect to work, Mauss himself noted the affinity of the labour contract with the gift: 'The producer . . . is giving something of himself – his time, his life. Thus he wishes to be rewarded, even if only moderately, for this gift. To refuse him this reward is to make him become idle or less productive' (ibid.: 77; see also Gregory 1994: 920). Options, when they are 'in the money', appear to return a gift of surplus, restoring a sense of positive reciprocity between labour and capital. Though Mauss's model of a socialist society would surely deem the surpluses from options and the distributions of surplus to shareholders as both misplaced and overgenerous, these possible surpluses can be simultaneously undermined or offset by the negative impacts of takeovers – the risks and uncertainties, and the absence of planned and reasoned futures (cf. Guyer 2007).

In the case of oil-based accumulation by junior oil and gas firms, the labour theory of value is not, as in Marx, about the exploitation of labour through proletarianization and the alienation of labour from the products of work and surplus value. On the contrary, it is about the capitalization of labour through the use of the option. Labouring for (uneven) returns on capital is the hallmark of this flexible and neoliberal reinvention of the labour theory of value. Exploitation is not eliminated in this model, but is rather displaced to an elsewhere in time and space. Spatially, under oil-based accumulation, exploitation must be viewed in a much broader, global geopolitical context, which is beyond the scope of this chapter. However, in local terms, landscapes, landholders, field services and environments absorb the impacts of hydrocarbon exploration and extraction. Temporally, labour time is fashioned as a form of market time, a 'meantime' that is punctuated by periodic windfalls of lucky money (or unlucky losses), followed by the frictions of circulation. This model offers no particular vision of long-term working futures. The goal is liquidation of corporations and of hydrocarbon reserves. While the option and the takeover produce various forms of ambiguity and ambivalence, I suggest that an even greater entanglement of Mauss and Marx is needed: one that combines the moral and political project of the gift with surplus value, and public policy on sustainable carbon-based futures.

Notes

1 Stock options are a form of derivative that defers time while guaranteeing a specific acquisition price for an underlying asset (Maurer 2002; Arnoldi 2004; LiPuma and Lee 2004). In other words, stock options exchange labour time for the right to purchase equity in a corporation at a future date, at a price set in the present. Options have vesting periods. Portions of options become exercisable over time. In most cases, however, a 'liquidity event' or change in corporate control triggers an automatic vesting of company stock options and renders them immediately exercisable. While the stock option is a fairly humble device compared to other derivatives deployed in the markets, they nonetheless have wide-reaching impact in the arena of work. Other derivatives were also used in the workplaces described in this chapter. In particular, they used financial derivatives, or 'price hedging', in order to produce commodity price and therefore cash-flow stability. While this observation is beyond the scope of this chapter, it is noteworthy that derivatives were not sites of speculation, but rather instruments deployed for stabilization: cash-flow protection/labour retention.

2 For definitions of flexible capitalism, see Lash and Urry (1987), and LiPuma and Lee (2004). See also Thrift (2005) and Leyshon and Thrift (2007).

3 Options are 'in the money' when the market price of the optioned share exceeds an employee's exercise price.

4 As Tsing (2005) has shown with respect to Indonesia's junior mining industry, entrepreneurial start-ups such as these work to attract capital through spectacle (investor presentations and marketing efforts of investment bankers) in order to differentiate themselves from other similar firms competing for that capital, and from other market sectors offering promises of accelerated returns. This spectacle, which Tsing refers to as an 'economy of appearances' (ibid.: 57) is normative in the junior oil and gas sector as they must compete with multiple similar firms for both capital and the sought-after sub-surface oil and gas leases, which together comprise the conditions of possibility for operations.

5 Boepd is a measure for crude oil, natural gas liquids and natural gas. The equivalency of these hydrocarbons is calculated on the basis of a ratio where one barrel of crude oil is equivalent to 6,000 cubic feet (6 mcf) of natural gas.

6 During the period under study, concerns over future supply constraints dominated market discourse. There was widespread concern that Alberta's conventional crude oil reserves had only a decade or more of remaining 'reserve life'. Questions of supply were routinely discussed with reference to Hubbert's peak and peak oil theory, which became a legitimating discourse alongside rising prices for emergent and accelerated forms of unconventional methods of extraction, such as bitumen mining and deep sour wells to grow crude oil production. 'Reserve life' in Alberta's deep WCSB has since been considerably extended due to such methods as well as the more recent adoption of horizontal drilling in the deep basin. Presently, such concerns have shifted. Climate change and environmental concerns are entering corporate energy discourse as constraints to future oil based accumulation. For an overview, see reports by the Canadian Association of Petroleum Producers (CAPP) at: www.capp.ca.

7 As reported in the *Daily Oil Bulletin*, 'The Darwinian nature of the business can be seen in the corporate names listed in trade journal *Oilweek* magazine's Canadian producers ranking from 1995. Of the top 100 firms that year, half are now gone, mostly absorbed by bigger players' (*Daily Oil Bulletin*, 7 April 2000).

8 In 2007, the federal government of Canada banned energy companies from trusting, and thereby eliminated the 'exit strategy' of the junior energy market. In 2008, the Alberta Government changed its formula for calculating oil and gas royalty payments to increase the government take, which further destabilized junior energy corporations. Since that time, M and A activity among juniors has radically decelerated (see Wood n.d.).

9 In this chapter, all names of companies and employees are pseudonyms.

10 Cash-flow multiple refers to a simplistic form of standard valuation that compares a peer group of publicly traded corporations on the basis of

their annual cash flow per share. A valuation of 2x cash flow, for example, refers to a stock that has a market value of two times its annual cash flow per share.

11 While hostile bids are rare in Calgary's oil and gas market due to the intertwined nature of business and the fact that 'everyone knows everyone', they do occasionally occur. A hostile takeover refers to an attempt to purchase a controlling interest in a corporation by means of a solicitation to shareholders without the support of management and the board of directors. In such cases, the offered price is often lower than management would agree to. A friendly acquisition (or takeover) is one that is recommended by management and by the board of directors.

12 All currency is expressed in Canadian dollars.

13 The employees who sold off large portions of their holdings in the company were later investigated by Canada's Securities Commission, though no charges were laid as a result of the investigation. They had not been 'offside' in their trades, but the trades of insiders are reported to the commission and are also part of the public record. Insider sell-offs tend to make other investors nervous.

14 At the time of research, the Bullboards were a popular list hosted by Stockhouse, where shareholders debated the performance of particular stocks online.

15 By 'frack', the speaker is referring to hydraulic fracturing, which is a method of creating permeability in deep tight rock by injecting high pressure fluid into a wellbore, which causes multiple fractures or fissures in the targeted geological formation that allow hydrocarbons to flow.

16 The literature in 'change management' is replete with testimonials about how people tend to resist organisational change. Literature in this field suggests that change must be managed, or 'driven' by a process of deliberate leadership, and appropriate employee incentivisation. For one example of this literature, see Anderson and Anderson (2010).

17 The notion of labour as collateral is inspired by Riles (2011) and her work on collateral knowledge.

References

Anderson, D., and L.A. Anderson. 2010 [2001]. *Beyond Change Management: How to Achieve Breakthrough Results through Conscious Change Leadership*. San Francisco: Wiley.

Appadurai, A. 1986. 'Introduction: Commodities and the Politics of Value', in A. Appadurai (ed.), *The Social Life of Things: Commodities in Cultural Perspective*. Cambridge: Cambridge University Press, pp. 3–63.

——— 2011. 'The Ghost in the Financial Machine', *Public Culture* 23(3): 517–536.

Arnoldi, J. 2004. 'Derivatives: Virtual Values and Real Risks', *Theory, Culture and Society* 21(6): 23–42.

Bloch, M., and J.P. Parry (eds). 1989. *Money and the Morality of Exchange*. Cambridge: Cambridge University Press.

Cefkin, M. 2009. *Ethnography and the Corporate Encounter: Reflections on Research in and of Corporations*. New York: Berghahn Books.

Gregory, C.A. 1994. 'Exchange and Reciprocity', in T. Ignold (ed.), *Companion Encyclopedia of Anthropology: Humanity, Culture and Social Life*. New York: Routledge, pp. 911–939.

Guyer, J. 2007. 'Prophecy and the Near Future: Thoughts on Macro-economic, Evangelical and Punctuated Time', *American Ethnologist* 34(3): 409–421.

Hertz, E. 1998. *The Trading Crowd: An Ethnography of the Shanghai Stock Market*. Cambridge: Cambridge University Press.

Ho, K.Z. 2009. *Liquidated: An Ethnography of Wall Street*. Durham, NC: Duke University Press.

Lash, S., and J. Urry. 1987. *The End of Organized Capitalism*. Cambridge: Polity Press.

Lee, B., and E. LiPuma. 2002. 'Cultures of Circulation: The Imaginations of Modernity', *Public Culture* 14(1): 191–213.

Lépinay, V.A. 2011. *Codes of Finance: Engineering Derivatives in a Global Bank*. Princeton: Princeton University Press.

Leyshon, A., and N. Thrift. 2007. 'The Capitalization of Almost Everything: The Future of Finance and Capitalism', *Theory, Culture and Society* 24(7/8): 97–115.

LiPuma, E., and B. Lee. 2004. *Financial Derivatives and the Globalization of Risk*. Durham, NC: Duke University Press.

Martin, E. 1994. *Flexible Bodies: Tracking Immunity in American Culture from the Days of Polio to the Age of AIDS*. Boston: Beacon Press.

Marx, K. 1990 [1867]. *Capital: A Critique of Political Economy, Vol. I*. London: Penguin.

Maurer, B. 2002. 'Repressed Futures: Financial Derivatives' Theological Unconscious', *Economy and Society* 31(1): 15–36.

——— 2005. *Mutual Life, Limited: Islamic Banking, Alternative Currencies, Lateral Reason*. Princeton: Princeton University Press.

——— 2006. 'The Anthropology of Money', *Annual Review of Anthropology* 20(4): 474–505.

——— 2012. 'Payment: Forms and Functions of Value Transfer in Contemporary Society', *Cambridge Anthropology* 30(2): 15–35.

Mauss, M. 1990. *The Gift: Forms and Functions of Exchange in Archaic Societies*, trans. W.D. Halls. London: Routledge.

Miyazaki, H. 2007. 'Economy of Dreams: Hope in Global Capitalism and its Critiques', *Cultural Anthropology* 21(2): 147–172.

——— 2013. 'The Gift in Finance', *NatureCulture* 2: 38–49.

Preda, A. 2009. *Framing Finance: The Boundaries of Markets and Modern Capitalism*. Chicago: University of Chicago Press.

Riles, A. 2004. 'Real Time: Unwinding Technocratic and Anthropological Knowledge', *American Ethnologist* 31: 392–405.

——— 2011. *Collateral Knowledge: Legal Reasoning in Global Financial Markets*. Chicago: University of Chicago Press.

Tsing, Anna. 2005. *Friction: An Ethnography of Global Connection*. Princeton: Princeton University Press.

Thrift, N. 2005. *Knowing Capitalism*. London: Sage.

Welker, M., Partridge, D., and R. Hardin. 2011. 'Corporate Lives: New Perspectives on the Social Life of the Corporate Form: An Introduction to Supplement 3', *Current Anthropology* 52(S3): S3–S16.

Williams, R. 1976. *Keywords: A Vocabulary of Culture and Society*. New York: Oxford University Press.

Wood, C. N.d. 'Inside the Halo Zone: Geology, Finance and the Corporate Performance of Profit in a Deep Tight Oil Formation'. Unpublished article.

Zaloom, C. 2006. *Out of the Pits: Traders and Technology from Chicago to London*. Chicago: University of Chicago Press.

——— 2009. 'The Yield Curve, Affect, and Financial Prediction', *Public Culture* 21(2): 243–266.

5

How to Stay Entangled in a World of Flows

Flexible Subjects and Mobile Knowledge in the New Media Industries

Hannah Knox

At the end of the 1990s and the beginning of the 2000s, the city of Manchester was gripped by the promise that the much heralded knowledge economy might hold the key to the transformation of its fortunes as a post-industrial city. Emboldened by its own history as the birthplace of the Industrial Revolution, aware of the role the city had played in the development of modern computing, and drawing on the (in)famous music scene that had emerged in the 1980s and 1990s, perhaps the greatest excitement revolved around the idea that Manchester might be developed as a hub for an emerging new media economy.

As the 1990s drew to a close and the promise of a new century beckoned, Manchester City Council facilitated several meetings with local and regional development agencies, university departments and local business partners to discuss the best way forward for the city, and various funding bids were submitted to national and international bodies in order to bring money into the city to support this vision of a new media future for the city. One such bid went to the European Regional Development Fund, outlining the case for the establishment of a business support organization that would be oriented towards making and supporting the creation of a new media city. The bid was successful, and in the summer of 2000, the doors of MediaNet opened, with the aim of tethering the flexible, mobile workforce of an emerging new media industry to the hope of a sustainable future for Manchester and its surrounding regions.

This chapter focuses on the ways in which the ambition to generate a new media industry in the city worked with and revolved around a preoccupation with skills, training and the production and capture of knowledge. I suggest that conventional anthropological literatures on learning and enskillment prove limited in their ability to describe and analyse the combination of aspiration and ambivalence that pervaded attempts to make a link between educational training and local economic success in the context of a global knowledge economy. Instead, I draw upon insights and ideas from anthropological exchange theory to rethink the ways in which training, and the production of knowledge, was envisaged as both a panacea for economic stagnation, and the basis of a perceived risk of economic isolation. Focusing on the ways in which knowledge, learning and embodied capacity became articulated as descriptions of their relative alienability or inalienability from subjects, places and histories, I suggest that certain insights from exchange theory allow us to re-approach 'flexible' capitalism as a contested form of value production. Claims to knowledge and the importance of skills in what has come to be known as 'flexible' capitalism are shown to be caught up not only with the question of technical or intellectual competence, but equally with relational claims which recast the question of the impact of flexible capitalism on contemporary subjects as a process which revolves around tensions in the relationship between public and private forms of action.

Intimately linked to technological change and alterations in working patterns, the way in which industrial restructuring has been linked to human experience has often been through a preoccupation with skills (e.g. Braverman 1975). Yet in anthropology, discussions of skill and enskillment have been largely divorced from a consideration of the part that they are supposed to play in processes of economic transformation. Instead, skilled practice has permeated the anthropological discourse in relation to investigations regarding the embodiment of knowledge and the theorization of craft practices and tool use (Mauss 1973; Ingold 1993, 1995; Keller and Keller 1993; Suchman and Trigg 1993). Less has been said about the exalted position of skills in the 'development' of contemporary Western society, though some have tangentially dealt with more general cultural ideas about skills through discussions of human and machine agency (Bloomfield and Vurdubakis 1997). Harvey's (1997) edited collection provides a variety of perspectives on the relationship between the domains of the technological and the social, and a cultural sensitivity to the ways in which the separation between the technological and the social is maintained through ideas of skilled practice (Costall 1997; Graves-Brown 1997; Strathern 1997).

My specific aim in this chapter is to extend an analysis of skills to incorporate the ways in which a notion of 'skill' is mobilized in relation to ideas about economic practice. Rather than focusing on skill as a neutral categorical descriptor of a particular kind of practice, using skilled practice as an object of study to elucidate ideas concerning the embodiment of knowledge through practice, I look at the way in which skilled practice comes to operate as a somewhat unsettling kind of economic object. Narotzky's consideration of skill comes closer to articulating the perspective which I adopt to understand its place in the new media industry (Narotzky 1999: 20–21). She concentrates her analysis on the idea of skill as a socially recognized form of knowledge, thereby making apparent the divisive potential of such a categorization in the consideration of economic practice.

Narotzky helpfully reminds us that 'skill' is not an 'objective' quality incorporated in labour, but that it expresses the struggle over access to and the value of knowledge as a means of production. Indeed, the construction of power relations in the labour process is often expressed in the language of 'skill' (ibid.: 25). According to Narotzky, skill is: 'at once both ideological and material, and therefore critical to the understanding of the social relations of production. However "skill" can only be a valuable conceptual tool if clearly distinguished from technical capacities and specific and general knowledge of a labour process' (ibid.). Narotzky also highlights the historical nature of the use of skill as a politicized concept. As long ago as the nineteenth century, the 'ownership of skill' was a 'core ideological concept used by workers to organize the first unions' (ibid.: 20). She goes on: 'Only after the Taylorist battle to expropriate "skill" from workers did other concepts for the organisation of solidarity acquire force . . . The acknowledgement of technical capabilities is not homogeneous in society . . . It expresses lines of struggle over social relations of production' (ibid.: 20). Nowadays, in the context of the 'new economy', the reappropriation of skill by the individual has once again gained forcible power, yet, rather than being articulated in a communitarian ethos, the ownership of skill, as we will see, is played out to reinforce and reproduce flexible capitalism as it is manifested in the proliferation of short-term contracts, freelance activities and the presence of sole traders, shifting terrains and the necessity of keeping up with technologies.

The aim of this chapter is to explore the ways in which exchange theory can help re-politicize the anthropological interest in skilled practice by rendering the current appeal to the importance of skills and training in flexible capitalism a matter of historical rather than philosophical relevance. The focus of this chapter then is not the analysis of skilled practices as such – that is, the particular practices which by virtue of their place as embodied and technical activities acquire a privileged status in analysis as 'skilled'. Instead, my focus is on the importance attributed to the notion of skill as a particular kind of knowledge, and an attempt to understand the implications of contestations over skill versus other kinds of knowledge in economic development. By considering skill from this perspective, I suggest that insights can be gained into the processes by which such an idea both draws on and acts to reproduce the condition of work within flexible capitalism. In settings of economic development, exchange theories can provide us with a helpful theoretical language for approaching the tensions that exist in discussions surrounding the relative value of skills and knowledge to economic transformation, and in doing so they represent a means of looking at the role of reciprocity, relationality and potentiality in the reformulation of working relationships in a contemporary context.

Skills for Development

At the time when MediaNet was being set up, the political landscape was full of the rhetoric of the importance of skills, education and training for a robust modern economy. The British Labour Party, relabelled under the term 'New Labour', had been elected three years earlier to the mantra 'education, education, education', and the government had been responsible for establishing a series of organizations oriented towards the nurturing of business expertise. Skills were being identified as the biggest limitation in the development of local economies in a global context. In particular, changes in technologies were producing new anxieties over whether the population was going to have the correct skills to work with new computing technologies.

The relationship between technologies and skills, made explicit in government rhetoric about skills for the country in general, emphasized basic skills (literacy and numeracy) and notably information technology (IT) skills. This focus on IT skills had come about as a response to the fact that many people who did not have access to information and communication technologies (ICTs) when they were at school were increasingly being expected to use them in their jobs, and the government had been involved in ensuring that people, particularly those who had come from industrial backgrounds where the need for IT skills was limited, were able to get jobs in the 'new economy'. The UK government seemed to have truly committed itself to the importance of skill as the panacea to economic development, and the cross over between knowledge, training and education, and industry and markets could be derived from even the most perfunctory look at contemporary government directives concerning technological and economic change. Crossovers between the work of the Department of Trade and Industry and the Department for Education and Skills were common, resulting in the publication of such white papers as 'Our Competitive Future' (DTI 1998) and 'Opportunity for All in a World of Change' (DTI and DEE 2001), both of which make explicit the need to relate skills and training to the economy. The challenge of precisely how to develop a skilled population was taken up by a number of government-led organizations and initiatives, including the University for Industry, 'lifelong learning' initiatives, the Learning and Skills councils (formerly Training and Enterprise councils), the Technologies for Training scheme, UK Online and UK Online for Business.

The common assumption in all of these initiatives was that skills are simultaneously generic and neutral objects. A direct relationship was assumed between the emergence of a 'skilled' workforce and the societal effects that would result. It is in this way that the feared 'digital divide' was expected to be resolved through training. The foreword to the 1998 White Paper entitled 'Our Competitive Future' read: 'Our success depends on how well we exploit our most valuable assets: our knowledge, skills, and creativity. These are the key to designing high-value goods and services and advanced business practices. They are at the heart of a modern, knowledge driven economy' (DTI 1998: 5). This kind of approach to skills mirrors the ways in which scholars like Goody and Watt (1963) have written about literacy. Goody and Watt saw literacy from the perspective of what Street calls an 'autonomous' view (Street 1984: 542) conceptualizing it as a technical ability and believing that 'the advent of literacy in a society will have the same social and psychological effects, no matter which society is being studied' (Ahearn 2001: 127). Critics of this conceptualization of literacy argued that literacy should be seen as form of social practice (Kulick and Stroud 1990; Street and Besnier 1994; Gee 2000). Whilst this has been convincingly demonstrated by anthropologists who have studied skills as a form of social practice, the question then remains as to why the 'autonomous' view of skill remains so powerful. It is here that the anthropological literatures on exchange are useful.

The basic premise of exchange theory as derived from Mauss's essay on the gift (Mauss 1966) is that the difference between commodity transactions and gift transactions can be understood through the relative capacity that people have to make alienable their possessions (Weiner 1992). Commodity transactions supposedly operate on the basis of transactions which leave no residue of connection between the producer or owner of an object and its buyer or receiver. Gifts, on the other hand, involve delayed reciprocity, whereby something of the giver remains in the transaction (Gregory 1982). In this sense, gifts remain inalienable from the giver, always requiring a return at some point in order to sever them from whence they came, whereas commodity exchange involves the severing of relations at the point of the transaction. Commodities are in this sense alienable from their producers or buyers. This is not an essay on the relative strength or weakness of exchange theory, or the various positions of its different proponents over the years, though there has been much contestation over the ways in which the differences between gifts and commodities have become simplified or read as typologizations of different societies. For the purposes of this chapter, I merely want to take the notion of the relative alienability/inalienability of objects from bodies of different kinds under conditions of exchange to think about claims that are made for the relative value of skills and knowledge as facets of a new economy.

One thing that government documents like those mentioned above seem to do is to disembody or alienate the notion of 'skill' from the person. Given the amount of ink that has been spilt in anthropological writings on the social constitution of skill, the very pervasiveness of the idea that technical skill could be disembodied is an intriguing ethnographic observation. The need to resolve the perceived risk of a digital divide between those who have the skills to access information and those who do not, focuses on what are called 'basic' skills. The idea of basic skills requires that we imagine the population as needy and receptive to such forms of enskillment. It also requires that we see skill as a de-socialized category, suitable and necessary for all. In such documents, skills are non-specific and seem to take on characteristics of commodities which the person can gain to add to a list of marketable capabilities on their curriculum vitae. In the specific context of business development, more specialist skills come to be the focus of political discourses.

At this point, I turn to the way in which these discourses were engaged in practice. MediaNet's engagement with these political discourses was at the level of ensuring competitiveness through techniques which would nurture the development of specialist skills, rather than an articulation of their activities in terms of the provision of basic skills. Much of MediaNet's staff's time was spent organizing seminars, holding workshops, disseminating information, writing for their website, establishing training events and putting people working in new media in touch with training organizations. We will come back to some of these activities in more detail below. The question for now, is: How did the political discourses described above actually figure in the daily practices in which MediaNet were involved?

Firstly, it must be noted that government documents were not taken on board unquestioningly by those implementing projects of development. It would be too simplistic and straightforward to suggest that these documents simply informed MediaNet's activities by informing them about the needs of the population, and the ways in which these needs should be dealt with. In fact their importance lay less in the intricacies of their content as their role as legitimizers of MediaNet's activities. Documents such as government white papers were largely considered dull and unhelpful, and the way they were written was seen as so self-congratulatory and superficial that they were considered limited as a source of information, and hence predominantly uninteresting on a day-to-day level. Furthermore, the content of such documents was treated with scepticism. Although supposedly based on neutral research, these texts were produced by government, and were therefore considered by MediaNet staff to have a particular partisan agenda. MediaNet staff were aware that such objects are created as forms of public communication, and the style in which they present information is highly rhetorical and riddled with 'sound-bites'. In MediaNet's offices, such government information was generally found on the internet by a member of staff, printed off, placed in a file, put on a shelf and left there, evidence that it had been acknowledged, albeit often not read.

If it was not in the specificities of the content of these documents, then the question remains: Why was it that these texts were still deemed to have importance to organizations like MediaNet? One thing they did was to situate the local setting in a larger macro 'context'. Although treated with distance and scepticism with regards to their content, their very presence acted as evidence of an important context for their work enabling the people working at MediaNet to juxtapose the local need for skills with wider trends of economic change. These texts were a necessary part of the process through which the local could be situated in relation to the nation. Wastell suggests that the effect of scaling is to make us think that we must 'accept each manifestation of a local context as a constituent element of a global whole, a subjective position in an objective reality' (Wastell 2001: 186). In this way, these documents worked to create a macro context, of which the local could then be seen to be a constituent part. It may appear paradoxical that documents that were treated with scepticism could be a part of the legitimization of a project like MediaNet. However, it was less the partisan fact of their production and more the 'public' audience to whom they were directed that I suggest had the effect of legitimizing MediaNet's activities and situating them in a national milieu. Furthermore, such documents provided a reference point and a mutually comprehensible language through which support for business could be publicly articulated in discussions between public and private sector organizations.

Recognition of the wider discourses exhorting the importance of skills and training provides one part of our understanding of the importance that MediaNet staff ascribed to ensuring a provision of some sort for the issue of a potential skills shortage. However, the government concern with skills extends far beyond the new media industry that is the focus of my research. A more specific framework within which support organizations like MediaNet operate can be identified by considering the demands of the European Union (EU), and particularly the manifestation of those demands in the documents which condition the allocation and use of EU monies in particular regional locales.

Rather than dealing directly with the EU, responsibility for the regulation of projects like MediaNet in the north-west of the UK was delegated to regional intermediaries, to whom each EU-funded project in a particular region became directly accountable. The intermediary organization was responsible for producing a document which outlined the rubric within which projects like MediaNet's work fitted. This document, called the Single Programming Document (or SPD), was much more directly mobilized in MediaNet staff acts of self-description than the generic government initiatives described above. This was due to the fact that organizations like MediaNet were funded by the EU, and thus were expected to deal expressly with issues outlined in this document. Furthermore, the SPD explicitly stated that it 'has been developed taking full account of European Union, national, regional and local policies' (EC 2000: 181). Even a cursory look at the SPD can help us understand part of the reason for the centrality of skills and knowledge to the definition of the general field of economic development, echoing the assertions of government documents, and creating a much more tangible link to the specific problem of skills shortages within the new media industry. According to the north-west England SPD, one of the main objectives of funding in the region is, 'To contribute to the creation of a 21st century economy through the development of new and high growth employment sectors as well as supporting the competitiveness of existing businesses, where the key features are enterprise and knowledge' (ibid.: 231).

The SPD had a more direct influence on the project's activities as it provided a basis for auditing and direct justification for the project's activities. As such, the SPD was used as a source of reference in the writing of quarterly reports. Such documents became useful in the practice of bid writing, where applications for funds demanded that certain criteria were addressed. The managers of the project encouraged members of staff to read this documentation, but in reality the staff who had most contact with companies and were in direct communication with local companies were not inclined to read such documents unless explicitly instructed to do so by their superiors.

MediaNet's articulation of the SPD's aim with regards to the new media industry was through the model of 'sectoral convergence' which would be resolved with recourse to the resolution of skills problems. The problem facing the new media industry was set up as a problem of miscommunication and misunderstanding between different professional 'tribes' that had been brought together in the invention of new media technologies, namely 'techies', 'creatives' and 'management'. MediaNet staff were encouraged by the director to think of the new media industry as a sector made up of companies that were formed through the fusion of technical, creative and managerial staff. In this light, Manchester was considered to represent fertile ground for a possible new media industry considering its creative and technical past, alluded to above, alongside four universities in the city, which would provide the 'skills base' for its future. The issue of skills, from the beginning of the MediaNet project, was central to the idea of convergence inasmuch as the employees of new media companies would have to be highly skilled if they were going to compete on a global stage. However the responsibility that MediaNet took in the provision of such skills for the region was not as might have been expected, through the training of individuals, but through the provision of already trained people to the industry, and in providing support in dealing with such skilled workers.

Skills: A Means to an End

One of the mechanisms through which MediaNet publicly hoped to bring about a convergence of creative, technical and managerial skills within the new media industry was through the technique of 'action learning'. This management technique had been included in the original bid for money from the European Union, and was to be a key aspect of MediaNet's work with new media companies. A delay to the start of the MediaNet project meant that by the time the project was up and running, action learning had already been piloted by another group who were part of the wider support organization. This group had attempted to effect action learning for local new media companies, with a particular emphasis on companies who were producing digital learning materials. The group who carried out these action-learning sets were employed as researchers, therefore the learning process was not just restricted to the companies who were involved in the research but extended to the team who were facilitating this learning opportunity. The focus of the group was on providing support for companies, but through this form of business support the team of researchers would be in a privileged position to find out the issues facing companies and, in particular, difficulties facing managers of companies who were having to deal with change and the 'convergence' of individuals with different skills within their own organizations.

The purpose of action learning was not only to bring about sectoral convergence however. Action learning was chosen as a form of business support for a number of reasons. Firstly, MediaNet was not funded to provide training, as this was the remit of organizations which were funded by the European Social Fund and not the European Regional Development Fund. However, it was important for MediaNet's director that the project was able to be seen to be tapping into not only European directives but also national and regional concerns. According to the project director, the convergence of people with different capabilities required a mutual understanding of different ways of working, divergent occupational histories and more specifically the emergence of techniques for 'managing creatives'. Action learning was supposed to provide a means through which managers could come together and share stories about their experiences of managing creatives in the context of new media. Thus action learning presented a means of bringing together people to articulate a discourse of skill through which the hype of political rhetoric could be grounded in daily experience.

As well as having a theoretical basis, the decision to pursue action-learning sets as a form of business support was also influenced by much more mundane and practical considerations, or what Narotzky (this volume) calls 'tactical needs'. The involvement of managers in such a learning process not only meant that they could be counted as an 'assist' – the auditable unit that MediaNet was being measured by – but also provided a way of counting their contribution to the action-learning set as 'match funding'. One of the ways in which match funding could be achieved was by encouraging people to give their services for free or at a discounted rate. The money that business managers would have charged for their time and knowledge in normal circumstances could then be considered a private sector contribution to the project. Whilst it was put to the managers that they would learn from their involvement in action learning, it was argued to funders that such managers were not only taking something from the experience, but also giving something to others in the process of their involvement. In this respect, a principle of exchange based on a particular form of reciprocity was being articulated as key to the process of business engagement and industry development. Managers were considered to be providing a service in the form of anecdotes of their own experiences, and thus it could be argued that they were contributing to the construction of a concept of 'best practice' which could then be disseminated to the industry as a whole.

Here we start to see how the different kinds of value attributed to knowledge were being articulated in a language of relative entanglement or detachment from business managers, MediaNet and the industry. Systems of accountability had the effect of extracting knowledge from the everyday flow of interactions in order to make it into an objectifiable entity like 'best practice', which could then be counted, compared and circulated. Action-learning sets combined a view of learning, whereby knowledge could be produced out of collective social relations, and would be a personal asset to the individual participant in the action-learning set who would nurture and develop their understandings of their business and the industry through conversations with others, whilst simultaneously rendering knowledge a circulating object which could form the basis of transfer of value from businesses to the support organization.

There are interesting parallels here with Narotzky's description of the way in which contemporary capital relations turn norms of reciprocity into a form of social capital (Narotzky, this volume). In the case of action learning, the effect of this activity was to blur the line between skills, training and knowledge sharing. The managers' ability to manage 'creatives' and 'technical staff' was articulated by the director of the project to be a form of tacit and skilled practice, but the means through which managers' embodied experiences could be transformed into a model of 'best practice' required a transformation of their embodied and socially acquired skill into transferable and capitalizable knowledge for the greater good of the region. The capacity of knowledge in this case to be both valuable because of its entanglement in social relations and valuable because of its capacity to be detached from those relations was a means by which it was possible for the twin aims of private profit and public good to be pursued. However, the lines of division between alienable/inalienable knowledge and its public/private status were far from clear cut. The ambiguity and slippage surrounding the relations that were being set up around knowledge was to have dire consequences for MediaNet's original ambitions over the capacity of action learning to square the circle of knowledge's capacity to act simultaneously in the public and the private interest.

This first attempt at action learning had mixed success. Company managers had complained that they had too little time to engage in such learning exercises, and although a series of feedback questionnaires indicated that most companies had found the experience of action learning in some way useful, various problems had been brought to the fore. As this initial round of action-learning sets had been carried out as a pilot scheme to test the viability of this method of learning for local new media companies, the subsequent difficulties raised in the evaluation of the training meant that action learning was slow to be taken up by MediaNet. The difficulties included lack of time, confidentiality, the size of the groups of companies involved in the action-learning sets, different levels of knowledge and issues of trust between participants, based largely on whether or not they knew each other before they met at the sets.

The issues which made action learning problematic were intimately entwined with the relationship between the conceptualization of skills which I have described and its relationship to wider discourses of globalization and information society, of which it was a part. In discussions of how to achieve a place for Manchester and the north-west UK in the information society, skills had been positioned and articulated as privately learnt, embodied, often tacit and most importantly personal, individualized resources. People's ability to gain skills had been considered a means of competitive advantage, and, as such, skills were very much considered a private 'asset' of the person. Action learning appeared to undermine the private status of 'skill' because of the expectation of transforming aspects of different people's skilled practice into mobile and circulating 'knowledge' which it was hoped would benefit the city and region through dissemination to local companies. This was nothing less than an attempt to make alienable that which had been inalienable – a highly political and contentious process with profound consequences for the relationship between new media company employees who were supposed to be recipients of support, and MediaNet staff who were attempting to provide that support. Due to these contradictions and some internal conflicts within MediaNet, a second round of action leaning did not occur. Instead, a training organization was brought in towards the end of the project in a last-ditch attempt to accrue some extra funding. The action-learning sets were outsourced to a training company, who reworked what were originally supposed to be collaborative workshops into a series of seminars addressing particular issues which local companies would find interesting. What had proved to be a problematic model of accumulation through reciprocity was here replaced by a more straightforward system of circulation based on the provision of information to businesses by a public sector organization that derived their funds through public subsidy.

As Graeber (2011) has recently pointed out, the main effect of the action of alienability, a process which tends to be effected through monetary transactions (but in this case occurred through the mediating technology of auditing), is to force a severing of the relationship between producer and consumer so that each can proceed after the transaction without any residue of obligation to one another. If we consider the commoditization of skill, however, alongside anthropological literatures on enskillment which have shown how skills are intrinsically social phenomena (Lave 1988), we can start to understand some of the difficulties that MediaNet faced as they attempted to fulfil the political ambitions of a knowledge economy by transforming complex relational histories into traceable lines of cause and effect.

The initial approach to business support, which had managed to reconcile the widespread recognition of the importance of skill in industrial development with the fact that MediaNet could not resolve the issue of skills through training, was eventually replaced. Instead, MediaNet put in place an approach which forfeited the organization's role as a skills provider, moving first to a role whereby they could facilitate the transformation of skills into knowledge or 'best practice' through action learning, to a final position where they were simply disseminating knowledge in the form of a unidirectional model of learning. This was done not because of a straightforward ideological adherence to the idea of enskillment, or because of a sense that the central needs of new media companies revolved around getting skilled individuals to work there. Rather, MediaNet staff and the director of the project negotiated decisions surrounding what kinds of support to provide through a combination of engagement with contemporary political discourses and the need to follow accountability procedures, which required that they simultaneously forged ongoing relationship with companies whilst at the same time rendering these relationships the basis of objective measures which would demonstrate certain kinds of productive outputs for the project.

Here we can see therefore that the provision of advice to deal with training and skills was not simply a value-free response to the capabilities of a pool of employable individuals in the locale. The way in which MediaNet dealt with the idea of skills involved a constant negotiation between ideas about the value of different kinds of skill and knowledge, a value that largely derived from their capacity to be held in place relative to their capacity for circulation. At the same time, micro-political decisions within the support organization required engagement with these discourses to legitimate or delegitimate the value of providing support for skills provision. The importance of skills to the development of the industry that was embedded in the original enthusiasm for action learning at the beginning of the project endured even when action learning was not followed through. In the following section, I build on the observation that systems of accounting and accountability had rendered skills as potentially alienable objects to explore the kinds of contexts for action that this rendering of skills helped produce.

Talent Match

Although action learning was abandoned as a collaborative and situated form of learning and skills exchange, the idea that skills were key to the development of the industry was engendered in other ways in the project. Rather than being involved in the creation of the right 'skills set' through the provision of training, MediaNet's staff shifted their attention towards the provision of people who already had the right skills for the companies which needed them. Focusing largely on graduates from local universities, but also with a parallel consideration of the large number of freelancer new media designers and programmers in the city, much of MediaNet's work came to be concerned with matching skills as located in individuals to skills as abstracted, technologically defined entities that were desired by the companies they were supporting. The role of the support organization was thereby configured as that of broker or facilitator, rather than that being the provider of the setting in which skills could be developed.

Looking back to the project SPD, it was therefore much easier for staff at MediaNet to justify their involvement in such activities as fitting into the remit of 'Re-engineer[ing] the industrial and commercial structure to develop a sustainable economy' (EC 2000: 216). The privatization of enskillment was not in this case compromised as skills were not transformed into knowledge which could then be shared or made public. Instead, people's skills were seen much more unproblematically as residing in the individual. The intervention of MediaNet took the form of creating a market for such skilled people, rather than creating a public for specialized knowledge. The region would be 're-engineered' through activities which enabled the 'natural' process of supply-and-demand economics. What was being sold was no longer knowledge but the well-known commodity of labour time, whilst skills were firmly relocated as the inalienable possessions of individual bodies. In fact, attention to attempts to match up a market for skills to skilled people reveals once again that the terms upon which people were situated as valuable assets involved not a commitment to an inalienable relationship between skills and persons, but rather the irresolvability of this opposition.

This notion of 're-engineering' the region drew on the idea of a 'skills gap'. This 'skills gap' referred to the relationship between the new industries which constituted part of this re-engineering process, and the availability of people to work in them. One of the fears was the possibility that the 'pool' of skills in the area was being bled dry by the lure of better employment prospects, either overseas or in London and the south-east through a perceived sense of the flows of a 'globalized' world. The need for skills represented a need for a particular pool of individuals with those skills which companies could draw on when needed, rather than the enskillment of individuals within the context of the work that they were engaged in. This conceptualization of a local skills shortage was only possible through the discursive articulation of space, whereby people could create local and global as opposed domains (Knox et al. 2012: 32–46).

The means through which MediaNet worked to resolve this much more market-oriented notion of skills was through an event called a 'talent match'. The talent match, as the name suggests, was an attempt to match graduates with particular skills to companies with particular needs. One part of the half-day event was a panel discussion between Nick, the director of a local business support organization, and members of staff from four new media companies in Manchester. Rows of chairs that had been set up facing the speakers gradually filled with local students who had come to the event in the hope of finding a job. A brief introduction giving the reason for such an event was given by Nick, and was articulated predominantly in terms of geography and the located nature of skill in the maintenance of an industry sector. Some of the speakers made suggestions as to the ways in which graduates from local universities could be encouraged to work in Manchester after leaving university. Partnerships between companies and particular degree courses, the sponsorship of academic modules by local companies and the placement of students in companies as part of their degree were all put forward as suggestions for the resolution of the movement of graduates away from the city.

The powerful connection between geography and skills has much to do with the way in which markets and economies are envisaged within regional development agendas. In a meeting between MediaNet, the local Regional Development Agency (RDA) and various new media companies, the director of ICT and new media at the RDA made continuous reference to the skills gap in the north-west. Acknowledging that there was a 'brain drain' from the region, he argued that there were ways in which Manchester could stem the flow of people from the city to the south-east. Using the example of Scottish 'clusters' of new media companies which had managed to attract graduates from other areas of the country to come and work for them, he reinforced the view that Greater Manchester, with its four universities, was well placed to have such an industry. Ensuring that the 'right' skills would be locally available was articulated in terms of trying to 'create, trap, and retain skilled and talented people', something implicitly considered much easier than having to attract already skilled people from elsewhere. The retention of 'local talent' was expressed alongside the common idea of 'inward investment'.

In economic development discourses, regional development is frequently seen to require inward investment. This sets up a penetrative view of the local economy that relies on a movement into the region from the outside. This idea draws heavily on globalization theses, which see global markets in terms of flows of goods and people. The role of development agencies is to channel these flows into the city or region through whatever means possible. Retention of skilled people on the other hand is concerned with the notion of being 'home grown'. 'Home grown' refers to those people who were trained or educated in the region rather than just those who are born there, and includes those people who come to the region to go to university. This very educational model of home-grown talent is prevalent in local development discourses, and it involves an attempt to introduce a relationship of obligation among graduates of local university courses towards the fortunes of the region where they study. The way in which the notion of being 'home grown' was used in local development discourse often jarred, however, with people's own sense of identity, which put much greater emphasis on birth and family residence as a criteria of belonging. As people often pointed out, being educated in Manchester does not make you a Mancunian. At the same time, it is striking, as we think about issues to do with reciprocity and exchange, that the use of the term 'home grown' to refer to 'talent' played on this local sense of belonging in order to give greater credence to calls for 'local' talent to stay in the region.

Much of the work to keep graduates in the region to work in ICT and new media was based on the idea that graduates needed to be made aware of the jobs available. Against the push of movement inevitable in a dynamic and globalized world, skills had become a mechanism by which a claim could be made for the importance of regionality, locality and the necessity of geographical affiliation achieved by evoking a sense of locality which was potentially missing from the educational or vocational experiences through which people gained skills.

The suitability of skills as a discourse through which the project could be implemented was further complemented by the fact that MediaNet were audited on the basis of various indicators of success, including the number of new jobs the project had created. The number of jobs created by the presence of MediaNet in the city was almost impossible for the project's staff to quantify. However, activities which confronted the skills issue engaged critically with the idea of employment, and as such they provided a basis by which MediaNet were able to locate their effect on the local industry in a very obvious and visual way. The graduate placement scheme which matched graduates from the north-west with companies in the local area and 'brokering' activities like 'talent match', gave MediaNet a means by which they could be seen to be responsible for the creation of employment, and solid proof (in the form of micro-economic indicators) of the relevance of the support organization to the local industry.

So far we have seen the ways in which the discourse of skills was a means through which skills were imagined as commoditized aspects of people's selves, and how this came to be reproduced through the activities of organizations like MediaNet. Engagement with contemporary discourses surrounding skilled practice resulted in the abandonment of a form of business support which drew predominantly on the idea of communication with a public to a more economically oriented form of support which had the effect of creating a market for the skills which people in the area were imagined to have. Furthermore, the discourse of skills located in texts produced for global and national publics was incorporated into the processes by which economic development was legitimized, and by bringing about an imagined relationship between the different scales of local, national, European and global.

Just as MediaNet's staff were engaged in the tension between skills as something owned by people and skills as a circulating commodity, so too did new media companies articulate their experiences through recourse to the same discourse of skill. Many company managers discussed the skills of their staff in highly market-oriented terms, and made similar recourse to the same discourses of globalization and supply and demand. The manager of one of Manchester's new media companies very clearly articulated to me the importance of obtaining the people with the right skills, with the suggestion that it was only due to his foresight regarding the relative importance and redundancy of particular skills that they were awarded an important piece of work. Tying this need to constantly reshape the skills of his company's workers to fit the exigencies of the modern market economy, he explained:

> The market changes so fast and moves so quickly, it is sometimes confusing. Well, it is confusing for us, and we live in this hyper-state . . . For example, over the last four months, when NASDAQ has been going through the floor, we've lost money in three consecutive months, and it took us three months to change direction . . . This month we made money, and we've dumped four or five people who were doing whatever we were doing before, right? . . . I have to look ahead and say, 'Oh God, if this doesn't work, what we're doing now, we're really going to be in it'. You know? But as it happened, I can tell you the anecdote: We made a decision to let go of some people with some skills and employ one or two others with other skills because we felt that the market was moving in that way. And you know, as it turned out, one of our major clients has just sacked one of their other developers – well, they didn't sack them, they resigned, they couldn't do it. Four months late on the project and they resigned. And we got told yesterday we'd got the work. Christ, if

we hadn't done what we've done, we wouldn't have had the facility to do the work, and you can't just recruit people like that, it takes two or three months.

Once again, we can see that the relationship between macro notions of economic instability and the necessity for individuals to take responsibility for their own capabilities was a central aspect of new media practice. This highly market-oriented conceptualization of skill, however, often appeared to undermine attempts of new media workers and company owners to tie themselves to workplaces in ways that would make not just their skills inalienable possessions of their own, but would also have the effect of making their labour part of a reciprocal engagement with the organizations and cities within which they worked.

Exchange Potential

In the panel discussion at the 'talent match' event described above, a dialogue took place which highlighted the discursive nature of the skills problem as envisaged by companies. The following excerpt from my fieldnotes illustrates the main thrust of the argument:

> The two speakers from Magnetic seemed to agree with the idea of training new recruits up when they got into the company, and suggested that having specific skills beforehand was not as important as being willing and open to learn. But one of the other panel discussants interjected, explaining that he thought it was most important for people to make sure they had their own particular specialisms and keep it that way, so that whilst they could expand into other areas if they needed to, they always had something they were particularly good at.

Here we can see that the interest in skills lies less in the capabilities of individuals to carry out particular technical tasks than in exhibiting a particular kind of competence, which is judged by their ability to be flexible. In the retort given by the second speaker, the emphasis is on the value of an individual who has a particular specialism. This specialized knowledge is exalted as a valuable asset largely because of the unstable nature of the industry sector and an expectation that those working in that industry are likely to move from company to company. Having a specialism is shown here to be an important factor in obtaining employment, yet it only retains its importance by virtue of the fact that a constant re-evaluation of one's position and an expectation of movement between companies is woven into the language of work within this industry. What matters is not so much technical ability in and of itself but the potential to be technologically capable. This is not to say that technological expertise is not valued, but that there is a very conscious awareness of the intransigence of particular technological skills, and a recognition that, in order to be successful, having the ability to change one's personal competencies is of central importance.

> By the end of the discussion there was little agreement as to whether it was better to have one major skill or several at a lower level. However, everyone seemed to agree that, as the industry was growing so rapidly and it was thus a popular career choice for graduates, it was important for people to make themselves stand out. Everyone on the panel had got into the industry at a time when it was in its infancy and there were less people interested in it, but it has become increasingly associated with large salaries and unbelievable success stories, particularly in relation to the dotcom companies, so that now it is not enough to simply 'be enthusiastic' about getting into new media, you have to have something tangible to offer which will make you stand out from other applicants.

Informing these perspectives was the core notion of the company as a sustainable economic unit. However, in many new media companies, the need to be able to make money was paralleled by a need to make the workplace a desirable place for people to work. Managers of new media companies frequently distanced themselves from the potential accusation that their relationship with their employees was merely about the extraction of value. Instead, they worked hard to create seemingly new working practices which provided some kind of 'freedom' or self-determination for employees, and they were often frustrated when they found that the old pressures that they had faced in previous jobs had come back to haunt them in new workplaces that were supposed to operate according to different principles. Ross (2003) has provided a robust critique of the emancipatory benefits of the 'no collar' workplace, but nonetheless, the construction of a particular kind of workplace identity was a central preoccupation in the recruitment and retention of staff. In this light, the centrality of actual skills that was so evident in national and supranational discourses was frequently played down by people working in new media. The employment of new members of staff was often articulated in terms of people having the 'right personality' for the company, which was seen as a more important concern than what skills they had. In terms of the training that they were offered, instead of engaging in formal training, individuals were expected to engage in a process of trial and error through which they would gradually learn how to achieve a particular effect using a combination of different pieces of software. This was seen to give the designer, for example, a sense of freedom, enabling them to explore their own capabilities.

This way of working tends to be posited in opposition to Tayorlized forms of work activity, which have been widely criticized for being overly rigid, structured and non-creative (Braverman 1975). Through processes of 'experimentation' at work, staff could learn how to use a piece of software whilst simultaneously developing ideas that could potentially be used in a future job, a proposal for work or on the company's website as a marketing tool. The 'freedom' afforded to these workers in the development of their own capabilities, however, meant that they were supposed to fit such experimentation in and around other pieces of work. They would play with ideas for sites by surfing the internet, reading industry magazines and communicating with other members of staff. The experimental creative process was thus simultaneously a learning experience, an economic activity and a creative way through which people could express and thus develop their selves through notions of creative authorship. The terms upon which enskillment was read as any one of these kinds of activities depended in part on how it was rendered as a form of knowledge or practice that could or could not be alienated from the person, the company or the location where training took place.

Whilst a level of skill was clearly important for the completion of particular contracts, skills were largely considered by new media company employees to be something which could be learnt when needed, and the close relationship between skill and constantly changing technologies meant that an ability to learn and fit in with the company rather than the specific knowledge of how to use a particular program was generally considered more important. Certain skills were taken for granted, and were seen as so ubiquitous as to not require mention. Literacy, numeracy and the ability to use a computer were all expected prerequisites of employment. These were not even categorized as skills and were considered to be a form of basic ability rather than expert knowledge or specialist competency. When people talked about skills in new media companies, they referred very specifically to the technical knowledge of how to manipulate a particular computer program. Most people working in the technical or design areas of new media development were able to reel off a list of software and programming languages which they were familiar with. 'Creative' ability was not usually categorized as a skill in such discussions, and an ability to be creative was more likely to be considered to be as a talent that a person either had or did not have.

What emerged out of conversations with new media companies then was not the importance of simply matching skilled individuals with positions which required specific skills, as in the 'talent match' model, but rather the requirement of employees within new media companies to be constantly aware of the need to manage themselves as a portfolio of more or less generic capacities which would make them employable in an uncertain and shifting market.

One example of this was the large online community of 'Flash' designers, who shared expertise, on various discussion sites, about how to manipulate the software to achieve different effects with the software. People who had 'creative' ideas but did not know the intricacies of coding to create them into animated movies would post a message on a message board for advice on how to achieve the effect they desired. In a popular critique of modern marketing, Locke (2001) identifies 'communities of interest', as he calls them, as one of the most important features of the internet. Whilst his manifesto is aimed at marketing managers, his observation that such communities are indicative of the most powerful potential of the internet supports the notion that skills are increasingly understood as the responsibility of the private individual. Such online communities represent a move away from apprenticeship – where a lineage of knowledge, both explicit and tacit, is established in particular settings (Sigaut 1993) – to a collection of individuals characterized by a communitarian logic rather than hierarchical responsibility who share their own technical expertise with others in the expectation that their collaborative sensibilities will be reciprocated.[1]

Once again, the tension between the individualization or inalienability of skill and the capacity to put knowledge into circulation for the greater good in the case of software programmers points us towards the reworking of the relationship between the public and the private under flexible capitalism. As Kelty (2008) has pointed out, the open-source movement has been a powerful force in rethinking the terms upon which contemporary forms of public expression are being enacted. No longer can the individual be seen to be the autonomous site of authorship and invention. Rather, public forms of knowledge reconfigure the status of the individual in flexible capitalism. For Kelty, this takes the form of membership of what he calls a 'recursive public' (ibid.: 3). Meanwhile, the same calls for openness can be seen simultaneously to require the re-establishment of the terms by which claims to inalienability can be made as a form of resistance to the fluidity of a liquid modernity where jobs, opportunities and prospects are increasingly conceived of, rightly or wrongly, as decoupled from the entanglements of geography and history.

I suggest that the importance of recognizing skill as a potential rather than an actual capacity which could be measured in the way in which MediaNet's systems of accountability required was one way in which people recovered something of the sociality which was erased by the way in which a discourse of skills had the effect of apparently objectifying skill into a market commodity. Designers and programmers saw themselves as simultaneously agents of change and innovation, and at the same time subjects of forces of transformation which they were having to respond to in their practices of retraining and re-skilling. Critically, it was more important for people to be able to demonstrate certain abilities of enskillment and flexibility than it was for them to have already learnt how to use a particular piece of equipment.

Conclusion

By moving away from an analysis of skill and knowledge as inherently human capacities towards an analysis which focuses on the ways in which the relationship between skills and knowledge in contemporary economies concerns the relative alienability or inalienability of knowledge from persons, organizations and places, I suggest that we have had to shift the terms of analysis of the new economy onto new terrain. I have paid attention to the ways in which discourses regarding the relative importance of skills and knowledge to economic improvement have come to produce difficulties, ambiguities and contestations over the power, freedom and control of workers in a global new media industry in ways that make it difficult to fall easily on the side of support for the emancipatory effects of new forms of work, or wholeheartedly embrace critical accusations of domination and relations of exploitation that they might be seen to entail. Instead, I have suggested that the way in which the relative alienability or inalienability of knowledge and capacity has been, and continues to be, negotiated in the context of new media work raises important questions about how public and private domains are being navigated, and social and political responsibility is being articulated in relation to processes of economic change. As the knowledge economy continues to be mobilized as a trope through which education and business are brought together to generate new forms of governance, accountability and responsibility, I suggest that using anthropological insights such as exchange theory so as to remain attuned to the specific ways in which capacities and persons become entangled and detached at different scales can provide us with a powerful means of remaining attuned to the politics of economic transformation under shifting terrains of flexible capitalism.

Whilst exchange theory has concentrated primarily on the way in which exchange relations entail the negotiation of social relations of debt and obligation as they pertain to the circulation of objects within communities, an investigation of the commoditization of skills under what has come to be known as 'flexible capitalism' introduces the question of how the intrinsic sociality of enskillment is dealt with in a system of exchange which increasingly attempts to render skill an alienable quality. Whilst Narotzky (this volume) suggests that these forms of social reciprocity have become increasingly made available as a resource for (flexible) capital accumulation, I have emphasized the ambiguities inherent in this process by demonstrating that reciprocity remains a complex issue which continues to produce confusion and uncertainty, particularly at the interface of public and private sector organizations. In this respect, I have variously shown: how an individualized conception of the embodied nature of skills is re-socialized through attempts to transform personal skills into generic or 'best practice' examples of knowledge in a way that allows the collective basis of training and learning to return to society in the form of a publicly available form of knowledge; how the exchange of knowledge is itself complicated by expectations about the proper forms of reciprocity that should be manifested in a relationship between public sector and private sector organizations which are situated in different positions vis-à-vis their relative roles and responsibilities for producing industry-level sectoral development; and how attempts at the implementation of a market for skills raises the question of both who it is that must take responsibility for ensuring a pool of skilled individuals to service the needs of a high-tech industry, and what kinds of skilled practice count as the responsibility of the individual vis-à-vis those skills that remain the responsibility of the state.

In the final section, I suggested that the idea that a pool of individuals is needed to fill a corresponding pool of jobs misses a key dynamic in people's experiences of flexible capitalism, one which is revealed by paying attention to exchange – that is, the importance of being receptive to the uncertainty of the future and demonstrating a capacity for transformation (Knox et al. 2007) in the face of shifting environments. I have suggested that we might see this attention to the importance of personal potential as a particular means by which people working within flexible capitalism negotiate the sociality of a market system which works to transform complex histories of personal relations into marketable commodities. The experience of work in flexible capitalism is thus shown to be neither primarily a matter of new forms of exploitation, nor of increasing autonomy and worker control, but rather a site for working out what kinds of exchange relationships are appropriate as people try to negotiate the (re)constitution of a division between public and private modes of social organization.

Note

1 See Adkins (2005) for a discussion of the de-differentiation of culture and economy in labour relations in the new economy.

References

Adkins, L. 2005. 'The New Economy, Property and Personhood', *Theory, Culture and Society* 22(1): 111–130.

Ahearn, L.M. 2001. 'Language and Agency', *Annual Review of Anthropology* 30: 109–137.

Bloomfield, B.P., and T. Vurdubakis. 1997. 'The Revenge of the Object: On Artificial Intelligence as a Cultural Enterprise', *Social Analysis*, special issue, 41(1): 29–45.

Braverman, H. 1975. *Labor and Monopoly Capital: The Degradation of Work in the Twentieth Century.* New York: Monthly Review Press.

Costall, A. 1997. 'The Meaning of Things', *Social Analysis*, special issue, 41(1): 76–85.

DTI. 1999. *Our Competitive Future: Building the Knowledge Driven Economy.* London: Stationery Office.

DTI and DEE. 2001. 'Opportunity for All in a World of Change', White Paper. London: Stationery Office.

EC. 2000. 'North West England: Objective 2 SPD 2000'. E. Commission. Luxembourg: Office for Official Publications of the European Communities.

Gee, J.P. 2000. 'The New Literacy Studies: From "Socially Situated" to the Work of the Social', in R. Ivanic, M. Hamilton and D. Barton (eds), *Situated Literacies: Reading and Writing in Context.* London: Routledge, pp. 180–196.

Goody, J., and I. Watt 1963. 'The Consequences of Literacy', *Comparative Studies in Society and History* 5: 306–326.

Graeber, D. 2011. *Debt: The First 5,000 Years*. New York: Melville House.

Graves-Brown, P. 1997. 'From Highway to Superhighway: The Sustainability, Symbolism and Situated Practices of Car Culture', *Social Analysis*, special issue, 41(1): 64–75.

Gregory, C.A. 1982. *Gifts and Commodities*. London: Academic Press.

Harvey, P. (ed.). 1997. 'Technology as Skilled Practice', *Social Analysis*, special issue, 41(1): 3–14.

Ingold, T. 1993. 'Tool-use, Sociality and Intelligence', in K.R. Gibson and T. Ingold (eds), *Tools, Language and Cognition in Human Evolution*. Cambridge: Cambridge University Press, pp. 429–445.

———— 1995. 'Building, Dwelling, Living', in M. Strathern (ed.), *Shifting Contexts: Transformations in Anthropological Knowledge*. London: Routledge, pp. 57–80.

Keller, C., and J.D. Keller 1993. 'Thinking and Acting with Iron', in S. Chaiklin and J. Lave (eds), *Understanding Practice: Perspectives on Activity and Practice*. Cambridge: Cambridge University Press, pp. 125–143.

Kelty, C.M. 2008. *Two Bits: The Cultural Significance of Free Software*. Durham, NC: Duke University Press.

Knox, H., D. O'Doherty, T. Vurdubakis and C. Westrup. 2007. 'Transformative Capacity, Information Technology, and the Making of Business "Experts"', *Sociological Review* 55(1): 22–41.

———— 2012. 'Enacting the Global in the Age of Enterprise Resource Planning', *Anthropology in Action* 19(1): 32–46.

Kulick, D., and C. Stroud. 1990. 'Christianity, Cargo and Ideas of Self: Patterns of Literacy in a Papua New Guinean Village', *Man* 25(2): 286–304.

Lave, J. 1988. *Cognition in Practice: Mind, Mathematics and Culture in Everyday Life*. Cambridge: Cambridge University Press.

Locke, C. 2001. *Gonzo Marketing: Winning through Worst Practices*. Oxford: Capstone Publishing.

Mauss, M. 1966. *The Gift: Forms and Functions of Exchange in Archaic Societies*, trans. I. Cunnison. London: Routledge and Kegan Paul.

———— 1973. 'Body Techniques', *Economy and Society* 2(1): 70–88.

Narotzky, S. 1999. *New Directions in Economic Anthropology*. London: Pluto Press.

Ross, A. 2003. *No Collar: The Hidden Cost of the Humane Workplace*. New York: Basic Books.

Sigaut, F. 1993. 'Learning, Teaching, and Apprenticeship', *New Literary History* 24(1): 105–114.

Strathern, M. 1997. 'A Return to the Native', *Social Analysis*, special issue, 41(1): 15–27.

Street, B. 1984. *Literacy in Theory and Practice*. Cambridge: Cambridge University Press.

Street, B., and N. Besnier. 1994. 'Aspects of Literacy', in T. Ingold (ed.), *Companion Encyclopedia of Anthropology*. London: Routledge, pp. 527–562.

Suchman, L., and R.H. Trigg. 1993. 'Artificial Intelligence as Craftwork', in S. Chaiklin and J. Lave (eds), *Understanding Practice: Perspectives on Activity and Practice*. Cambridge: Cambridge University Press, pp. 144–178.

Wastell, S. 2001. 'Presuming Scale, Making Diversity – On the Mischiefs of Measurement and the Global: Local Metonym in Theories of Law and Culture', *Critique of Anthropology* 21(2): 185–210.

Weiner, A.B. 1992. *Inalienable Possessions: The Paradox of Keeping-while-Giving*. Berkeley: University of California Press.

6

The Payoff of Love and the Traffic of Favours

Reciprocity, Social Capital and the Blurring of Value Realms in Flexible Capitalism

Susana Narotzky

In an inspiring critique of 'flexibility', Anna Pollert (1991) pointed both to the ideological aspect of the concept of flexibility as it was voiced by proponents of industrial restructuring in the 1980s and early 1990s, and to its force as a reality performing the transformation of relations in the labour market and in the labour process. She also underlined how the argument of change that dominated the flexibility debate often presented the saliency of new flexible organizational, work and labour-market arrangements against the background of a particularly simplistic characterization of the past (that is, Fordism), where these types of relations were deemed to be absent. In this chapter I want to engage with this critique by trying to address 'flexible capitalism' not as something 'new' but as a persistent aspect of capitalism that acquires different expressions depending on history and place. Moreover, I will try to show how concepts that become part of a particular structure of the social reproduction of capitalism, and give form to a dominant moral economy at a particular moment and place, have to be articulated to the material transformations of relationships of exploitation and domination that structure the political economy of that time and place (see also Neveling, this volume). From this perspective, the alienable aspect of labour power in capitalism is always dependent on its inalienable ties to a social environment that constitutes its specificity (Narotzky 2009; see also Garsten, Knox, this volume).

   This chapter is based on two ethnographic experiences in Spain, the first in a farming area of rural Catalonia (where I undertook research from 1986 to 1988), the second one in a regional economy in the south of the autonomous community of Valencia (where I carried out research in 1995/6 with Gavin Smith). A historical perspective, central to both analyses, has enabled a better understanding of historical transformation, particularly in relation to changes in production relations and to related emergent conflicts. By comparing these two instances, I wish to underscore the productive tension between two apparently distinct domains of social and moral obligation: that of personal and intimate relations (in the home, among friends and kin), and that of production relations (clearly linked to a market logic). Although in both cases a similar entanglement of values pertaining to different realms occurs, the degree and manner in which this situation seems to become structural to capital accumulation differs. I will propose that we need different categories from those that have characterized the social sciences since the rise of modernity. Instead of discrete, differentiated abstractions often opposed in pairs, we need methodological instruments that allow for pervasive ambiguity in order to understand present-day processes of value production, circulation and accumulation. Instead of an evolutionary understanding of temporality, we need historical complexity devoid of any form of teleology.

The general theoretical argument I want to make is about a shift away from distinct confronted realms of value creation, material production and social organization (reproduction/production; emotional/rational; non-capitalist/capitalist) that would be dialectically intertwined or 'articulated'. I suggest we think instead in terms of an ambivalent value realm, predicated on the ambiguity of simultaneously experiencing these domains of social interaction. This value realm allows agents greater flexibility and opportunism, and a wider scope for reconfiguring relations according to tactical needs. It is also highly arbitrary, and morally shifting and contradictory.

By using both the framework of 'moral economy' and that of 'political economy' in approaching the ethnographic cases, I intend to point to the ambiguous logic that sustains economic practice. Thus my contention is that this overlapping of realms of value enables a particular form of exploitation by capitalist firms and a particular mode of governmentality that continuously shifts and blurs conflict locations and obscures knowledge about the localized and globalized processes of capital accumulation.

Moral Economy and Political Economy

In present-day anthropology, moral economy is making a strong comeback in the conceptual arena, with analyses stressing the centrality of moral values, practices and emotions in channelling economic and political behaviour.[1] Scott's argument for reconfiguring 'moral economy' as a central concept for understanding the emergence or lack of peasant rebellion was strongly based on a critique of Marxist political economy's idea of exploitation (Scott 1976). Scott criticized the abstract universal aspect of the concept of exploitation that produced a measurable value (surplus value), itself a result of relations of production based on forced cooperation (expressed in terms of contract and exchange) between owners of the means of production (capital) and a workforce (labour) lacking the means of livelihood. From the perspective of a Marxist critical approach to political economy, then, this situation would account for inevitable class conflict, unless ideology obscured this reality with the veil of false consciousness. What Scott (and before him E.P. Thompson and Moore) underscored was the historical and place-bound specificity of social relations in actually existing social formations on the one hand, and the centrality of diverse modes of obligation that sustained the structure of social reproduction in a particular place and time on the other. What was especially interesting in Scott's view was his insistence that the social and cultural framework of subjective experience and obligation was not an ideology producing false consciousness. It was instead a concrete reality, the *only* reality, and had to be explained in its own terms. He then produced the two moral principles of 'securing subsistence' and 'claiming reciprocity' as the basis of his moral economy concept, in turn making it a universal explanatory tool for understanding conflict.

However, this did not explain why social relations of production changed in such a way that a disjuncture appeared between the existing moral economy framework of expectations and the new practices of landowners and middlemen, which did not follow traditional forms of behaviour and then triggered rebellion. In sum, it did not explain the logic of the economic transformations that led to exploiters going against the grain of moral economy practices. In order to understand these, a Marxist political economy framework was still much more useful. Here, the logic of transformation was based on an abstract objective law: capital accumulation, a particular form of increasing wealth production and appropriation through exchange. The finality of capital accumulation seemed to constrain equally, although in different and unequal ways, both the owners of capital and the owners of labour power. This objective structured production physically, spatially and ideologically. Workplace and home were increasingly separated and gendered: producing goods and obtaining an income became commoditized and contractual, while housework and caring for kin and dependents was defined as emotional and natural activities. The realm of commoditized value was disconnected from that of non-commoditized values. Ideologically, if not always in practice, industrial capitalism established clearly defined and opposed realms of life: the private domain of household reproduction, with its internal hierarchies and power differentials; and the domain of commodity production, public in its aim of providing an optimal allocation of resources, although private in its authority structure. This narrative was couched in a teleological time frame, but was often disproved in the here and now by the many expressions of capitalist accumulation that did not conform to it. Indeed, a number of conceptual instruments were produced in order to explain the pervasiveness of instances where capitalist exploitation hinged on the blurring of commoditized and non-commoditized relationships of exchange.[2]

In theory, the need remained to bridge the abstract dimension of the economic structure developed through the logic of accumulation and the concrete dimension of the practical processes that enabled its continuity in real life situations (political institutions, culture and so on). This dilemma has produced some of Marxism's most interesting recent contributions to political economy. While the abstraction of a logic of accumulation has proved very useful in explaining historical transformations through the production of a theory of the laws of motion of capitalism, in order to connect this general movement with concrete historical locations other concrete, on-the-ground institutions and practices have to be considered.

Here Gramsci's stress on the power of reflexive culture to produce the tools for transforming the 'good sense' of concrete historical experience into a 'historical bloc'[3] capable of confronting hegemony expresses the need to resolve the tension between abstract and concrete movements (Gramsci 1987). In his definition of a 'philosophy of praxis', the general problem that Gramsci tries to address is how to produce a coherent conception of the world that empowers subaltern classes as agents of history. This is also set as a necessary superseding of a mechanical determinism that would fatalistically reproduce subaltern positions in a particular structure. To underscore the activity of the will present within subaltern classes was in itself a political act: 'if yesterday the subaltern element was a thing, today it is no longer a thing but an historical person, a protagonist; . . . an agent, necessarily active and taking the initiative' (ibid.: 337). For Gramsci (ibid.: 323–77), the forces defining the arena of struggle are: first, a particular structure of the economic and social forces that constitutes the environment of people's practical activity and produces in them, through that practice, a latent conception of the world; second, a 'philosophy' becoming the norm of collective action for a historical epoch which expresses 'nothing other than the "history" of that epoch itself, nothing other than the mass of variations that the leading group has succeeded in imposing on preceding reality' (ibid.: 345); and third, a 'creative philosophy' critically emergent from practical activity and corresponding to the objective historical necessities of ordinary people ('the many') (ibid.: 345–46). This creative philosophy's strength is predicated on its 'rationality', on its correspondence with 'objective historical necessity', which makes it acceptable to the many:

> It comes to be accepted by the many, and accepted permanently: that is, by becoming a culture, a form of 'good sense', a conception of the world with an ethic that conforms to its structure . . . [It is] diffused in such a way as to convert itself into an active norm of conduct. Creative, therefore, should be understood . . . as thought which modifies the way of feeling of the many and consequently reality itself, which cannot be thought without this many. Creative also in the sense that it teaches that reality does not exist on its own, in and for itself, but only in a historical relationship with the men who modify it, etc. (ibid.: 346)

As a consequence of this insight, Marxist social scientists found a way to articulate scale, thereby encompassing intimate experience in relation to institutional transformations and structural movements. Raymond Williams (1977) spoke of 'structures of feeling' in order to capture the tension of emerging understandings tied to immediate experience that were simultaneously structured at intimate and institutional scales. Bourdieu (1980a) developed the concept of 'habitus' while trying to resolve a similar breach between structure and concrete practice. Anthropologists in particular (e.g. Wolf 1982; Roseberry 1989, 1994; Roseberry and O'Brien 1991; Smith 1999, 2004) were able to underscore the agency of concrete subaltern positions within hegemonic frameworks.

While all of these approaches were trying to make sense of the tension between abstract and concrete realities simultaneously reproduced at different scales, the moral economy/political economy divide was set in a historical-evolutionary framework that entailed a particular teleology. As it appears in Thompson (1971) initially, and later in Scott (1976, 1985), the moral economy is captured in the historical process of its demise, when its breach by the powerful classes causes the subaltern to revolt, demanding the return of a *status quo ante* that provided relative security in times of crisis (see also Hobsbawm 1965). The moral economy, then, as a historical reality and as an analytical concept, is construed in opposition to classical political economy (also as both a description of historical reality and a concept). It is defined as a situation where moral obligation (forms of social and political dependencies), rather than contractual obligation (individual autonomy to engage in a commitment freely), sets the framework for the transfer of resources and structures the economy (including surplus extraction) (see also Neveling, this volume).

This dichotomous and evolutionist view has been challenged by various scholars, starting with Thompson himself pointing to a methodological problem (Thompson 1993; see also Zelizer 1988; Booth 1994), one which has been mostly resolved by granting an abstract status to the analytical concept and detaching it from its original concrete historical basis, enabling it to float freely as an intellectual commodity. Instead, in my opinion, we need to preserve the tension between the various scales of analysis that are in fact simultaneously experienced by actual historical subjects, and which emerge more clearly in moments of rupture. These moments underscore a mismatch between the processes of surplus extraction and the moral frameworks of obligation that sustained the continuity of particular forms of production and unequal distribution. Moreover, we need to keep the tension between abstract and concrete realities in our analysis instead of choosing one or the other.[4]

Therefore, I want to point to the key articulation between the concrete historical manifestation of the moral economy on the one hand, and the concrete historical manifestation of processes of so called 'primitive accumulation' on the other. Both in Thompson's and Scott's original analysis, the revolt of peasants is tied to the emergence of a new hegemony that, while eroding some types of paternalistic reciprocal obligations, supports a different set of obligations – mostly between an incipient bourgeoisie and power elites – which become central to the development of capitalism. For Thompson, 'The "nature of things" which had once made imperative, in times of dearth, at least some symbolic solidarity between the rulers and the poor, now dictated solidarity between the rulers and "the Employment of Capital"' (Thompson 1971: 131). Moreover:

> The breakthrough of the new political economy of the free market was also the breakdown of the old moral economy of provision ... One symptom of its final demise is that we have been able to accept for so long an abbreviated and 'economistic' picture of the food riot, as a direct, spasmodic, irrational response to hunger, a picture which is itself a product of a political economy which diminished human reciprocities to the wages-nexus. (ibid.: 136)

It has been cogently argued by other scholars (Perelman 2000) that the intellectual construction of the corpus of classical political economy was a central aspect in the production of particular institutional frameworks that supported capitalist development. Likewise, various paternalistic institutions and practices of Ancien Régime moral economy in pre-capitalist Europe were supported by a corpus of discourses, mostly but not only religious ones, which never completely disappeared (Clavero 1990; Hespanha 1993; Guerreau-Jalabert 2000).

The analytical concept of 'moral economy', therefore, cannot be separated from its concrete emergence as the expression of a clash of material forces and cultural constructs vying for hegemony at a particular historical conjuncture of primitive accumulation. It is interesting to note, moreover, that the present-day resurgence of the 'moral economy' discourse parallels what some scholars have underscored as a new primitive accumulation process (De Angelis 2007), the persisting relevance of processes akin to primitive accumulation such as accumulation by dispossession being recognized as central to capitalism (Harvey 2005). Therefore the 'moral' aspect emerges with force again in the concrete conjuncture of the neoliberal expression of present-day capitalism which seems to have shattered a certain moral arrangement of capitalism based, first, on relatively Keynesian distribution of wealth policies, and, second, on the belief that the process sustained by the capitalist objective of expanded accumulation was part of a process of political 'democratic' inclusion and relative social 'convergence' (Smith 2011). The framework of capitalist morality was supported by the enlightenment liberal project of equality and freedom for all.

The perspective I will use in this chapter is one that attempts to understand moral aspects of economies as integral to political economy processes and to the drive to expand capital accumulation, a methodology close to Gramsci's philosophy of praxis.

In particular, what seems to emerge from the two ethnographic cases I present is a situation where moral obligation is an asset for capital accumulation. It is also a situation where 'embeddedness' and 'reciprocity' are central to the operation of capitalist social relations of production (see also Cross, this volume). In these two cases, we observe a growing tension between two apparently contradictory processes. On the one hand, the technical aspects of productivity and competition focus on enhancing skills through endless training and obtaining a flexible labour market through the elimination of legal or institutional protection. This is viewed as the necessary liberalization of the labour market, and produces a particular moral environment where responsibility is shifted to the entrepreneurial self of the worker. Flexible capitalism is about enhancing the individual qualities of the worker (adaptable skills for flexible organization) and fully disembedding the labour market from society as expressed by state regulations. On the other hand, requirements of trustworthiness and good character are simultaneously at work in the labour market, relying on embedded social networks or patronage links (see also Garsten, this volume). These are integral to work relations and employment opportunities, and are the other face of flexible capitalism.

The classical concept of 'reciprocity' as developed in anthropology presents an interesting inroad into the observed practices of embeddedness in capitalism. I will explore this avenue in order to underscore two issues that have emerged from my ethnographic experience: first, ambivalence in subjects' evaluation of responsibilities, and, second, anxiety in assessing and judging appropriate moral behaviour. The concept of 'reciprocity', stressing the social value of exchange relations, will be contrasted to that of 'social capital', stressing the exchange value of social relations. These two concepts appear as the mirror image of each other, and stress different aspects of real life experiences that blur various value domains.

After a brief review of the concepts of 'social capital' and 'reciprocity', I will present these issues as they appear in the ethnographies of my two different field sites in Spain. Here, the anxiety caused by the clash or the blurring of boundaries of different value regimes (structures of obligation) becomes apparent. Historical specificities add nuances to the modalities of tension, however. It seems to me that both the generality of the tensions arising from ambivalent responsibilities and the specificity of their localized expression need to be understood as active principles of capitalism's social reproduction in different historical conjunctures.

Two Concepts: Social Capital and Reciprocity

The concept of 'social capital' as defined by Bourdieu (1980b) originally refers to one of the various fields (*champs*) of capital: economic, social, cultural and symbolic. Capital is here understood as a social relation, a social energy that can be put to play and accumulated in different fields by social actors constrained by their habitus but free to strategize. Each field has a specific logic to it that determines the incorporated and 'objectified' capital resources to be used efficiently in each field's 'market' (Bourdieu 1988: 112–13). The concept of social capital, here, seeks to explain the specific logic of the social field and its articulation with the system of social reproduction. It highlights how certain forms of sociability are knowingly used and produced as long lasting, non-contractual mutual obligations.[5] As such, they create a particular sense of belonging to a group that will recurrently provide access to valuable resources (material, symbolic). These in turn will be articulated to other forms of capital, within a general logic of accumulation specific to each field. Although it appears as an abstract concept of universal applicability, social capital in Bourdieu is tied to a concrete economic system, namely capitalism, and its social reproduction (Bourdieu 1980b, 1988). Bourdieu's methodology is linked to his critique of capitalism. Nevertheless, Bourdieu's work is partially guilty of the extension of capital as a metaphor to all fields of social interaction, creating the potentiality for the misappropriation of the concept of social capital that subsequently took place.

The concept of social capital that has become hegemonic in the social sciences is based on the premises of rational action theory – a theory that was explicitly rejected by Bourdieu (see Wacquant 1989: 42–43). Coleman's social capital concept seeks to reintroduce 'social *context*' in rational action, premised on the autonomous individual and freedom of choice. Indeed, he asserts, 'the conception of social capital as a resource for action is one way of introducing social structure into the rational action paradigm' (Coleman 1988: S95) Following this trend, social theorists have developed a concept of social capital attuned to a new development paradigm, one where community relations and values are used as productive 'capital' to forward economic development.[6]

Finally, the work of Putnam (1993) is key to the articulation of an instrument of economic development – social capital – with the development of civic political responsibility, in a new governance agenda. For Putnam, the kernel of the concept expresses two elements: 'norms of reciprocity' and 'networks of civic participation' (ibid.: 167). Here, 'social capital refers to those aspects of social organization such as trust, norms and networks that might improve the efficiency of society through enabling coordinate action' (ibid.: 167). Putnam's work has been strongly criticized, and I will not go over the extensive literature here (see e.g. Portes and Sensenbrenner 1993; Portes and Landolt 1996; Tarrow 1996; Newton 1997; Putzel 1997). However, it is important to note that in this political project the state is to be substituted by social capital as the main regulatory instrument.[7] From this perspective, the concept appears as part of a neo-liberal governance agenda. Indeed, social capital as an instrument of power points, firstly, to instances where moral obligation ('reciprocity') substitutes for the legal or contractual obligation sanctioned by the state as a guarantor, and, secondly, to instances where unelected private networks of individuals ('networks of civic participation') set the objectives of the 'common good' and exercise control over their implementation.[8]

Ben Fine (2001) presents a devastating critique of the concept of social capital and of the use international agencies such as the World Bank have made of it in their post-Washington Consensus development policies. His main critique, from a political economy point of view, is that the concept rests on a previous conceptual separation between the realms of 'economy' and 'society' and a refusal to understand capital as a set of social relations of production. In that context, the concept of social capital is used to recapture the social and cultural component that had been previously conceptually expelled from capitalism, but was always there. The idea of social capital, on the one hand, adds to the reification and fragmentation of the concept of capital (that is, natural, production, human, social) and obscures our ability to understand our present day political economic reality in terms of connected social relations. On the other hand, as an ideological concept, it points to the direct value of social relations and moral obligation for the purposes of capital accumulation.

Reciprocity is a concept almost as vague and undefined as social capital, and it is also politically charged (Narotzky 2007). It has a particular history in the social sciences that derives, originally, from Enlightenment views of the social and political community as a pact between individuals. Subsequently it has been somewhat elaborated by anthropologists seeking to explain patterns of resource circulation and social cohesion in non-capitalist societies.[9]

The concept of reciprocity has been central to anthropological analyses of social interaction for a long time (e.g. Mauss 2002a; Polanyi

1957; Sahlins 1965; Malinowski 1961, 1971; Weiner 1992; Godelier 1996), and has been revived recently as a sociological concept with an 'alternative economy' political agenda through the writings of the Mouvement Anticapitaliste en Sciences Sociales (MAUSS) group (Godbout 1992; Caillé 2007). The concept describes and seeks to explain transfers that are embedded in social and cultural domains. Cultural values defining moral obligation are crucial to the production of the relationships that support these transfers. In the realm of the economy, reciprocity refers to exchanges taking place within decision-making processes other than those guided by market logic (that is, gift, charity, solidarity, mutual help, filial care). Reciprocal transfers are supported by previously existing social bonds that they in turn strengthen (Sahlins 1965; Gregory 1982). In the realm of politics, reciprocity refers to relations of mutual obligation that are supported by conceptions of justice and injustice, and moral imperatives (Hobsbawm 1965; Thompson 1971; Scott 1976, 1985; Moore 1978; Bourdieu 1980a). In most societies, transfers of resources and sentiments of mutual obligation (legal, customary, moral) depend on multiple and different logics (material accumulation, prestige increase, religious duty, kinship obligations, love) that contribute to simultaneously reproducing a particular system of domination.

For Gudeman (2001), reciprocity occurs at the boundaries of communities and between communities. It is a means for 'extending the base' by creating commensurable value out of the incommensurable value that is shared by the members of a community, and produces the 'base' for reproducing the community. In this sense, reciprocity could be said to correspond to 'binding' social capital, while sharing the base corresponds to 'bonding' social capital (Woolcock 1998). Social scientists, however, have alerted us to an excessive optimism regarding the nature of reciprocity as invariably expressing a positive aspect of social relations. Indeed, the highly contested and extreme relativity of moral domains of reference that support these transfers are especially subject to unequal, exploitative and speculative social processes such as patronage, corruption and mafias, or to be interpreted as unjust by a part of society that holds different moral frameworks (Bourdieu 1980a; Bugra 1998; Narotzky and Smith 2006). In my view, reciprocity does not represent a communitarian mode of beneficial social interaction found in small, closely knit locations or social environments such as local communities, neighbourhoods or ideologically bound communities. Rather, the concept expresses a particular dimension of social relationships that is found in any kind of society. What seems interesting in Gudeman's perspective on reciprocity is the tension between incommensurable and commensurable values as they emerge prior to, or unconnected to, commoditization, but always connected to exchange. This tension, however, might be the foundation that enables non-market regimes of value to be co-opted by capital accumulation.

Reciprocity has both a material aspect expressed in the actual transfers of political and economic resources that take place between people or groups, and a cultural aspect expressed in the discourses that support diverse morals of mutual obligation. From this perspective, it attempts to capture the ambivalence in the construction, legitimization and practice of mutual obligation and responsibility in economic and political terms. It seeks to unpack social relations located simultaneously in market and non-market circuits of provisioning, in universal and particularistic modes of claiming, and between beneficial and predatory outcomes of redistribution processes.

Reciprocity, however, is also the concept that describes the personal and concrete quality of social relationships that build up into social capital in Putnam's view (Narotzky 2009). While economists and sociologists trying to use a (post-Washington Consensus) social capital approach to development policies have tried to measure discrete elements of these useful social relationships, they have admitted to the inadequacy of the results, explicitly pointing at the qualitative and embedded nature of most of the elements under scrutiny. Their inability to fully approach these 'other' forms of regulation and obligation that sustain material transfers stems from a flawed methodological proposition: that social relationships can be cut into discrete pieces, and their concrete qualities described as measurable categories subject to aggregation and disaggregation. That is, it stems from positing that social relationships can be treated as 'things'.[10] Instead, a concept of reciprocity, in contrast to social capital, expresses an irresolvable entanglement of social values and material interests that need to be addressed in their ambivalence and tension.[11]

The concept of reciprocity seems to address exchange from a moral economy perspective. However, for our purposes we need to link the concept of reciprocity to a political economy framework while retaining its moral economy aspects. From this perspective, several questions emerge: How do we analyse social relations that sustain flows of transfers (of goods, information, services) that become incorporated in the value of commodities but are not commoditized in market exchange?[12] How are these 'other' relationships incorporated in capitalist relations while at the same time being reproduced as something different,[13] more primordial and emotional

than contract or market relationships? Are all present-day social relations subsumed in a capitalist global structure of articulations and
dependencies? Should we think of them as distinct from or, on the
contrary, as a fundamental part of the social reproduction of capitalist accumulation? Would reciprocity be better than social capital
for the understanding of how mutual obligation is produced and
sustained between individuals, groups and institutions while giving
us an insight into how it serves surplus value extraction? Would it
help us make theoretical sense of the often ambivalent evaluation
that ordinary people make of the social relations they depend on for
obtaining a livelihood? What I find most appealing in the reciprocity
concept is its underscoring of a generalized system of mutual dependencies and obligations that contribute to forms of collective social
belonging. However, as these get thoroughly subsumed under capitalist imperatives, we might find that the social capital concept is a
better description of what is taking place.

Two Ethnographic Vignettes

I will now present two ethnographic vignettes from different field
sites. The first will consider the 'payoff' of care giving in a rural
setting in Catalonia, where love and interest are the two sides of a
morality of domestic social reproduction and petty commodity production facilitated by land inheritance and access to family labour.
This case shows how the entanglement of moral obligation and value
production change with the demands of an increasingly liberalized
market and the pressure from competition.

The second vignette will consider the 'traffic' of favour networks
in an informal semi-rural regional economy where providing work in
a context of high unemployment is perceived simultaneously as a gift
of support, as a market transaction or as a form of exploitation by the
subjects involved in the relationship.

In both cases, flexible capitalism is based not only on the opportunistic use of existing reciprocal relations and moral obligations for
the purpose of capital accumulation, but on their transformation into
a new kind of ambivalent reality.

The Payoff of Love

The area where I did fieldwork in the mid 1980s is the *comarca* of Les
Garrigues in the interior of Catalonia. This is a dry-land farming area

specializing in olive oil production. Small and medium landowner-ship (5 to 20 hectares) is the main form of access to land, and property enables membership in the processing cooperative producing olive oil for export.[14] Relations to the means of production within the family farm household (*casa*) show strong differentiation even as the cultural concept of *casa* stresses the common objective of all members of the household toward the collective family farm project.[15] In the 1980s, the pressure of entry into the European Economic Community (Spain joined the EEC in 1986) forced investment to be made in the agricultural means of oil production and transformed social relations of production in order to increase productivity and enhance quality.

Traditionally, the collective productive and reproductive endeav-our of household members was not based on a naturalization of mutual obligations: *casa* members were bound by contract, often a notarized document.[16] Therefore, they explicitly set in commensu-rable terms the value of their various activities, some of which are strongly entangled with affect. The institution of marriage contracts in this area expressed access to the means of production: it explicitly set material returns for labour invested in the *casa* project, including the loving care of elderly parents. Although few *casas* drew up mar-riage contracts after the 1950s, every household with some landed property (over 90 per cent of the total) referred to it as the local framework of moral obligation.

The heir's marriage contract served to re-establish privately and explicitly the cultural assumption of a community of interest and *casa* identity as the basis of social reproduction.[17] Simultaneously, it created lines of differentiation between generations (predecessors versus successors in ownership), between siblings (heir versus non-heirs) and between genders (male and female spouse obligations, and male preference in inheritance). These lines constructed specific power relations and revealed intra-household differentiation embed-ded in the meanings of such words as work, care and love: they defined what 'working for the *casa*' meant for different household members, and what they would get for it.[18] Within this framework, support networks were developed, often full with tension and contradictory objectives and meanings, especially when urbanized, nuclear-family-centred, domestic moral economies became hegemonic in the late twentieth century as the competitive injunctions of the EEC came into play. Institutionalized modes of defining economic responsibili-ties and exchanges between household members (through customary law) and of producing the *casa* as an economic unit (a family farm) are increasingly overlapped by non-institutionalized modes of defining filial responsibilities (through affects and flexible moral obligations) and by technical modes of organizing the agricultural business.

Still, recent informal support and care practices must be understood against the background of the institutionalized process of past marriage contracts (Narotzky 1991). The commitment to reproduce the *casa*, constrains the younger couple into dependent, sometimes exploitive relations with an older couple in exchange for a sharecropping income and other resources such as shelter, babysitting or food-produce donations. Care of the elderly predecessor couple is, in the end, the factor determining the transfer of property assets to the next generation, and is the responsibility of the woman of the younger couple. This creates opportunities for non-inheriting siblings that take care of propertied elders without direct heirs. As time goes by, the priorities of the elderly couple change with care work becoming increasingly important as compared to farm labour. The power balance between younger and older couple, and between genders in the younger couple is thus transformed. Property ownership is the definitive sanction of the transfer of control between generations, and the transfer is not completed until the older couple both die.[19] Property transfer is also the proof of 'love' coming from the older couple, and reciprocates the caring 'love' given by the younger couple. The marriage 'love' bond between the younger couple presents the young woman's care work as a joint endeavour and glosses over her exploitation as a care giver, especially when she is not the daughter and will not inherit. The *casa* will benefit from her work as a care giver which will be acknowledged as a contribution to that collective aim.[20]

The picture that is drawn here is one where support provided in the language of love and moral obligation consolidates claims on material resources that are conceived of as part of entrepreneurial assets oriented toward the capitalist viability of the farm, while maintaining a family centred reproduction priority.

In the mid 1980s, the effort to make farms viable and competitive before entry into the EEC pushed women into informal garment production networks, producing for such international brands as Benetton, which provided additional income for the household. Capitalization of the farm was supported by work that relied heavily on personalized social networks. This work went mostly unaccounted for in terms of the moral framework of the *casa* project. In contrast to the traditional institutionalized care work of household women that provided access to farm assets, income from garment work was viewed as individual and aimed at personal consumption, and the term used for it was the morally tainted *malgastos*, literally 'bad expenses'. But women used this personal income for family and household expenses (food, clothing, minor repairs) that had previously been covered by agricultural income.[21] This practice freed farm income from being used for household reproduction and transformed it into capital for investment in the agricultural business. Love and care for the family channelled women's personal income into 'working for the *casa*' without properly being acknowledged doing so (Narotzky 1990). The embeddedness of women's moral commitment to the *casa* became the reason for their work in informal garment manufacture. Their labour was simultaneously incorporated and exploited in the agricultural and the garment commodity chains of capital accumulation, while their aim was to 'work for the *casa*'.

The Traffic of Favours

The fieldwork for the following vignette was carried out by Gavin Smith and myself during 1995/6 in the Vega Baja, a region in the autonomous community of Valencia. This is a predominantly shoe-manufacturing area with over 40 per cent footwear production in the informal sector and declining agricultural production of citrus and other garden produce for export (Bernabé 1975; Ybarra 1991; Ybarra et al. 2004; Narotzky and Smith 2006; Narotzky 2009). The structure of production is fragmented and decentralized, and it relies heavily on family, kin and neighbourhood networks that alternatively provide access to income and labour. This takes a form resembling the Italian 'industrial districts', although with a clear hierarchical subcontracting articulation nested in networks of personalized relations centred on large commercial firms that often only retain marketing and packaging processes (Sabel 1989; Ybarra 1991; Becattini 1994; Ybarra et al. 2004). The traffic of favours is ubiquitous and permeates the entire social fabric. Here I wish to highlight the tensions that arise when feelings of shared belonging, structured by values and obligations (kinship, friendship, other forms of mutuality) that are not referred to in terms of the market become crucial to the organization of production in a very competitive global footwear market. Here, the experience of work is deeply embedded in other social relations and regimes of value that are distinct from market values. What happens, then, when labour and capital relations forgo 'contracts' and, instead, rely heavily on the personal attributes and social circumstances of workers, middlemen and sweatshop owners? What happens when different regimes of value overlap in such a way that a pervasive ambiguity seems to be the basis of the local structuring of production? The situation in this case seems to mirror that of the previous case: instead of drawing up a contract of relations of production supported by affective ties (rendering commensurable the incommensurable), here theoretically contractual ties – such as the wage relation part of the labour market – eschew contracts and are substituted by personalized ties (rendering incommensurable the commensurable).

For the small shoe-manufacturing entrepreneur or middleman in the Vega Baja, subject to the demands and tensions of a highly competitive global market, the use of affective relations for the construction of production relations is a necessity. Their claim over other people's work are based on shared notions of belonging and mutual responsibility that refer to non-market domains (family, neighbourhood, friendship) and are morally qualified (Narotzky 2004). However, these claims occur in a context where the hegemonic model for labour relations is the contractual model of the free labour market. This ambiguous situation generates strong tensions and anxiety, both in the realm of the organization of the labour process as well as in the realm of affective relations and the structuring of personal and collective responsibilities. Deep tensions are generated or aggravated by the present-day embeddedness of production relations in the social fabric of the community, the family and the self. These tensions arise from conflicting obligations towards those around whom personal and collective identities are constructed and security against uncertainty is intimately built. Conflicting responsibilities are experienced as part of a unique morality with two clearly differentiated and potentially contradictory aspects: firstly, economic interest; and second, care responsibilities. Both aspects are experienced as simultaneously part of the substance that builds proximity relations between kin, neighbours and friends, but the danger of their incompatibility is always lurking and emotionally stressful (Narotzky 2006). The moral aspect of the obligation both supports and contradicts exchange relations and exploitation. The permanent articulation of these split responsibilities is similar to that described for patronage moral economies and clientelist systems of power. This is often rendered in the language of 'favours', where people situated in very different social and economic positions try to make sense of the moral obligations that frame responsibility (Wolf 1966).

Ambiguous Responsibilities between Care and Profit

The two cases sketched above bring out different articulations of economy and morality. The first case exposes the entanglement of different levels and meanings of provisioning, linking love and care to the material devolution of property and production work for the farm. It shows how domains of morality, exchange and power overlap in the social reproduction of the family farm, where the moral obligation to give care secures the right to property, and where positioning in regard to property legitimates power cleavages and exploitative relations in agriculture within the *casa*. The situation has changed in the context of growing involvement by local family farms in competitive global markets that demand increased investment, shifting family income to capital. This in turn has led to a diversification of income provisioning strategies, such as informal garment manufacture. As a result, the clearly defined obligations of past marriage contracts (moral obligations sanctioned by law) have become blurred. In local discourse, the reproduction of the *casa* is still acknowledged as the most important objective of all household members. However, the idiom of value has shifted almost unnoticed from the kinship-oriented reproduction of the *casa* to a market-oriented idea of the farm's viability in market (money-making) terms.[22] In the context of the farm as a market enterprise that has to produce an income for the family and reproduce or accumulate capital in order to ensure viability in market terms through investment, two complementary sets of responsibilities emerge as indissolubly tied, one that addresses the creation of profit, the other that of family income and care (Narotzky 1990). But the two contexts have fuzzy boundaries in practice: care has to be given for capital assets to be transferred, and farm viability needs to be maintained for family income to enable urbanized forms of consumption. Simultaneously, women's personal income from wages needs to be lovingly devoted to domestic consumption in order to enable capitalization of the farm and its viability.

The overlapping of these different domains of value seems central to the creation and appropriation of surplus value both in agriculture and the garment industry. Stephen Gudeman speaks of 'debasement' when the 'base' of community reproduction is co-opted by the 'market'. He defines this process as one where 'joining the un-priced and the priced, or community resources, labor and relationships, with capital, can lead to debasement' (Gudeman 2001: 126). The Catalan farmers' case that I have just described could be interpreted as 'debasement' (ibid.: 121–43), where shifts between different value regimes effect a conversion of value that is appropriated by and accumulates in the market realm (the incommensurable 'base' being dispossessed by the commensurable 'market'). It seems to me, however, that these differentiated 'regimes' appear as the consequence of our categories of analysis, but are not relevant in practice to real subjects. Instead, what seems to be relevant for practice is the ambiguity that we can capture in the 'love' idiom that links care, moral obligation and material transfers, which are central to involvement in the market by farmer entrepreneurs and to the provisioning of cheap and docile labour in garment manufacture. Base and market appear as two faces of the same coin, and ambiguity becomes the stuff of social practice: we seem to be closer to Gudeman's concept of reciprocity, which incorporates the tension between incommensurable and commensurable values in exchange. Here, the social value of exchange structures and takes precedence as the argument for social organization: working/caring for the casa.

The second case study would seem to involve a much clearer case of 'debasement'. However, I would like to address these ambiguous categories directly instead of thinking in terms of different value regimes (gift and commodity) or distinct domains of the economy (base and market). Indeed, what seems to be happening in the Vega Baja's decentralized and heavily informal footwear production industry is that social actors cannot easily separate their everyday practices into distinct value regimes. Thus my contention is that this overlapping of value regimes is precisely what enables a particular form of exploitation by capitalist firms. The blurring of value boundaries also produces a particular mode of governmentality that shifts conflict locations and obscures knowledge about the localized and globalized processes of capital accumulation. In the present conjuncture it might be useful to think about a regime of value constituted by both incommensurable and commensurable kinds of value, with personalized, affective, moral obligations and rational, contractual ones operating simultaneously. Reciprocity turns into social capital as an asset for accumulation. The moral economy arena is losing the sharp boundaries that seemed to differentiate a non- or pre-capitalist 'moral economy' based on reciprocity from the 'political economy' of capitalism based on free contractual exchange relations.[23] Rather than a process of 'conversion' between distinct value domains, as Gudeman proposes, we might be witnessing a process of value creation within an ambiguous value regime that enables accumulation in present-day capitalism, and simultaneously the reproduction of social and identity values through commodity consumption.[24] If the central tenet of the Marxist labour theory of value is the dual nature of labour in the commodity – the *form* of exchange value and the real use value *content* – then the unity of opposites of this dual reality results in a situation whereby, 'the transaction between the capitalist and the worker is as much an exchange of equivalents as of non-equivalents' (Grossman 1977: 36). In the case of the Vega Baja, mystification directly addresses the 'form' of exchange: the form of relations between capital and labour is that of non-equivalent, personalized, localized and unique reciprocity ties, but it is simultaneously that of a commoditized, labour-market exchange equivalent. Here the 'exchange of equivalents' aspect of the commodity of labour power is in turn mystified by a non-commoditized form (social capital). The content remains its use value capacity to produce concrete goods (see also Knox, this volume).

In the present conjuncture, forms of market value extraction seem to increasingly favour a fully embedded labour force, one whose economic alienation is predicated on its linkage to other forms of reciprocal obligation and value regimes (in fact, to its non-alienation). It is often embedded in such a way that 'love labour' and wage labour are impossible to separate, different moralities are not easy to distinguish, and the tensions of the constant overlapping of value realms produces useful forms of cooperation but often also acute distress (see also Cross, Garsten, this volume). It is also embedded in such a way that capitalist firms directly or indirectly rely on the growing ambiguity of the relation between capital and labour to extract surplus value. Keane has described the ambiguity involved in exchange processes as a result of semiotic volatility and the temporal dimension of most exchange processes where 'the boundaries among regimes of value are always vulnerable to slippage and retrospective re-categorization' through the mediating role of metalanguages of action, reflexively characterizing and disciplining systems of exchange (Keane 2008: 33).[25] This is an insightful perspective on the variability of value regimes, but it rests on the assumption that actors operate with set categories of value regimes that can be discursively defined and are often discrete. Instead, I propose that present-day values are increasingly ambiguous as categories and ambivalent as moral guides for action, but seem to have become central in the discourse of capitalism and in its practice.

Conclusion

The argument I want to make is about a shift in perspective away from conceiving distinct, confronted regimes of value producing antagonistic forms of moral obligation that would guide practice according to dissimilar categories of good or bad, clearly apparent to the social actors concerned and potentially producing struggles over value. Rather, I suggest we listen to the anxiety of the subjects in our ethnographic experience and to their inability to define their actions in terms of stable categories and moral options regarding their economic practices. The entanglement of care and profit values might not be a novelty, as our Catalan farmers know from their past moral economy of the *casa* and the reciprocal obligations of 'working for the *casa*'. But care and profit then appeared as complementary aspects of a coherent morality centred on the household as a social entity and identity to be reproduced.[26] It was a household moral economy, instituted in customary law, that created its own anxieties, but was unambiguous as to its objectives and obligations. In present-day farming households, this clarity is disappearing as market capitalization obligations compete with family reproduction obligations (and individual consumption becomes the main driving force of younger generations) within the apparently stable and coherent idiom of the *casa* project.

For the footwear manufacturers of the Vega Baja, the informal structure of production and subcontracting that replaced large Fordist factories in the late 1970s has strongly re-embedded production relations in personal networks of reciprocity, in turn embedded in market-oriented objectives. Sabel (1991) has described this as a Möbius strip-like situation, where different value regimes form the obverse and reverse sides of an undistinguishable continuum.

We must now ask what characterizes this new ambiguous value regime. First, uncertainty: the semiotic volatility described by Keane has materialized in Sabel's Möbius strip-like framework. As a consequence, the reconfiguration of actions according to different idioms is not so much an instrumental discursive shift that develops in time; for many, it is a permanent ambiguous reality producing anxiety, while for others it remains mostly an opportunistic arena where this ambiguous value regime becomes an instrument of exploitation within a clearly defined market value orientation.

Second, class demobilization: it is increasingly difficult to understand market imperatives as different from livelihood ones, so that the entrepreneurial self appears as the universal identity model (see Garsten, this volume). It is increasingly difficult to experience commonality in the practices of exploitation and dispossession, as every individual takes responsibility for their social position and sees it as crucially embedded in their personal assets, now transformed into 'capital' assets ('human capital' and 'social capital' being classical examples). The collapsing of a 'household morality' into 'capitalist morality', two realms of value that had initially been carved out as different with the rise of industrial capitalism during the nineteenth century,[27] impedes the production of spaces of autonomy, convergence and dissent around moral values such as 'respect' or 'responsibility' not directed by money-making objectives (Sennett and Cobb 1972; Rancière 1981).[28] Following De Angelis (2007), it is worth keeping in mind the discursive and practical production of distinct regimes of value in the eighteenth and nineteenth centuries as the outcome of a value struggle. However, the situation I am describing seems to be one of value collusion, which is different from that of social movements that attempt to create values distinct from capitalist-driven ones through value struggle.

Here I want to make a brief excursus around the value concept as differently framed by moral economy and political economy approaches. From a political economy point of view, value is inextricably linked with the commoditized aspect of social reproduction through the production and exchange of the commodities that are needed to sustain life. The double aspect of value (use value and exchange value) emerges as a consequence of this, and the simultaneous exchange of equivalents and non-equivalents gives rise to the Marxist labour theory of value. Thus value is a fundamentally contradictory dimension that human relations adopt in capitalism. Worth is what accrues as profit individually and socially from this fundamental contradiction. From a moral economy viewpoint, value relates to responsibility and mutual obligation in a social and cultural environment that appears as coherent, albeit unequal. Worth comes from seamless compliance to formally instituted or tacit norms that contrive to ensure social reproduction. In the classic moral economy approach (Thompson 1971; Scott 1976) and the newer version of value struggles (De Angelis 2007), what is analysed is the clash between these two modes of measuring value in particular historical conjunctures of primitive accumulation or the expansion of enclosure.[29]

In my hypothesis, present-day capitalism rests on a new moral hegemony based on the blurring of value regimes that were previously clearly defined and instituted.[30] If, as Marx and Engels envisioned it,

the 'constant revolutionizing of production, uninterrupted distur-
bance of all social conditions, everlasting uncertainty and agitation
distinguish the bourgeois epoch from all earlier ones' (1848, Ch 1),
we might be witnessing one of these revolutions in the Möbius strip-
like compression of value regimes that increasingly pervades social
relations of and in production, and guides the reproduction of the
system. The uncertainty and anxiety that is thus produced in ordinary people becomes a powerful ideological means of domination
for economic and political elites. Marxist political economy understood that the exchange value of labour power realized in the market
obscured the concrete aspect it had as a use value able to incorporate
concrete value into commodities and produce surplus value through
exchange. An important part of the concrete aspect of labour power
stems from the various moral obligations set by a historically produced cultural and social reality. This is used as an asset by capitalist
firms both large and small in a global conjuncture. As a result, the
equalizing aspect of the market exchange form of labour power is
obscured with the underscoring of its extremely particularized assets.
Present-day capitalism destroys society not so much through disembedding the economy from other social relations and value realms,
but rather through pervasively embedding capitalist objectives in all
spheres of responsibility, blurring distinctions, inhibiting the emergence of alternative value spaces and preventing struggle – in fact, by
turning reciprocity (a nineteenth-century concept) into social capital
(a late-twentieth-century concept).

   In the Catalan farmers' case, the *casa* moral economy is not
devoid of contradiction and anxiety. It is strongly articulated with
the money-making realm through labour and produce markets, farm
investment needs and family and individual consumption patterns
that express social position in a class-based society. Even so, value
is strongly oriented toward family-*casa* reproduction rather than
capital accumulation, although this is mediated by the competitive
market. What the Vega Baja case seems to show more clearly perhaps
is that capitalist relations of production often co-opt spaces and networks of intimate belonging directly for profit-making objectives,
and entangle moralities of a very different sort in a unique practice
of earning a livelihood. This situation should be compared to the
proto-industrial entanglement of merchant capitalism and independent producer figures, which has generally been described as petty
commodity production patterns of capitalist encroachment (or the
articulation of different 'modes of production'). If we free ourselves
from the 'transition' model framework and look at these realities as

paradoxical, non-rational, albeit reasonable aspects of capitalist production relations, we might be in a better position to analyse some of the mechanisms that sustain capitalist reproduction in the long term. Ambivalent value regimes and ambiguous categories increase the ability of both discretionary and arbitrary decision making by those in power.

As the ambivalence of moral regimes grows, so does the totalitarian aspect of capitalist relations expand into the intimacy of the entrepreneurial self, closing spaces for thinking and acting according to other sets of obligations. This is closely related to a round of accumulation by dispossession, whereby enclosure attacks the most intimate boundaries of personal support and solidarity, and uses these relationships as assets in the market. As a result, non-equivalent exchange in the labour market gets incorporated into the surplus value extraction process in production. While this has been described and theorized at the 'formal subsumption' stage of capitalist development, I would suggest that it is central to present day flexible capitalism as well. Flexible capitalism appears to refer to a situation where 'real subsumption' often adopts the mystified form of personalized, reciprocity-based, non-commoditized relations for the labour power commodity. This is a process of 'paradoxical alienation' where capitalist exploitation – the accumulation of surplus value – hinges on not fully commoditizing the labour force.

Rather than presenting a totally new phase of capitalist accumulation, flexible capitalism can be described as 'change within continuity', a situation where some practices of entanglements and moral obligations that sustained work transfers and work organization (kinship, patronage, ritual, customary law and so on) in other circumstances (for example, merchant capitalism, proto-industrialization, Fordist capitalism) are transformed into something similar yet different in present-day globalized free-trade capitalism. The tension between the concepts of reciprocity and social capital as they can be used to describe the present-day situation of flexible capitalism seems to capture both the ambiguity of the value of social relations in exchange and the ambivalence surrounding the final objective of exchange.

Acknowledgements

This chapter has been a long time in the making. A first version was presented in 2008 at the Max Planck Institute for Social Anthropology,

Halle, and I thank Tatjana Thelen and Chris Hann for inviting me there to discuss my work. Another version was presented in 2011 at Manchester University, and I thank Karen Sykes and Chris Gregory for their kind invitation. Several aspects of this chapter stem from various intellectual debates with many colleagues over these years, and it would be impossible to name them here. I wish to thank the reviewers and the editor of the volume for their helpful comments. Various funding agencies have given me support to carry on my research and writing: Ministerio de Economía y Competitividad project CSO2011–26843; Ministerio de Ciencia e Innovación grant CSO2009–08059–E/SOCI; Ministerio de Educación y Ciencia project SEJ2007–66633SOCI. Finally, I want to acknowledge the invaluable support of the Generalitat de Catalunya Fellowship Program ICREA-Acadèmia, which has allowed me to have time to think.

Notes

1 Although some authors have proposed an extension of the concept to other domains of life (e.g. Fassin 2009), stressing the moral in the 'moral economy' concept and adopting a very general understanding of 'economy', I think that the particular force of the concept rests in the articulation of moral values and obligations with material provisioning and resource allocation.

2 In the Marxist tradition, concepts such as 'formal subsumption' and 'articulation of modes of production' are examples of this difficulty; in the neo-classical tradition, 'modernization' and 'underdevelopment' are also attempts to address this difficulty; more recently the concepts of 'informal economy' and 'social capital' also tackle the issue.

3 In Gramsci's terms, the 'historical bloc' refers to the articulation of material realities and ideological constructs. He stresses the need for organic intellectuals to produce knowledge that corresponds to the actual feelings of the 'popular element' and to the material structure they live in. The historical bloc thus formed can then become a force of change (Gramsci 1987: 360, 366, 377, 418): 'If the relationship between intellectuals and people-nation . . . is provided by an organic cohesion in which feeling-passion becomes understanding and thence knowledge . . . then and only then is the relationship one of representation. Only then . . . can the shared life be realised which alone is a social force – with the creation of the "historical bloc"' (ibid.: 418).

4 For expressions of this tension, see both Garsten and Knox (this volume).

5 The concept is defined as 'the ensemble of actual or potential resources that are tied to the possession of a durable web of relationships, more or

less institutionalized, of inter-acquaintance and inter-acknowledgement' (Bourdieu 1980b: 2).

6 See the Social Capital Initiative at the World Bank: http://web. worldbank.org/WBSITE/EXTERNAL/TOPICS/EXTSOCIAL DEVELOPMENT/EXTTSOCIALCAPITAL/0,,contentMDK:201947 67~isCURL:Y~menuPK:401035~pagePK:148956~piPK:216618~theSite PK:401015,00.html, accessed 4 May 2010. For a critique, see Fine (2001).

7 'In all societies, to summarize our argument so far, dilemmas of collective action hamper attempts to cooperate for mutual benefit, whether in politics or in economics. Third-party enforcement is an inadequate solution to this problem. Voluntary cooperation (like rotating credit associations) depends on social capital. Norms of generalized reciprocity and networks of civic engagement encourage social trust and cooperation because they reduce incentives to defect, reduce uncertainty, and provide models for future cooperation. Trust itself is an emergent property of the social system, as much as a personal attribute. Individuals are able to be trusting (and not merely gullible) because of the social norms and networks within which their actions are embedded' (Putnam 1993: 177). For a critique of the perverse effects of the application of the social capital concept in the development programmes of international agencies, see Bretón (2005).

8 For a critique, see Greco (1996), Bologna (1997), Supiot (2000) and Bretón (2005).

9 It is interesting to note, however, that the concept of reciprocity is ambivalent from the start. First, it relates to 'organic solidarity' (Durkheim), that is, to heterogeneous societies (*sociétés polysegmentaires*, or complex societies) and explicit norms and obligations, while, second, it is assumed as the main characteristic of 'primitive' closely knit societies, of communities sharing a 'base' homogeneously glued by 'culture' (Durkheim 2008); but see Mauss (2002b) for an early critique.

10 See Knox (this volume) for the case of skill.

11 It is interesting to note in this respect that Lévi-Strauss's reading of Mauss was particularly harmful to the idea of reciprocity as developed in the latter's essay on the gift. Mauss's proposition (one that has been subsequently recaptured by many Melanesianists, e.g. Weiner 1992) is tied to his idea of the 'total prestation' – that is, to a mode of social interaction where people and things are not detached from each other a priori, often are never fully detached even when changing hands in circulation, and where the movement of objects participates simultaneously in different value regimes in the society as well as being key to the social reproduction of the total structure. In Lévi-Strauss's reading, there is instead an 'exchange' which means that individuals or groups are detached from the things they give to each other, and that it is the action of giving and taking things that produces social cohesion (Lévi-Strauss 1989).

12 This debate brings to mind the domestic labour debate of the 1970s, which attempted to understand how domestic housework was incorporated as

value through the commodity of labour power (Dalla Costa and James 1972).

13 This brings to mind Harvey's idea of the centrality of the process of accumulation by dispossession in capitalism, and how an 'outside' has to be produced and reproduced in order to keep the process of accumulation going (Harvey 2005).

14 During the nineteenth century, however, large numbers of day labourers (up to 50 per cent) and a substantial number of sharecroppers constituted the productive structure, although the size of properties was on average similar. Private oil mills were then the only means available for transforming the crop into oil and, patronage relations with large land- and oil-mill owners were pervasive.

15 The same concept – *casa* – is used by Catalan political representatives as a metaphor of the nation, building on a nineteenth-century corporatist and Catholic understanding of the social body, but simultaneously based on the contractual tradition of the Catalan customary law of medieval origin (Terradas 1984; Prat 1989).

16 This system of household production and impartible inheritance developed in relation to a particular emphyteutical organization of feudal production in this area of Catalonia (Terradas 1984). Emphyteusis is a usufruct system whereby rights to land are hereditary held on a piece of land that is the property of another person.

17 This identity includes all people originally belonging to a certain *casa*, even after founding another *casa* in the case of non-heirs.

18 'Working for the *casa*' is a formula found in all marriage contracts, and the central argument justifying transfers of property and services.

19 As the death of the propertied parent approaches, a notarized donation *inter vivos* will probably transfer the main property assets to the younger couple, reserving use rights to both parents until their death, in order to make sure that they will receive proper care.

20 A man in his late sixties told me the following about his father, who had died aged ninety: 'I loved my father very much and I respected him . . . But I never knew if he really loved me until he died and left me all the property. I thought he didn't love me because he had never demonstrated it, he had never said, "I will leave you everything". But he did, and this proves that he loved me. I thought he didn't love me, you understand, he never expressed it'. In a further elaboration of the intertwining of love, morality and material transfers of care and property, this man, whose wife had taken care assiduously of his father 'until the last minute', explained: 'That person who takes care of you until death is the one who should get a compensation (*recompensa*) . . . The heir (*hereu*) has to care for his parents until the last minute, that is the reason why then the parents give the biggest share to the one who stays with them, who is good with them. Being good (*portarse bien*) means one should take care, and if the parent is sick [it means] to keep company and cook the food, to wash the clothes, to take care of the house – that is being good . . . The

person who is with you in the house (*casa*), who has to clean you if you dirty yourself, has to clean the bed, do everything for you, feed you in the mouth and push the wheel chair. I suppose this is the one who should get the larger part'.

21 For a similar case, see Neveling (this volume).

22 I refer here to Gudeman's concepts of the 'base' as oriented toward the reproduction of the community's resources, and the 'market' as profit oriented (Gudeman 2001). Here the concept of petty commodity production used in the peasant studies literature might be particularly appropriate.

23 Here I am using Hann's definition of moral economy: 'moral economy is primarily a nexus of beliefs, practices and emotions among the folk, rather than an analytical concept designed to register only those beliefs, practices and emotions which conduce to action which the observer considers to be progressive. . .' (Hann 2010: 195).

24 For buyer-driven commodity chains such as footwear, clothing and so on, Foster speaks of a 'value chain' that encompasses two poles of value creation, part of a unique process. He points to branding in consumption processes, in the context of commodity chain structures of production as a form of value creation and accumulation that is based on the articulation of surplus value extraction in a classical labour–capital relationship, and a 'work of love' in consumption practices which also produces value that is extracted and accumulated by capital (Foster 2008: 20). A similar argument is made by Thrift about the centrality of 'affects' in the added value creation process (Thrift 2005) and in politics (Thrift 2004).

25 Keane has argued that 'the boundaries among regimes of value are always vulnerable to slippage and retrospective recategorization. This is due both to the semiotic ambiguity inherent in material things themselves, and in the temporal dimension of virtually any exchange that extends beyond barter for immediate use. Both the ambiguity and temporality provide openings for social intervention and individual opportunism. For instance, a loan that is never returned can become a 'gift' – or a 'theft'. Goods given by one party in an ethos of generalized reciprocity ('we never calculate among brothers'), if never reciprocated, may in time become subject to a bitter reckoning of accounts after all. An incomplete marriage exchange may register as the Maussian debt that creates solidarity among affines – or, in time, produce a shameful relation of subordination. If transactions are events, they are geared to exerting control over definitions and outcomes in the future, beyond the event. They thus contain within themselves metalanguages of action, that is, reflexive characterizations (explicit but more often implicit) of the kind of event now taking place, and the kinds of participants entering into it. Distinctions among regimes of value require indigenous forms of objectification and self-consciousness that tell people, for instance, "this now is a case of swapping, not selling", and so forth' (Keane 2008: 33). He adds: 'It is, I want to suggest, in the very nature of social institutions and

actions that the mediating role of semiotic forms in systems of exchange, of the metalanguages that discipline them, and thus of the social relations they continue to reflect and even reproduce, should play a critical role even in the newest economic formations' (ibid.: 36).

26 People were known through the name of the *casa* they were born into, or by the name of the *casa* they married into.

27 This was often conceived as a 'natural economy' or a 'pre-capitalist economy' by Marx, one that set the conditions of possibility for primitive accumulation through enclosure and formal subsumption. This carving out of clearly differentiated value regimes seems to be as much the result of confrontation and struggle between the powerful as the result of organic intellectuals' strategies of defending spaces of autonomy (Humphries 1977; Reddy 1987).

28 See also Humphries (1977) for labourers' struggle to maintain a 'separate' space in the home.

29 Enclosure is defined as 'the action of surrounding or marking off (land) with a fence or boundary; the action of thus converting pieces of common land into private property' (OED).

30 This can also provide a useful perspective on the related transformations of the liberal state into its present form of overlapping responsibilities, and its fuzzy – rational-emotional – justifications for regulation (devolution of responsibilities, overlapping of jurisdictions, legal pluralism and the cunning state). Cf. Randeria (2007).

References

Becattini, G. 1994. 'El distrito marshalliano: una noción socioeconómica', in G. Benko and A. Lipietz (eds), *Las regiones que ganan*. Valencia: Alfons el Magnanim, pp. 39–57.

Bernabé, J.M. 1975. *Indústria i subdesenvolupament al País Valencià*. Mallorca: Editorial Moll.

Bologna, S. 1997. 'Dieci tesi per la definizione di uno statuto del lavoro autonomo', in S. Bologna and A. Fumagilli (eds), *Il lavoro autonomo di seconda generazione*. Milano: Feltrinelli, pp. 13–42.

Booth, W.J. 1994. 'On the Idea of the Moral Economy', *American Political Science Review* 88(3): 653–667.

Bourdieu, P. 1980a. *Le sens pratique*. Paris: Les Editions de Minuit.

——— 1980b. 'Le capital social: notes provisoires', *Actes de la Recherche en Sciences Sociales* 31: 2–3.

——— 1988 [1979]. *La distinción: Criterio y bases sociales del gusto*. Madrid: Taurus.

Bretón, V. 2005. *Capital social y etnodesarrollo en los Andes: La experiencia PRODEPINE*. Quito: Centro Andino de Acción Popular.

Bugra, A. 1998. 'The Immoral Economy of Housing in Turkey', *International Journal of Urban and Regional Research* 22(2): 303–307.

Caillé, A. 2007. 'Un quasi-manifeste institutionnaliste', *Revue du MAUSS* 30(2): 33–48.

Clavero, B. 1990. *Antidora: Antropología Católica de la economía moderna.* Milan: Giuffrè Editore.

Coleman, J.S. 1988. 'Social Capital in the Creation of Human Capital', *American Journal of Sociology* 94: S95–S120.

Dalla Costa, M., and S. James. 1972. *The Power of Women and the Subversion of the Community.* London: Butler and Tanner.

De Angelis, M. 2007. *The Beginning of History: Value Struggles and Global Capital.* London: Pluto Press.

Durkheim, E. 2008 [1893]. *De la division du travail social.* Livre I, electronic version by Jean-Marie Tremblay for 'Les classiques des sciences sociales': http: //www.uqac.uquebec.ca/zone30/Classiques_des_sciences_sociales/.

Fassin, D. 2009. 'Les économies morales revisitées', *Annales Histoire, Sciences Sociales* 6: 1237–1266.

Fine, B. 2001. *Social Capital versus Social Theory.* London: Routledge.

Foster, R.J. 2008. 'Commodities, Brands, Love and Kula: Comparative Notes on Value Creation', *Anthropological Theory* 8(1): 9–25.

Godbout, J.T. 1992. *L'esprit du don.* Paris: Editions de la Découverte.

Godelier M. 1996. *L'énigme du don.* Paris: Fayard.

Gramsci, A. 1987 [1929–1935]. *Selections from the Prison Notebooks.* New York: International Publishers.

Greco, R. 1996. 'I diritti nella crisi della società del lavoro', in M. Bascetta et al. *Stato e diritti nel postfordismo*, Rome: Manifestolibri, pp. 103–20.

Gregory, C. 1982. *Gifts and Commodities.* London: Academic Press.

———. 2009. 'Whatever Happened to Householding?', in C. Hann and K. Hart (eds), *Market and Society. The Great Transformation Today.* Cambridge: Cambridge University Press, pp. 133–159.

Grossman, H. 1977 [1941]. 'Archive: Marx, Classical Political Economy and the Problem of Dynamics, Part I', *Capital and Class*, 1(2): 32–55.

Gudeman, S. 2001. *The Anthropology of Economy: Community, Market and Culture.* Oxford: Blackwell.

Guerreau-Jalabert, A. 2000. 'Caritas y don en la sociedad medieval occidental', *Hispania, Revista Española de Historia* 60(1): 27–62.

Hann, C. 2010. 'Moral Economy', in K. Hart, J.-L. Laville and A.D.Cattani (eds), *The Human Economy.* Oxford: Polity, pp. 187–198.

Harvey, D. 2005. *The New Imperialism.* Oxford: Oxford University Press.

Hespanha, A.M. 1993. *La gracia del derecho: Economía de la cultura en la edad moderna.* Madrid: Centro de Estudios Constitucionales.

Hobsbawm, E.J. 1965. *Primitive Rebels.* New York: Norton.

Humphries, J. 1977. 'Class Struggle and the Persistence of the Working-class Family', *Cambridge Journal of Economics* 1(3): 241–258.

Keane, W. 2008. 'Market Materiality and Moral Metalanguage', *Anthropological Theory* 8(1): 27–42.

Lévi-Strauss, C. 1989. 'Introduction à l'oeuvre de M. Mauss', in M. Mauss, *Sociologie et anthropologie*. Paris: Presses Universitaires de France, pp. IX–LII.

Malinowski B. 1961 [1922]. *Argonauts of the Western Pacific*. New York: Dutton.

———— 1971 [1926]. *Crimen y costumbre en la sociedad salvaje*. Barcelona: Ariel.

Marx, K. and Engels, F. 1848. *Manifesto of the Communist Party*. Marxist Internet Archive, marxists.org: http://www.marxists.org/archive/marx/works/download/pdf/Manifesto.pdf, accessed 12 May 2011.

Mauss, M. 2002a [1923/24]. 'Essai sur le don: Forme et raison de l'échange dans les sociétés primitives', *Année Sociologique, seconde série*, electronic version by Jean-Marie Tremblay for 'Les classiques des sciences sociales': http: //www.uqac.uquebec.ca/zone30/Classiques_des_sciences_sociales/index.html, accessed 12 May 2011.

———— 2002b [1931]. 'La cohésion sociale dans les sociétés polysegmentaires', *Bulletin de l'Institut français de sociologie*, I, 1931, electronic version by Jean-Marie Tremblay for 'Les classiques des sciences sociales': http: //www.uqac.uquebec.ca/zone30/Classiques_des_sciences_sociales/index.html, accessed 12 May 2011.

Moore, B. 1978. *Injustice: The Social Bases of Obedience and Revolt*. New York: Macmillan.

Narotzky, S. 1990. '"Not to Be a Burden": Ideologies of the Domestic Group and Women's Work in Rural Catalonia', in J.L. Collins and M. Gimenez (eds), *Work Without Wages: Comparative Studies of Domestic Labor and Self-employment*. Albany, NY: State University of New York Press, pp. 70–88.

———— 1991. 'La renta del afecto: ideología y reproducción social en el cuidado de los viejos', in J. Prat et al. (eds), *Antropología de los Pueblos de España*. Madrid: Taurus.

———— 1997. *New Directions in Economic Anthropology*. London: Pluto Press.

———— 2004. 'The Political Economy of Affects: Community, Friendship and Family in the Organization of a Spanish Economic Region', in A. Procoli (ed.), *Workers and Narratives of Survival in Europe*. Albany, NY: State University of New York Press, pp. 57–79.

———— 2006. 'Binding Labour and Capital: Moral Obligation and Forms of Regulation in a Regional Economy', *Etnográfica* 10(2): 337–354.

———— 2007. 'The Project in the Model: Reciprocity, Social Capital and the Politics of Ethnographic Realism', *Current Anthropology* 48(3): 403–424.

———— 2009. 'Regulation and Production in a Globalized World: What Ethnography Brings to Comparison', *Ethnology* 48(3): 175–193.

Narotzky, S., and G. Smith. 2006. *Immediate Struggles: People, Power and Place in Rural Spain*. Berkeley: University of California Press.

Newton, K. 1997. 'Social Capital and Democracy', *American Behavioral Scientist* 40(5): 575–586.

Perelman, M. 2000. *The Invention of Capitalism: Classical Political Economy and the Secret History of Primitive Accumulation*. Durham, NC: Duke University Press.

Polanyi, K. 1957. 'The Economy as Instituted Process', in K. Polanyi, C. Arensberg, and H. Pearson (eds), *Trade and Market in the Early Empires: Economies in History and Theory*. New York: The Free Press, pp. 243–270.

Pollert, A. 1991. 'The Orthodoxy of Flexibility', in A. Pollert (ed.), *Farewell to Flexibility?* Oxford: Blackwell, pp. 3–31.

Portes, A., and P. Landolt. 1996. 'The Downside of Social Capital', *American Prospect* 7(26): 18–21. http://www.prospect.org/print/V7/26/26-cnt2.html, accessed 26 November 2005.

Portes, A., and J. Sensenbrenner. 1993. 'Embeddedness and Immigration: Notes on the Social Determinants of Economic Action', *American Journal of Sociology* 98(6): 1320–1350.

Prat, J. 1989. 'El pairalisme com a model ideològic', *L'Avenç* 132: 34–53.

Putnam, R. 1993. *Making Democracy Work: Civic Traditions in Modern Italy*. Princeton: Princeton University Press.

Putzel, J. 1997. 'Accounting for the "Dark Side" of Social Capital: Reading Robert Putnam on Democracy', *Journal of International Development* 9(7): 939–949.

Rancière, J. 1981. *La nuit des prolétaires*, Paris: Fayard.

Randeria, S. 2007. 'The State of Globalization: Legal Plurality, Overlapping Sovereignties and Ambiguous Alliances between Civil Society and the Cunning State in India', *Theory, Culture and Society* 24(1): 1–33.

Reddy, W.M. 1987. *The Rise of Market Culture*. Cambridge: Cambridge University Press/Maison des Sciences de l'Homme.

Roseberry, W. 1989. *Anthropologies and Histories: Essays in Culture, History and Political Economy*. New Brunswick, NJ: Rutgers University Press.

——— 1994. 'Hegemony and the Language of Contention', in G. Joseph and D. Nugent (eds), *Everyday Forms of State Formation: Revolution and the Negotiation of Rule in Modern Mexico*. Durham, NC: Duke University Press.

Roseberry, W., and P. O'Brien. 1991. 'Introduction', in J. O'Brien and W. Roseberry (eds), *Golden Ages, Dark Ages: Imagining the Past in Anthropology and History*. Berkeley: University of California Press, pp. 1–18.

Sabel, C. 1989. 'Flexible Specialization and the Re-emergence of Regional Economies', in P. Hirst and J. Zeitlin (eds), *Reversing Industrial Decline? Industrial Structure and Policy in Britain and Her Competitors*. Oxford: Berg, pp. 17–70.

Sabel, C. 1991. 'Moebius Strip Organizations and Open Labor Markets: Some Consequences of the Reintegration of Conception and Execution in a Volatile Economy', in P. Bourdieu and J. Coleman (eds), *Social Theory for a Changing Society*. Boulder, CO: Westview Press, pp. 23–54.

Sahlins M. 1965. 'On the Sociology of Primitive Exchange', in M. Banton (ed.), *The Relevance of Models for Social Anthropology*. London: Tavistock, pp. 139–236.

Scott, J.C. 1976. *The Moral Economy of the Peasant: Rebellion and Subsistence in Southeast Asia*. New Haven: Yale University Press.

——— 1985. *Weapons of the Weak: Everyday Forms of Peasant Resistance*. New Haven: Yale University Press.

Sennett, R., and J. Cobb. 1972. *The Hidden Injuries of Class*. New York: Norton.

Smith, G. 1999. *Confronting the Present: Towards a Politically Engaged Anthropology*. Oxford: Berg.

——— 2004. 'Hegemony', in D. Nugent and J. Vincent (eds), *A Companion to the Anthropology of Politics*. Oxford: Blackwell, pp. 216–230.

——— 2011. 'Selective Hegemony and Beyond – Populations with "No Productive Function": A Framework for Enquiry', *Identities* 18(1): 2–38.

Supiot, A. 2000. 'The Dogmatic Foundations of the Market (Comments Illustrated by Some Examples from Labour Law and Social Security Law)', *Industrial Law Journal* 29(4): 321–345.

Tarrow, S. 1996. 'Making Social Science Work across Space and Time: A Critical Reflection on Robert Putnam's Making Democracy Work', *American Political Science Review* 90(2): 389–397.

Terradas, I. 1984. *El mon històric de les masies*. Barcelona: Curial.

Thompson, E.P. 1971. 'The Moral Economy of the English Crowd in the Eighteenth Century', *Past and Present* 50: 76–136.

——— 1993. 'The Moral Economy Reviewed', in *Customs in Common*. New York: New Press, pp. 259–351.

Thrift, N. 2004. 'Intensities of Feeling: Towards a Spatial Politics of Affect', *Geografiska Annaler* 86B(1): 57–78.

——— 2005. *Knowing Capitalism*. London: Sage.

Wacquant, L. 1989. 'Towards a Reflexive Sociology: A Workshop with Pierre Bourdieu', *Sociological Theory* 7(1): 26–63.

Weiner, A.B. 1992. *Inalienable Possessions: The Paradox of Keeping-while-Giving*. Berkeley: University of California Press.

Williams, R. 1977. *Marxism and Literature*. Oxford: Oxford University Press.

Wolf, E.R. 1966. 'Kinship, Friendship, and Patron-Client Relations in Complex Societies', in M. Banton (ed.), *The Social Anthropology of Complex Societies*. London: Tavistock, pp. 1–22.

——— 1982. *Europe and the People without History*. Berkeley: University of California Press.

Woolcock, M. 1998. 'Social Capital and Economic Development: Toward a Theoretical Synthesis and Policy Framework', *Theory and Society* 27: 151–208.

Ybarra, J.A. 1991. 'Industrial Districts and the Valencian Community', International Institute for Labour Studies, Discussion Paper No. 44. Geneva: International Labour Organization.

Ybarra, J.-A., et al. 2004. *El calzado en el Vinalopó, entre la continuidad y la ruptura*. Alicante: Universidad de Alicante.

Zelizer, V.A. 1988. 'Beyond the Polemics on the Market: Establishing a Theoretical and Empirical Agenda', *Sociological Forum* 3(4): 614–634.

7

Flexible Capitalism and Transactional Orders in Colonial and Postcolonial Mauritius

A Post-Occidentalist View

Patrick Neveling

In the early 1970s, a series of crises struck Western advanced capitalist societies. As the number of workers in industrial manufacturing declined, it seemed as if the whole world was changing. Sociologist Daniel Bell's *The Coming of Post-Industrial Society* (1973) provided a catch-phrase for such sentiments. In Europe, Alain Touraine's *The Post-Industrial Society: Tomorrow's Social History* (1971) gave voice to a similar mood. Not least in the social sciences, those years would cast a long shadow. To this day, the early 1970s have been regarded as a turning point towards post-Fordism, flexible accumulation and so forth (see Harvey 1990). Nash (1995), however, has long pointed to the spatial and, hence, analytical limitations to the notion of 'post-industrial society'. Neither Bell nor Touraine took into account that changes in Western core areas had to do with the relocation of industrial manufacturing to other regions. The bigger picture was, indeed, a 'global shift' (Dicken 2003). From an analytical perspective, notions such as 'post-industrial society' thus emerge from what may be seen as a particular and limited conception of change, which is recurrent as Kjaerulff points out (see Introduction, this volume), and which has profoundly shaped recent 'end of work debates' (e.g. Strangleman 2007). Gloomy declarations of the end of a 'golden age' of manufacturing and the coming of flexible capitalism forget that only a few decades earlier the same societies had lamented the social disruptions caused by the advent of industrial manufacturing (ibid.: 91). Analytical engagement with capitalism at the scale of the global, the regional or the factory therefore has to consider spatial and temporal limitations of change. Caution is advised whenever the coming of a new era is declared, be this post-industrial, post-Fordist or flexible capitalism (cf. Baca 2005; Neveling 2006).

This chapter is an enquiry into anthropology's position regarding such processes. What can a discipline claiming understanding of a wide range of societies contribute to debates over the end of work, the flexibility of capitalism and its impact on social structures across the globe? To address this question, I focus on the long history of capitalist practice in Mauritius and how this history informed changes in the 1970s, when garment and electronics manufacturing was established in an export processing zone (EPZ) on a large scale. These developments were partly shaped by relocations from Western and Asian regions, as many companies expanded their business ventures and set up new production sites in Mauritius. This small Indian Ocean island nation-state was not alone in using EPZs as an export-oriented development strategy. India (see Neveling 2014; see also Cross, this volume), Malaysia (Ong 1987), Mexico (Fernandéz-Kelly 1983), South Korea (Kim 1997) and many other nation-states have done so since the 1970s or earlier. EPZs have become a market where nation-states bid for manufacturing relocation to their territories. Central features of this market are investment incentives, including tax and customs duty holidays, special labour laws, low-cost factory space, credit portfolios and so on. Such particular relations of exchange between capital, state and labour mean that EPZs are one focal point in global, flexible capitalism (cf. Neveling forthcoming).

My concern is thus with the coming rather than the departure of large-scale industrial manufacturing in the 1970s, because this is the flipside of developments captured in debates about the end of work and post-industrial society. But rather than establishing a synchronic juxtaposition of regions 'giving' away manufacturing jobs with regions 'receiving' those jobs, I do not take for granted that EPZs (sometimes also called special economic zones or free trade zones) are 'cornerstones of flexibility' that have 'made informality and precariousness an integral part of ... many global commodity chains' (Cross 2012: 4). Analysing Mauritian developments requires diachronic enquiry as well, and I go back in time and juxtapose the advent of new industrial manufacturing in the 1970s with the development of the colonial sugar industry. The latter was established after 1810 and, as I will show, has dominated Mauritian socio-economic relations ever since, creating highly flexible and precarious labour relations embedded in a competitive global capitalist system.

The chapter, then, extends Garsten's observation (Garsten, this volume) that change is 'an everyday constant' (in the labour process at Apple Computer), to the long history of capitalism in Mauritius. This move requires a reconsideration of those conceptual tools that economic anthropology uses to understand the advent of industrial manufacturing in a particular location. That reconsideration provides the analytical bracket for the three sections below, and is grounded in the following reflections which are expanded on in the course of the chapter. The relocation of industrial manufacturing to non-Western regions has often been portrayed as the advent of commoditized exchange relations in places that had so far been dominated by gift exchange, barter and, on a different analytical level, by what Scott (1976) has identified as a 'moral economy of the peasant'. This juxtaposition essentializes both 'Western societies' and 'non-Western' societies. The notion of the latter as gift-driven and the former as capital-driven is core to 'Occidentalism' in anthropology (cf. Carrier 1992). As I will show, such Occidentalism is also latent in the distinction between long-term and short-term transactional orders (Bloch and Parry 1989), when long-term transactional orders become synonymous with pre-capitalist ways for securing 'the reproduction of the cosmic and social order', and short-term transactional orders are seen as synonymous with capitalism's 'individual competition' (ibid.: 24). In this view, individual competition contradicts the cosmic and social orders of many non-Western societies and therefore needs 'cosmic purification' – as in India, for example, 'where even wealth acquired through the most devious means by merchants, bandits and kings is unproblematic so long as a proportion of it is gifted to Brahmans as part of the long-term cycle' (ibid.: 25). This ignores the fact that most societies, if not all, have for long been integrated into global capitalism, and that a long-term transactional order may well offer the 'greatest potential for capital accumulation', particularly so if it is coupled with development efforts and monetary exchanges (Gregory 1980: 627).

I build on the latter insight to explore how religion and cosmic order may serve as ideological foundations for flexible, capitalist exploitation. To do so it is necessary to go beyond a traditional anthropological conception of a 'native's point of view' that assumes coherent social formations. Instead, my analysis of the historical trajectory of flexible capitalism concentrates on the conflicting views that a population, in a given space at a given time, holds about cosmic and socio-economic orders. The approach is mirrored in Zigon's work, which abandons normative distinctions of moral and immoral by introducing the concept of moralities (Zigon 2007). This approach links situated, individual points of view on events and actions to wider social settings as contested rather than coherent. Such concerns have largely yet to be developed for economic anthropology where the moral/immoral nexus prevails, though Narotzky (this volume) has made important steps in this direction. Likewise, economic anthropologists have begun increasingly to consider the coexistence of gift and commodity exchange in a given capitalist social order (indeed this is a general thrust of this volume). To further this analytical move, we need to go beyond normative views on exchange as either moral/pre-capitalist or immoral/capitalist. Such normative views are implied not only in Bloch and Parry's distinction of transactional orders and in Scott's conception of a 'moral economy of the peasant' (see above), but also in one of anthropology's core texts on women's work in EPZ factories, where Ong (1987) argues that spirit possession among women workers is driven by the painful transition from a moral economy of the peasant to an economy of commodities (see below). Building on an analysis of spirit possession in Mauritius, I contradict this view and show how spirit possession is an excellent example of the way workers criticize the ideological foundation of capitalism in long-term transactional orders.

The chapter correlates the historical establishment of a long-term, capitalist transactional order in the colonial and postcolonial Mauritian sugar sector with gendered exploitation in postcolonial EPZ factories, and the way that women have contested this exploitation by commenting on the ideological linkages and continuities between capitalism and religion, rather than lamenting radical ruptures. In other words, I introduce the problem of inequality and class struggle. This allows me to highlight the fundamental role that gifts and many other forms of supposedly non-capitalist exchange play in the expansion and maintenance of the capitalist system at all scales.

In order to develop these perspectives on solid empirical ground, the following section outlines how a capitalist, long-term transactional order was established as an integral part of global market adjustments affecting the Mauritian sugar industry throughout colonial times. The next sections analyse the establishment of the Mauritian EPZ in the 1970s, and how this rested on gendered exploitation and informed conceptions of short-term and long-term transactional orders. The final empirical section shows why spirit possession in Mauritian EPZ factories is best understood as a critique of the persistence of colonial capitalism's long-term cosmic-religious transactional order. In my concluding remarks I suggest how, in

Mauritius and elsewhere, flexible capitalism may be understood in terms of ambiguous practices of exchange which have been at work through centuries rather than being a sudden arrival, and how this is best framed in anthropological research.

The Flexibility of Capitalism in the Long-term Transactional Order: The Colonial Sugar Sector

Mauritius was one of the few uninhabited places colonized by Europeans. Possibly because there was no settled population to exploit, early capitalist ventures failed. The Dutch East India Company abandoned the island around 1710; French colonial rule lasted from 1735 until 1810. As the island had gained strategic relevance because of its proximity to major international shipping routes, new British and old French rulers struck a deal after takeover in 1810. Trade and privateering were to end. In exchange, Mauritius was incorporated into the West Indian Sugar Protocol in 1825. This meant preferential access to the British Empire's markets, and turned the island into a mono-crop economy. As subjects of the Empire, French settlers had to accept the abolition of slavery in 1835, albeit with financial compensation. The latter was invested in new production technology, banking capital and, not least, in importing contract labourers to replace slaves and sustain a cheap labour supply (Teelock 1998; Neveling 2013: 126). The cycle of sugar cane cultivation and processing now determined external relations, population structure and class divisions. French-British joint ventures mushroomed in agriculture, banking and transport, and would soon include Indian Ocean business communities. Chambers of commerce and agriculture were set up, while successive British governors facilitated the exploitation of labour within and beyond the legal limits. An overall racist consensus dominated everyday life, but otherwise this life was anything but stable. For one thing, the political battle over free trade or protectionism in Britain meant that preferences and export quotas for Mauritian sugar changed several times throughout the nineteenth century and well into the twentieth century (Neveling 2013: 123–29).

One crucial change came with the First World War. The war years meant stable prices for sugar, and were followed by a brief surge in prices before the global recession of the 1920s and 1930s hit the industry. This crisis was resolved with the ratification of the International Sugar Agreement (ISA) in 1937, which effectively ratified an existing long-term transactional order of capitalist, reciprocal exchange relations. The Empire's centre granted preferential quotas to the colonies for the import of sugar, and some of the customs duty collected by the United Kingdom authorities was handed back, trickling down the commodity chain of sugar to reach even small planters. Contradicting the common distinction between gift-based and commodity-based systems of exchange, the ISA thus facilitated the global movement of commodities by way of a reciprocal recognition of bilateral trading agreements. This, to some extent, ended a period of volatile macro-structural integration for Mauritius (ibid.: 129–36).

All the same, volatile macro-structural exchange relations continued to affect developments within Mauritian society, allowing significant room for Mauritians' manoeuvring. Investment in indentured labour, for example, created considerable turmoil. Being used to an abundant supply of cheap slave labour, Mauritian 'plantocrats' called for ever more indentured labourers, and ignored the fact that this new system of exploitation introduced factors beyond their control. One such factor was that indentured labourers sent remittances to their families. Around 1845, supplies of money fell short. Then the British banking crisis of the late 1840s hit the island and two out of three local banks went bust. Suddenly, there was no credit to fund the next harvest and, despite intervention from the colonial state, the structure of the sugar industry changed radically. Many plantations went bust, and landless white settlers filled the ranks of upper-management in those surviving enterprises that now modernized and built steam-driven mills. The shift from extensification to intensification is well captured in the number of sugar mills. This rose from 157 mills in 1823 (Teelock 1998: 96) to 303 in 1863, and then declined steadily to 43 just after the First World War (North Coombes 2000: 141).

While processing was increasingly centralized, cultivation moved in different directions. Large establishments took over fertile lands from bankrupt ventures, but other plots were parcelled out and sold off. Historians distinguish two periods of land sales, a *petit morcellement* from 1839 to 1859, and a *grand morcellement* following the crisis of the early 1870s. Mainly former indentured labourers bought plots of land, not least because this gave them rights of residence and protection from marauding hordes of the bourgeoisie hunting down everyone who had no residence permit. Thousands of land acquisitions meant a 'major restructuring of rural social and economic relations' (Allen 1999: 117). Postcolonial Mauritian nation-building ideology and academics alike interpret this restructuring as an emancipation and liberation of former slaves and indentured labourers.[1]

But the unfolding of events during the long crisis of the 1920s and 1930s suggests that the Mauritian *morcellement* was a process of out-sourcing market risks which, effectively, is an example of 'flexible capitalism'.

Indenture ended in 1923. Ideally, Mauritius would have seen rising numbers of free wage labourers. But developments on the ground set workers on a different trajectory. The highest number of land sales took place before and around 1920. Then, sugar prices were high and so were land prices. Once world market prices declined, many newly landed labourers fell short on their mortgage repayments and entered a debt spiral. Although classified as smallholders (*petits plan-teurs*), out of roughly 14,000 such businesses operating in 1930, more than 90 per cent held plots of land that could not sustain a house-hold. The result was that 'emancipated' planter households sent men, women and children to earn additional income as seasonal labourers on larger plantations, and dependency on the established bourgeoisie persisted. Around 2 per cent of *morcellement* plots were rather large. These households became wealthy. They sent their children to school to fill the ranks of bureaucrats and politicians in the late colonial and postcolonial state (cf. Teelock 2001: 323–50).

The colonial state played a crucial role in maintaining this depen-dency of labour on capital. It supported large planters and millers with subsidies and tax holidays throughout the 1920s and 1930s. In 1937, the island's first development bank provided a safe haven where larger businesses could move their debts (Neveling 2012: 161–91). Owners of small plots received no relief from hardship. Steady jobs with monthly incomes were scarce, and during the harvest season there was competition from an ever-growing semi-urban and urban population. Hiring was 'by task work or by day or if they were cutting canes by tonne. Those who loaded canes on trucks were paid by week' (Teelock 2001: 361). Such workers had next to no bargain-ing position, and wages fluctuated related to the prices sugar fetched on the world's markets. Rising demand for the right to unionize from workers in transport and in the mills, and deadly protests by small-holders in 1937, coupled with efforts to keep the population on the British side during the Second World War, meant minor improve-ments in the 1940s. But rights to unionization were confined to per-manently employed workers (cf. Allgoo 1985).

In short then, there is little empirical evidence for a 'Fordist' or Keynesian era with stable employment and a certain degree of pros-perity in Mauritius during these times (cf. Neveling 2012: 302). Instead, the lives of most Mauritians continued to be integrated into global capitalism in highly flexible ways. This is vividly illustrated in a report on the Mauritian economy written by the British economist James Edward Meade in 1960. It counts a total active workforce of 200,000 in 1958, with 75 per cent male workers and 25 per cent female workers, and an unemployment rate of 15 per cent. The vast majority of so-called permanent agricultural labourers were hired by 'job contractors' who sold their labour on to estate owners and millers. Meade concludes that there was a 'casualisation of labour' in the late 1950s (Meade 1961: 62).

But the preceding also suggests continuity and change in terms of what can be conceived as a long-term transactional order in Mauritius, shaped by various socio-economic factors. Mono-crop agriculture meant that changes in the global sugar commodity chain had particularly strong repercussions, and British imperial policies also delineated a succession of labour regimes. Class divisions on the other hand were rather stable, and only small fractions of the population enjoyed upward socio-economic mobility. These are all historically specific factors related to the production of sugar, which have profoundly shaped experience through time in Mauritius, and so outlooks in terms of social, political and cosmic order. The way the production of sugar cane marks the landscape in Mauritius even today may serve as a simple entry point for appreciating how this is so. Before the harvest season starts in June, the mountainous slopes are covered with green cane. As this is cut, the landscape turns brown and scraggy, only for the next generation of cane to blossom a few months later. Well into the 1960s, this cycle dominated social life in Mauritius. Household incomes varied according to harvest and planting/growing seasons. There was also a credit cycle for small and large estates alike that was completed only once the sugar cane had been processed and the final returns from customs rebates for sales on the London market had come in. That the crop cycle also has dimensions of a 'cosmic' transactional order is manifest in a ritual marking the beginning of the harvest season, known as 'La Coupe'.[2] In the first decade of the twenty-first century, when centralization had reduced the number of sugar mills to nine, La Coupe was held in a different mill each year. In 2004, the minister of agriculture was invited to the Savannah sugar mill as the main speaker. Addressing an audience of mill owners, managers, ordinary workers and journalists, he expressed hope that Mauritian sugar would continue to thrive, despite the World Trade Organization's efforts to abolish all trade preferences (to the effect of opening up Mauritius to competition from Thailand, Brazil and elsewhere). Heading an entourage of celebrities form the world of agribusiness and politics, he then walked up to start the crushing machine engine. Lower-ranking personnel sat and watched. Afterwards, there were drinks and snacks for the workers and the anthropologist, while celebrities rushed off in black limousines. In the days before, religious services had been held in Catholic, Hindu and Tamil houses around Savannah, and congregations had asked for a successful harvest season. La Coupe gives a condensed but vivid example of the way agribusiness, politics and religious leadership concur on affirming a kind of long-term transactional order with both cosmic and social dimensions, shaped by the history of sugar production and trade, as it has marked experience through time in Mauritius. I expand on the perspective below.

Sugar is thus an important pillar of colonial and postcolonial capitalism, and the industry itself has been a stable factor in much of Mauritian history. But, as the above shows, labour relations were highly flexible long before Mauritian independence in 1968 and the foundation of the EPZ in 1970. There was a large, free-floating proletariat in villages, semi-urban and urban areas, living precarious lives as unemployment peaked well above 20 per cent in the late 1960s.

Diversifying Flexible Capitalism in the Postcolonial State: The Mauritian EPZ

The colonial state provided capital with incentives, and this was continued by the postcolonial state. Building on advice from the World Bank and the United Nations Industrial Development Organization, as well as recommendations from local economists and business people, the Mauritian EPZ received significant financial input from 1970 onward. This state investment is important for an anthropological analysis of flexible capitalism and deserves attention. But this does not mean that the sugar sector and the EPZ can be treated as one and the same. The colonial plantocracy had sourced labour globally, buying slaves and indenturing labourers from Africa and Asia before outsourcing cane cultivation to small planters and generating fresh capital from land sales. Investments had been fixed in space, and it was the organization of production and the supply of labour that granted flexibility. In the EPZ, these spatial and temporal relations between capital and labour would be inverted to some extent. EPZ investors move factories and knowledge rather than labour around the globe. Their business strategy was and is to seek 'low-skilled, export platform assembly' work, and prototypical EPZ investors will be ready to relocate if another zone offers a higher surplus. In this sense, EPZ factories are 'world-market factories' (Fröbel, Heinrichs and Kreye 1981: 347).

The Mauritian state contributed to this by granting tax and customs duty holidays for periods of ten years. This was a significant step. On the one hand, expenses for industrial zones and other infrastructure were enormous. On the other hand, tax and customs revenues as a potential means for refinancing these expenses were waived. In order to understand why the state made such a significant gift to investors, it is instructive to look at how Mauritian politicians imagined export-led development.

In 1970, the Mauritian parliament debated EPZ laws and investment incentives. Whether it was necessary to set up an EPZ soon became a side issue. Instead, opinion was split over its negative impact on social order and morale. In parliamentary debates over the matter, some said that the arrival of foreign managers and new production processes would upset public order and undermine morals.[3] Free-market liberals instead imagined a prosperous future with jobs for everyone, and Mauritius joining the ranks of Taiwan, Hong Kong and Singapore as world-famous examples of rapid industrialization.[4] The latter arguments carried the day, not least because everyone agreed that mainly women would work in the EPZ. And because women would be part of a household with a male breadwinner who could make up for the low EPZ wages and ensure the enforcement of morals, the minimum wage for the EPZ was set much lower than for the national economy.

Interestingly, conservative members of the Mauritian parliament had little regard for the fact that their island had been integrated into a highly volatile world market for sugar all along, and that morals had been changing all the time. Similar to Western sociologists declaring the coming of post-industrial societies or an end of work, a stable past that is under attack and subject to rapid rupture was constructed in these parliamentary debates. Setting up an EPZ as a second pillar for the national economy thus had little to do with offering workers an alternative to the long-term transactional orders of the sugar sector and its flexible employment conditions.

On the investors' side, continuity rather than change prevailed as well. Throughout the 1970s, many joint ventures between Mauritian sugar companies and foreign corporations from the electronics and garment sectors were set up. Soon, the first fully Mauritian-owned factories emerged, and the local plantocracy could reap the full benefit of generous EPZ incentives. In this, they collaborated with established foreign businesses, which shifted to Mauritius with the explicit aim of exploiting a cheap labour force, whose wages were 30 per cent below the already low wages of Asian EPZs (World Bank 1973: 3).

In 1975, there were seventy-nine EPZs in twenty-five countries (Fröbel, Heinrichs and Kreye 1981: 306), and Mauritius competed with the Irish EPZ in Shannon, Taiwan's EPZ in Kaohsiung and *maquiladoras* in the larger cities along the Mexico–US border. For Mauritians entering EPZ factories, this maturing global labour market was a manifestation of how the 'historical geography of capitalism' (see Harvey 1990) cuts across space and time. Some factories hired training personnel from Hong Kong, German managers ran others and, as one company owner remembered, even retired officers of the British colonial army would be recruited to make workers meet production targets. Newspapers invited EPZ factory managers to talk about Mauritian workers' lack of productivity.[5] On the shop floor, line managers regularly repeated how much faster and better workers in EPZs in the Philippines and elsewhere operated.

The factory environment was a challenge in itself. Before 1970, labour had taken place mainly outdoors or in rather modestly sized manufacturing establishments, and only workers in sugar mills had experience of highly standardized and rhythmic production processes. In this sense then, work in EPZ factories was indeed a new experience. Those predominantly women workers who spent ten-hour working days in cheaply built and non-air-conditioned factories surely had new views on the subtropical Mauritian climate. Unfamiliar work routines, constant demand for high performance and precision, the noise of industrial machines and the smells and garment fibres filling the air on the shop floor added to the challenge. Considering that husbands and families often demanded household labour to be finished before and after factory shifts, these women workers indeed had to be highly flexible.

These demands could not always be met. A late 1970s study revealed that most workers were slim, malnourished and lacked both the financial means and the eating habits necessary to maintain the pressure on their bodies (Hein 1984: 256). The way this problem was dealt with is another example of how the long-term transactional order of colonial days extended into the new factories.

Milk and yoghurt are rather expensive consumer goods, as they have to be imported to an island whose agricultural sector is dominated by sugar. For EPZ businesses, they were surely affordable, as moderate estimates put the annual value added per worker around

$2,000 for the early 1970s (World Bank 1973: 21). But when it was evident that EPZ workers needed such additional nutrition, EPZ companies adopted the following stance:

> Past studies have revealed that an important factor responsible for low productivity, and illnesses leading to absenteeism has to do with inadequate or unwholesome nutrition . . . We believe that Government, with MEPZA [Mauritius Export Processing Zone Association, the association of EPZ employers] help, should seriously consider a meals-on-wheels type of operation freely supplying either 2 glasses of milk (a gift from some friendly country may surely be arranged) or 2 yoghurts and possibly be partly subsidising a well-balanced meal. (Forget 1983: 92, my addition)

This is quoted from a report financed by the Mauritius Commercial Bank Ltd. This is the island's oldest bank, and a stronghold of the 'native' Franco-Mauritian upper class, which still holds considerable economic power today. Although asking for 'a gift from some friendly country' was surely an inventive move, the above indicates that EPZ investors showed little flexibility in their approach to exchange relations with workers, the nation-state or Western countries. The latter were seen as outlet and culprit, ultimately responsible for the shortcomings of EPZ employment.

Continuity was also evident in paternalistic attitudes towards the workforce. The report further states that, 'there are also indications that wages earned in the free zone are substantially wasted on nonessentials like clothing and make-up while satisfactory diets are not achieved' (ibid.: 92).

So far, my analysis of the Mauritian EPZ highlights continuities with the sugar industry, except for the new experience of working in factories and working for highly mobile investors. I now turn to scrutinize whether EPZ employment changed the overall Mauritian social setting, enabling me to analyse whether or not there was the social rupture commonly associated with flexible capitalism.

Crucially, the above underlines how the establishment of the EPZ also established double moral standards. On the one hand, female labour was declared to be of lesser value and, hence, women could be paid lower wages. If EPZ employment posed a challenge that was too high for women workers, it was these women and their irrational spending habits that were to blame on the one hand, and Western consumer markets and their grip on the world market on the other. But then, the success of the Mauritian EPZ was crucial for sustaining the postcolonial developmental state and its government, which had invested huge sums to build a new industrial infrastructure and to ultimately change the island's historical geography of capitalism.

Anthropologists studying Mauritius have by and large focused on the issue of ethnicity (cf. Neveling forthcoming), and have thus paid little detailed attention to the phenomenon of large scale EPZ employment. Although 20,000 new jobs were created throughout the 1970s, and another 70,000 jobs were added in the 1980s, from 1995 onwards an increasing number of workers were laid off. Hein (1984) provides rich statistical material, and helps to put the impact of EPZ employment on women in perspective. Female participation in the labour force stood at 19.7 per cent in 1972 – a strong reminder that the sugar sector employed a significant number of women. This moved up to 26.9 per cent in 1982, and manufacturing generated nearly 90 per cent of this increase. EPZ manufacturing was, in short, a female domain (ibid.: 254).[6] The increasing participation of women in industry conflicted with a society that had an 'underlying belief that employment is much more important for a man who must support his family than for a woman who normally has a husband or father to support her' (ibid.: 253).

This 'myth of the male breadwinner' (Safa 1995) obviously not only distorted Mauritian reality in the 1970s, but also that of earlier periods. The following will show how the treatment of women as workers of lesser value added to the sustenance of inequality resting on what I conceive as a long-term transactional order. Some 70 per cent of respondents to a survey conducted by Hein in 1977 were younger than twenty-five. For many, factory employment was their first job. More than two-thirds of new entrants had been 'recruited' by friends or relatives already working in an EPZ factory. Although this at first indicates that respondents did not depend on wages, as they had not actively sought such income, most respondents contributed at least one-third of their earnings to their household (ibid.: 256). This belies the above-cited claims of employers that income was wasted on non-essentials. It also questions considerations in parliament that women's wages were insignificant as regards household incomes. Explicit sexism in the workplace added to these central ideological foundations for the devaluation of women's labour. Below I provide an indicative outline.

In the 1970s, most Mauritians seeking EPZ employment did not have birth certificates or identity papers. In order to check whether applicants matched the legal minimum working age of fifteen, women were subjected to what managers called a 'tit test'. As many underage women were highly dependent on wages and knew that managers would grab their breasts in this demeaning 'test', they would stuff their bras with tissue to make their breasts appear bigger and to decrease its intimacy. Similar to EPZ factories in Mexico (Fernández-Kelly 1983: 133–44), sexual harassment extended to everyday workplace relations in Mauritian factories. Outside the factory, women were discriminated against by right-wing groups that had voiced concerns over moral disorder in the parliamentary debates referred to above. Religious groups blamed workers for abandoning public morals by having affairs with their male co-workers. Similar to employers' claims, wages earned were denounced as 'lipstick money'. In other words, conservative public discourse actually sanctioned and naturalized low factory wages, branding it income used only for conspicuous consumption (cf. Neveling 2006). Women workers thus had to defend themselves against sexism inside and outside the factory.

But such sexism did not extend to all strata of the population. Although Hein maintains that 1970s Mauritius was 'a society where segregation of the sexes is considered desirable' (Hein 1984: 253), her data show that 43 per cent of parents expressed no concern at all about their daughters working in factories. Workers themselves also seemed to be anything but ashamed of their employment, expressed satisfaction with their work, were happy to earn money and to have the opportunity to establish social relations outside the household. Still, only a fraction of workers would continue work after marriage without the consent of their husband (ibid.: 256–57). This indicates that the majority of young women considered their employment temporary, a phase in their life that would end once they set up their own household.

Such flexible biographies are also documented for EPZ workers in South Korea (Kim 1997), where they were similarly denounced for conspicuously spending their income. South Korean workers supported their families and saved earnings to pay future dowries, hoping that marriage 'would free them from the burden of factory work' (ibid.: 67). Not every marriage involves dowry in Mauritius, but workers used their income for similar purposes. Looking back on their youth in 2004, many older women told me how EPZ employment was part of a larger strategy. This included wearing lipstick and nice clothes, saving for wedding-related expenses and spending money on education. One aim was to find a husband who would not be violent, not drink too much, who would have a good job and family background, and let them be who they wanted to be.

In light of my concern with long-term and short-term transactional orders, it is interesting to note that women in various locations around the world may well have similar ways of coping with EPZ employment. This indicates that, rather than cultural differences that derive from a spatial understanding of difference in human populations, working conditions, gender and class structures are much more relevant for understanding individual actions and notions of agency in EPZs. Only if we drop the victimization stance and consider the entry of women into world-market factories as a strategic decision taken within the limits set by capitalism can we acknowledge that these women are, so to speak, rational economic actors. This is not to say that their behaviour verifies the assumptions of neo-classical economics and the idea that humans are driven by the making of rational choices, but to say that these women are well able to set up short-term and long-term transactional orders for themselves within the said limits. In the above, gains from short-term factory employment are intended to provide long-term income security and happiness. Such calculations do not make EPZ labour less exploitative.

As I said, many women who had been working in EPZ factories for one, two or more decades are nowadays looking back on their work in light of these conscious choices. What was belittled as 'lipstick money' was an investment in finding a better marriage partner. Often, women stopped work when their first child was born. Later, they resumed factory labour once or several times to increase household income in order to qualify for mortgages, to pay for their children's higher education or, if marriages had not worked out, to make a living as single mothers. Work in EPZ factories was much more difficult and tiring as they got older. But they knew about differences in working conditions, distinguishing between established factories where pressure on the shop floor was lower, and runaway shops where pressure was high. Piece-rate work in runaway shops offered monthly salaries three times higher, and women would choose to work there if a larger sum of money was needed, being aware of all the difficulties this entailed.

These conscious choices of actors are important for assessing long-term and short-term transactional orders in factory labour. Bloch and Parry's (1989) notion of long-term transactional orders as bound to 'the reproduction of the cosmic and social order' (ibid.: 24), and opposed to short-term transactional orders informed by 'individual competition' (ibid.), falls short of capturing the experiences and motivations of all groups of actors in Mauritius's EPZ. It is tempting to follow their argument that morally questionable income from transactions of a short-term order is in need of 'cosmic purification', and to suggest that, for example, women workers' savings going into dowry payments or other morally sanctioned marriage-related activities are a purification of this kind. But such an analysis would portray EPZ workers as anxiously maintaining social stability in the same way as an Indian merchant is said to do by Bloch and Parry (ibid.: 25), and this understanding would come at a high price. It would imply that all workers are conservative traditionalists who consciously accept that their position becomes morally ambiguous as they enter the EPZ factories. Furthermore, it would mean that anthropology acknowledges the existence of a morally dubious sphere of individual competition and portrays this in the way that the paternalistic Mauritian state, investors and conservative religious groups do when they belittle the relevance of women's income and declare it 'lipstick money'. There is, however, an alternative to this view.

Bloch and Parry's distinction between short-term and long-term transactional orders resembles what Gregory (1980) distinguished respectively as 'gifts-to-men' and 'gifts-to-god' systems. The latter, argued Gregory in the context of Papua New Guinea, offers the 'greatest potential for capital accumulation in the context of a "modern cash economy aimed at development"' (ibid.: 627). The affinity between 'gifts-to-god systems' and the notion of long-term transactional orders as I develop it here enables us to see how capitalism operates and thrives in terms of long-term transactional orders. Such an approach to capitalist practice in Mauritius is convincing for various reasons.

It should by now be evident that gender inequality is an important feature of EPZ employment. Discrimination against women is also part of religious and other aspects of Mauritian everyday life, ideologically backed by right-wing groups, the early postcolonial government and capital. This discrimination is, however, contested by women working in EPZ factories. Also, it is contested at the household level, as there was a significant number of households that did not mind their daughters working in EPZ factories. Such differences in opinion and world-view are common in most societies, where conflicts over long-term transactional orders prevail, and neither the predominance of religious beliefs nor of sexism or capitalism goes uncontested. This has to do with inequality. In the Mauritian case, the insistence on the immoral nature of EPZ employment serves the interests of an alliance of political, economic and religious ruling classes who have vested interests in continued inequality among the population.

Economic anthropology knows many examples of societies where people in power have successfully established and continue to nurture those notions of cosmic and social order that portray the particular social matrix which produces inequality as the natural order of things. One excellent example that helps us understand the patriarchal underpinning of Mauritian EPZ capitalism is Godelier's analysis of the Baruya. Among this Melanesian group, similar relationships between gender inequality and long-term transactional orders are manifest and maintained with the aid of 'sacred objects and secret formulas' (Godelier 2007: 188). These are called *kwaimatnie* and they serve male elders (and thereby all men) to sustain the fiction of being able to create male life without the aid of women. Rituals, and particularly those rituals signalling the transition from one life cycle to another, were instituted to legitimize and naturalize gender inequality (see Godelier 1999). The developments in the Mauritian EPZ during the 1970s and afterwards can be interpreted in the same way. Events are of course somewhat less dramatic, as the issue in Mauritius is not the creation of life but the reproduction of households via monetary income, for example. Male dominance and female subordination was asserted as the postcolonial state supported the entry of young, lower-class women into factory labour as a rite of passage from adolescence to marriage. Sexist practices such as the 'tit test' can be regarded as rituals marking the entry of women into this sphere.

The material presented so far still carries implications that women accepted factory labour as a rite of passage. Although they made it part of their individual calculus and used some of their income to invest in longer-term reproduction, Mauritian workers still supported the overall workings of flexible EPZ capitalism. The Mauritian EPZ grew rapidly in the 1980s, and the island was awarded labels such as 'Africa's first tiger'. Therefore, some might object that women workers' individual ambitions could be read as compliance with the postcolonial government's aim of developing the nation and employers' aim of making profits. In order to address this question, it is important to assess how factory workers commented on and acted against gendered and capitalist subordination.

Spirit Possession as a Fight against the Legacy of Colonial Capitalism and Exorcism as a Naturalization of Capitalist Gender Inequality

Analysing a Malaysian EPZ, Ong has described how female factory workers' possession by 'evil spirit[s] of an archaic Malay world'

(Ong 1987: 7) brought factory production to a standstill on a massive scale. To show how such spirits mediate 'the conflict between [non-] capitalist and capitalist modes of objectifying the human condition' (Taussig 1980: xii, cited in Ong 1987: 9), Ong relates workers' possession to disciplining production regimes and to moral discrimination inside and outside EPZ factories. Possession, then, was an act of resistance, expressing what Raymond Williams has called a 'structure of feeling' (cited in Ong 1991: 281), in this case of Malaysian factory workers exposed to flexible capitalism, 'traditional' gender hierarchies and new lifestyle opportunities. As workers were possessed and shut down the production of multi-national corporations, they invoked 'spirits of resistance' to confront a regime that would otherwise not allow them to lay down their work. These spirits could only be expelled by a local *bomoh*, a male spirit healer (ibid.: 88). Spirit possession in Malaysian EPZ factories indicates that the employment of women interfered with the long-term transactional order, not least because male religious authorities could control the spirits. The following section reconsiders Ong's observation, and is based on the above critique of Bloch and Parry's Occidentalist model of transactional orders. It exemplifies how anthropological misrepresentations of EPZ workers as irrational actors locked in traditionalist worldviews can be avoided.[7]

Women in Mauritian factories knew how to react to shop-floor pressures. This is evidenced by the 'spirits of resistance' that haunted Mauritian shop floors in the 1970s, which led to similar work stoppages as in the Malaysian factories described by Ong. The two cases I consider offer grounds for comparison within the diverse Mauritian setting. One happened in 1973 in a factory employing mainly workers from an urban setting; the other occurred in 1978 in a factory employing workers from a rural setting.

In 1973, the total number of EPZ workers in Mauritius was around 3,000, and there was only one industrial zone, in Plaine Lauzan, just south of the capital Port Louis, where members of the free-floating working class had been rehoused in the 1960s. One day, machinists in one factory fell to the floor, experiencing cramps and screaming, and claiming they had seen a ghost. They refused to resume work, and perplexed factory managers called for support from a Catholic priest. The workers were mainly Catholic, and the priest called in was an influential figure in everyday life, even though Mauritian Christian churches have always been close allies of the ruling class.

When I spoke with this priest in 2004, he illustrated vividly how upon his arrival he found the Plaine Lauzan factory in a mess.

Although he recited a prayer and gave blessings to workers, panic prevailed. Knowing about the hardships of factory workers, he recommended that the factory close for some days so that everyone could get some rest. During this time he found out that the ghost of a French colonizer who lay buried underneath the factory had haunted the workers. The priest decided an exceptionally strong performance of God's power was needed: an exorcism. But to perform an exorcism and not violate the Vatican ordinance, he needed a psychologist or psychiatrist to confirm that matters went beyond those professions. The priest was a member of a private, upper-class club called Stella Clavisque, and this club's founder was a famous Algerian psychiatrist working in Mauritius.[8] A phone conversation was sufficient to obtain the psychiatrist's go ahead, and the exorcism commenced. In the priest's version of this, all workers and machines were carefully blessed and the ghost was not seen again.

Word spread, and over the following years, the priest was approached for advice on several other cases of spirit possession in factories. Based on what I heard from retired factory managers, the ghosts involved could be those of dead sailors roaming a factory building that had once been a brothel near the harbour, for example. According to the priest, factory managers and local religious authorities quickly became capable of handling spirit possession themselves. Only one other time was he called to exorcise a ghost. This was in a factory in the rural district of Moka. Expanding businesses had opened up subsidiary factories in such regions since the mid 1970s, when cheap labour became scarce in the urban belt around the capital. Inhabitants of the area had different legacies though: dependency on agriculture was high, and rural districts were strongholds of right-wing political and religious movements. Women EPZ workers therefore had to deal with much more rigid moral codes.

In 1978, workers in a large factory in St Pierre encountered a spirit. As word spread and the factory could no longer operate, this medium-sized rural centre and its Hindu inhabitants were in serious turmoil. Speaking in 2004, the Catholic priest recalled, with a certain *schadenfreude*, how local religious authorities – the local Hindu Pandit, the Kusari Tamil, and even a *longaniste* (a kind of freelance spirit healer offering anything from cursing one's neighbour at midnight on the graveyard to healing diseases at noon) – had failed to evict the spirit. As with the case in Plaine Lauzan, the priest 'went in strong' to show the workers that he was 'the man who can face the forces of evil'. But his initial success was jeopardized because factory operations continued. In Plaine Lauzan, a few days rest were crucial to give workers time off from the 'social revolution' that the establishment of new industries had caused in the 1970s, putting immense physical and psychological strains on women EPZ workers. Proving him right, possession ended once workers were given some leave. In the Moka case, the priest also had to obtain consent from the same psychiatrist to exorcise the ghost. But the priest's recommendation that the haunted factories be closed and workers given rest derived from his awareness that it was a 'social revolution' that put strain on workers' lives, not mean spirits. What are we to make of this apparent contradiction between his expertise and the way his approach was informed?

If spirit possession was a way for workers to resist, then we should consider what workers actually expressed during instances of possession rather than taking them as one of many 'weapons of the weak', as Ong (1987) suggests. Elsewhere I have argued that the spirits appearing in Mauritian factories in the 1970s were 'spirits of capitalism' (Neveling 2006). Here I will extend this understanding and show, on the one hand, how capital, politicians and religious leadership used the appearance of spirits to present a general social problem as an irrational sentiment. On the other hand, the actual comments that workers made amount to a critique of the persistence of capitalism's long-term transactional order. This perspective is suggested by the fact that the concrete possessive spirits (like the French colonizer and the dead sailors mentioned above) were from the same historical reactionary world as EPZ employers, the priests and moralist conservative groups.

Two further accounts appear to consolidate this perspective on spirit possession in the Mauritian EPZ. The first is a novel by the Mauritian writer Lindsey Collen (1991). Although this is a work of fiction, it is authoritative. Collen migrated from South Africa to Mauritius in the early 1970s, and became a leading figure in the Mouvement Militante Mauricien (MMM), a hybrid socialist movement influenced by the European uprisings of 1968, as well as anti-colonial and anti-imperialist movements in the Global South. Its union wing, the General Workers' Federation (GWF) organized strikes throughout the 1970s, and the Muvman Liberasyon Fam (MLF, 'Women's Liberation Movement') attracted many EPZ workers to the fight against gendered exploitation. In the MLF, Collen met many of those women and made their experiences central to her novel. The main character, Shiny Tiny, encounters sexism, high production pressure, tough working conditions and everything else that EPZ factories have to offer, not least an exorcism performed by a Catholic priest:

> A Roman Catholic Priest who specialized in exorcism was called in as an emergency by the boss. He and his sakristen [minister] arrived. Both were in full fancy dress. Long robes, gold crosses, purple cummerbund and what-nots.
>
> The unconscious Deomala was picked up first by the priest and his assistant, laid on a table, and hit firmly on each side of the jaw.
>
> 'O nom di-per, di-fis, di-sen-tespri' [In the name of the father, the son, and the holy ghost].
>
> Sign of the cross.
>
> Deomala came round.
>
> 'Next', bawled the priest . . .
>
> The piece rate for that day was drastically slowed down. (ibid.: 144)

Here again, the priest appears firm and as the man who can face evil. But the last sentence indicates a rationality on the workers' part that we have not encountered so far. Collen further recounts how Tit Albert, a common figure in Mauritian superstition, was consciously invoked to lower a day's piece rate and give workers some rest. Both the priest I interviewed and Collen were actively involved in the world of Mauritian EPZ labour throughout the 1970s, and their accounts are surely both fictitious and biased in their respective ways. All the same, we may say that the priest entered the factories on the management's side, and Collen on the side of women workers.

A second account, a survey of newspaper reports on events in the St Pierre factory discussed above, expands on Collen's rendering in this regard, and underlines how workers chose to be possessed by spirits instead of being taken over by them. In that factory, workers had been in a dispute with management over delayed wage payments, bad working conditions and sexual harassment. They had filed their complaints individually with the Ministry of Industrial Relations in accordance with the Industrial Relations Act of 1973. The ministry should then have negotiated on the workers' behalf, but nothing happened.[9] Less than four weeks later, Tit Albert indeed haunted the shop floor. On this, another Mauritian newspaper plainly reported, 'New industrial disease: P'tit albert in a factory in Saint Pierre?'[10] In this case, rather than irrational sentiment or moral outrage marking the transition from a moral economy to one of immoral capitalism, possession was a last resort in an industrial dispute.

My overall point here is that generalizing talk of a social revolution cannot capture such conjunctures as those experienced within single factories (cf. Narotzky, this volume). But neither can many

concepts in anthropology. Thus, for Ong, possession was 'spontaneous, carried out by individual workers independently of each other',
and such spontaneity expressed 'the dislocation experienced by
peasants in an industrializing world' that was commoditizing their
lives (Ong 1987: 210–13). This explanation is actually very close to
the images of a social revolution and of a moral order threatened by
the advent of EPZ employment that the Catholic priest or conservative Mauritian parliamentarians invoked. Given that commodity
production for global markets was a reality for much of the world
long before the 1970s, it seems rather odd to sustain a juxtaposition
between a moral economy of the peasant and an economy of commodities for this and for earlier decades. As my historical outline
of the colonial sugar industry has shown, Mauritius was part of a
global plantation complex where disputes over capitalist exploitation as well as 'social revolutions' were common in pre-EPZ times.
Equally common were ambiguous and unequal exchanges, as were
many other features now portrayed as defining contemporary flexible capitalism.

It is along such lines of historical continuity that spirit possession in Mauritian factories must be read. The appearance of a French
colonizer's ghost in the factory in Plaine Lauzan was informed by
beliefs in ghosts, of course. Many Mauritians consider burial sites
to be 'states of ghosts', ruled by kings who govern the souls of the
dead, for example (Jensen 1988). But such imaginings of a hierarchical social order among spiritual beings reflect upon the organization
of real-world society, which is likewise spatial in nature because economic power in Mauritius was for long defined by the ownership
of land, the main means of production. If EPZ workers then claim
that an EPZ factory was erected on the grave of a dead colonizer,
they refer to the concrete continuity of exploitation from the days
of French rule to the present. A more satisfactory interpretation of
events in early 1970s Mauritius would thus be that workers did not
perceive EPZ labour relations as contradicting a long-term transactional order, but rather as a continuation of this order. Stated differently, Mauritian workers used spirit possession not to lament a
disruption to the social stability of a 'moral' long-term transactional
order, but rather to lament a lack of disruption and the continuity of
exploitation.

Conclusion:
A Post-Occidentalist View of (Flexible) Capitalism

The findings from Mauritius presented here challenge widespread assumptions in anthropology that the global expansion of capitalism comes in conflict with stable, long-term transactional orders which are morally sanctioned and grounded in the shared cosmic-religious world-views of given places. Instead, this chapter has shown how such long-term transactional orders and their cosmic foundations are a backbone of capitalist exploitation. Gregory's conception of 'gift-to-gods-systems' exempted, various notions resembling Bloch and Parry's 'long-term transactional order' actually rehearse romantic fictions that are otherwise coined by conservative religious movements. They slight the fact that contemporary workers are descendants of earlier generations of workers who were exposed to similar well-established systems of control and exploitation. Building on Zigon's (2007) call for abandoning a distinction between the moral and the immoral, both capitalist and non-capitalist exchange are moral. Economic morality shifts over time as exploitation is adjusted to a changing global (capitalist) system. Labour regimes such as slavery, indenture and free wage labour rest on particular moralities. Anthropologists might not like any of these regimes – I certainly do not. But if scientific analysis takes on the guise of moralism, this comes at the high cost of misleading juxtapositions of an 'immoral' Western world of capitalism and a 'moral' non-Western world of pre-capitalist societies.

A secular, post-Occidentalist view avoids such purification of pre-capitalist societies. Instead it considers how capitalist market relations have influenced long-term and short-term transactional orders alike, in Mauritius and elsewhere. Women's investment of their EPZ wages in finding the right spouse, for example, should not be read as efforts to convert income from an 'immoral' capitalist, short-term transactional order into something from a 'moral', long-term transactional order. These, as much as spirit possession, are conscious acts whereby women 'keep sane' (Zigon 2007) in a highly flexible and strenuous work environment.

My insights have further analytical implications for anthropology's analysis of flexible capitalism. In the 1970s, Mauritius was a location for relocation. Because of a lack of attention to such relocations, scholars like Bell and Touraine declared the coming of post-industrial society. But this era was emerging neither in the West nor at a global level (cf. Nash 1995; Baca 2005). Instead, for many places, the 1970s onwards saw decades of accelerated industrialization driven by national export-oriented development strategies and the opening of EPZs and SEZs (Special Economic Zones). Recently, the International Labour Organization (ILO) counted 3,500 EPZs worldwide, employing more than 60 million workers in more than 130 nations (Boyenge 2007). If anthropologists want to understand individual and collective experiences in these socio-economic settings, they might reconsider how to deal with socio-economic change and the long histories of most regions' integration into the capitalist world system. As I have argued, to portray a given locations' inhabitants as holding on to a moral economy of the peasant or to long-term transactional orders in the sense of Bloch and Parry (1989) does them no justice. When workers contest flexible capitalist practice, they may effectively equate such practice with a cosmic-religious, long-term transactional order. I have shown that such equations are pertinent, for example, where gendered exploitation is a crucial feature of the long-term transactional order of global capitalism (other economic practices, as seen for the Baruya, bear resonance with the general perspective I have outlined). The concrete appearance of such long-term transactional orders may vary according to a given region's changing integration into global markets. But everywhere this integration is based on long-standing collaboration between local economic, political and religious leaders and their well-established alliances in wider trading networks. It is such alliances and their backbone in moralist and religious ideologies and practices of capitalism's long-term transactional orders that many people in the world contest, and even hope to overcome.

Acknowledgements

Research in Mauritius was carried out in 2003 and 2004 and funded by the Martin-Luther-University, Halle-Wittenberg. I am particularly indebted to the members of the Mauritian political party Lalit ('Struggle') and to the members of Ledikasyon pu travayer ('Education for workers') who generously supported my search for historical incidents of spirit possession. May there be a day when they see their dream of a truly postcolonial Mauritius come true. In Halle, Burkhard Schnepel has been a source of intellectual stimulation. His reminders that religion is an important dimension of global capitalism have been very influential on my work. I would like to thank Rosie Read for her thought-provoking comments on this, as well as Jens Kjaerulff, who has been the most generous editor one could wish for. Also, comments from three anonymous reviewers have been helpful, albeit to different extents.

Notes

1 Allen (1999) is the most prominent among historians supporting what I suggest to call 'the myth of the small-planters'. Teelock instead concludes on the *morcellement*, 'whether it was a "liberation", as has been stated, is a matter of further discussion' (Teelock 2001: 303).

2 Social anthropology has so far represented Mauritius as an island society whose main feature is ethnic and religious division. See Neveling (forthcoming) for a critique; Schnepel (2005) shows the multifariousness of identifications in the present. Accordingly, mainly ethno-religious ritual practices have so far been considered, and rituals related to economic activities have been ignored (e.g. Labour Day or La Coupe).

3 Debates of the Legislative Assembly of Mauritius, Third Session, Third Legislative Assembly, 10th March–30th June 1970, Debates Nos. 1–19, Vol. 1 (Port Louis: Authority of the Assembly, Mauritius Government Printer, 1970), pp. 1244–56.

4 Debates of the Legislative Assembly, pp. 939–45.

5 See e.g. 'La Floreal Knitwear Ltd. investit Rs. 225,000 dans l'entrainement des ses employés', *L'Express*, 23 June 1971.

6 Note that the total labour force in 1972 was around 139,000, according to Hein (1984). This would be a sharp decline from more than 200,000 in 1958, and seems unlikely given that those were years of population increase.

7 Parry has argued that this spirit possession indicates how women workers struggle with 'men and industry' rather than with capitalism (Parry 2005: 149–51). As I have shown above, it is not viable to distinguish between 'men and industry' on the one hand and capitalism on the other, particularly not for the case of EPZs, which build on the devaluation of women's labour and on gendered exploitation on a global scale. In my view, Parry's juxtaposition of capitalism and gender rather mirrors his earlier distinction between short-term and long-term transactional orders, introducing yet another normative distinction to the social and political practice of resistance.

8 The club's name means 'the star and the key', referring to Mark Twain's 1897 labelling of Mauritius as 'the star and the key to the Indian Ocean' (from Latin, *Stella Clavisque Maris Indici*).

9 See *L'Express*, 2 September 1978.

10 'Nouveau malaise industriel: P'tit albert dans une usine à Saint Pierre? *The Nation*, 27 September 1978.

References

Allen, R.B. 1999. *Slaves, Freedmen, and Indentured Laborers in Colonial Mauritius*. Cambridge: Cambridge University Press.

Allgoo, R. 1985. *Le mouvement syndical à l'ile Maurice*. Port Louis: Artisans and General Workers' Union.

Baca, G. 2005. 'Legends of Fordism: Between Myth, History, and Foregone Conclusions', in B. Kapferer (ed.), *The Retreat of the Social: The Rise and Rise of Reductionism*. Oxford: Berghahn Books, pp. 31–46.

Bell, D. 1973. *The Coming of Post-Industrial Society: A Venture in Social Forecasting*. New York: Basic Books.

Bloch, M., and J. Parry. 1989. 'Introduction: Money and the Morality of Exchange', in J. Parry and M. Bloch (eds), *Money and the Morality of Exchange*. Cambridge: Cambridge University Press, pp. 1–32.

Boyenge, J.-P. S. 2007. 'ILO Database on Export Processing Zones (Revised)', ILO Working Paper No. 251. Geneva: International Labour Organization.

Carrier, J.G. 1992. 'Occidentalism: The World Turned Upside-Down', *American Ethnologist* 19(2): 195–212.

Collen, L. 1991. *There Is a Tide*. Port Louis: Ledikasyon pu Travayer.

Cross, J. 2012. 'Sweatshop Exchanges: Gifts and Giving in the Global Factory', *Research in Economic Anthropology* 32: 3–26.

Dicken, P. 2003. *Global Shift: Reshaping the Global Economic Map in the 21st Century*, 4th edn. London: Sage.

Fernández-Kelly, M.P. 1983. *For We Are Sold, I and My People: Women and Industry in Mexico's Frontier*. Albany: State University of New York Press.

Forget, P.A. 1983. *Wishing a Future for the EPZ Is Not Enough*. Port Louis: Mauritius Commercial Bank.

Fröbel, F., J. Heinrichs and O. Kreye. 1981. *The New International Division of Labour: Structural Unemployment in Industrialised Countries and Industrialisation in Developing Countries*. Cambridge: Cambridge University Press.

Godelier, M. 1999. *The Enigma of the Gift*. Cambridge: Polity Press.

——— 2007. 'Death of a Celebrated Truth and Others Still Worth Re-stating', *Journal de la Société des Océanistes* 125(2): 181–192.

Gregory, C.A. 1980. 'Gifts to Men and Gifts to God: Gift Exchange and Capital Accumulation in Contemporary Papua', *Man* 15(4): 626–652.

Harvey, D. 1990. *The Condition of Postmodernity: An Enquiry into the Origins of Cultural Change*. Oxford: Blackwell.

Hein, C. 1984. 'Jobs for the Girls: Export Manufacturing in Mauritius', *International Labour Review* 123: 251–265.

Jensen, J. 1988. 'Synkretismus und Religiöse Konfession auf Mauritius', *Sociologicus* 38: 1–18.

Kim, S.-K. 1997. *Class Struggle or Family Struggle? The Lives of Women Factory Workers in South Korea*. Cambridge: Cambridge University Press.

Meade, J.E. 1961. *The Economic and Social Structure of Mauritius (Report to the Governor of Mauritius)*. London: Methuen.

Nash, J. 1995. 'Post-industrialism, Post-Fordism, and the Crisis in World Capitalism', in F. C. Gamst (ed.), *Meanings of Work: Considerations for the Twenty-first Century*. Albany: State University of New York Press, pp. 189–211.

Neveling, P. 2006. 'Spirits of Capitalism and the De-alienation of Workers: A Historical Perspective on the Mauritian Garment Industry', Graduate School Societies and Cultures in Motion Working Paper Series No 2. University of Halle, Germany.

——— 2012. 'Manifestationen der Globalisierung: Kapital, Staat und Arbeit in Mauritius, 1825–2005', PhD diss. Halle: Institute for Social Anthropology, Martin Luther University.

——— 2013. 'A Periodisation of Globalisation According to the Mauritian Integration into the International Sugar Commodity Chain (1825–2005)', in J. Curry-Machado (ed.), *Global Histories, Imperial Commodities, Local Interactions*. Basingstoke: Palgrave Macmillan, pp. 121–142.

——— 2014. 'Structural Contingencies and Untimely Coincidences in the Making of Neoliberal India: The Kandla Free Trade Zone 1965–1991', *Contributions to Indian Sociology* 48(1): 17–43.

——— forthcoming. 'Export Processing Zones and Global Class Formation', in J. Carrier and D. Kalb (eds), *Anthropologies of Class: Power, Practice, and Inequality*. Cambridge: Cambridge University Press.

North-Coombes, M.D. 2000. *Studies in the Political Economy of Mauritius*. Moka, Mauritius: Mahatma Gandhi Institute.

Ong, A. 1987. *Spirits of Resistance and Capitalist Discipline: Factory Women in Malaysia*. Albany: State University of New York Press.

——— 1991. 'The Gender and Labor Politics of Postmodernity', *Annual Review of Anthropology* 20: 279–309.

Parry, J.P. 2005. 'Industrial Work', in J. Carrier (ed.), *A Handbook of Economic Anthropology*. Cheltenham: Edward Elgar Publishing, pp. 141–159.

Safa, H.I. 1995. *The Myth of the Male Breadwinner: Women and Industrialization in the Caribbean*. Boulder, CO: Westview Press.

Schnepel, B. 2005. 'Inder auf Reisen', in K. Geisenhauer and K. Lange (eds), *Bewegliche Horizonte*. Leipzig: Leipziger Universitätsverlag, pp. 165–183.

Scott, J.C. 1976. *The Moral Economy of the Peasant: Rebellion and Subsistence in Southeast Asia*. New Haven: Yale University Press.

Strangleman, T. 2007. 'The Nostalgia for Permanence at Work? The End of Work and Its Commentators', *Sociological Review* 55(1): 81–103.

Taussig, M.T. 1980. *The Devil and Commodity Fetishism in South America*. Chapel Hill: University of North Carolina Press.

Teelock, V. 1998. *Bitter Sugar: Sugar and Slavery in 19th Century Mauritius*. Moka, Mauritius: Mahatma Ghandi Institute.

———— 2001. *Mauritian History: From Its Beginnings to Modern Times*. Moka, Mauritius: Mahatma Gandhi Institute.

Touraine, A. 1971. *The Post-Industrial Society: Tomorrow's Social History*. New York: Random House.

World Bank. 1973. 'Mauritius, Appraisal of the Coromandel Industrial Estate'. Washington: Development Finance Companies Department, World Bank.

Zigon, J. 2007. 'Moral Breakdown and Ethical Demand: A Theoretical Framework for an Anthropology of Moralities', *Anthropological Theory* 7(2): 131–150.

8

The Corrosion of Character Revisited

Rethinking Uncertainty and Flexibility

Jens Kjaerulff

Richard Sennett's *The Corrosion of Character* (Sennett 1998) is a widely cited contribution to a body of literature which has emerged over the past couple of decades on the social dimensions of recent trends in economic practice. Concisely stated, a major concern in this literature, and pre-eminently in Sennett's book, has been with the ways in which new practices of flexibility ostensibly bring about unprecedented experiences of uncertainty. In her introduction to a special issue of *Ethnos* focused on 'risk', Boholm nicely summarizes this concern:

> A central thought . . . is that modern society has entered a new phase in its historical development. Industrial production and the market assume novel structural features emerging from the mobility of capital, people and technology over the globe. Traditional social relationships, groupings and identities erode along with the progression of late modernity . . . The embeddedness of the individual in a firm order of meanings and expectations is disappearing. Certainty has given way to uncertainty, resulting in a state of collapsing ontological security and a sense of fundamental vulnerability and lack of faith. (Boholm 2003: 157)

Likewise, in a more recent review concentrated specifically on key contributions to newer studies in the sociology of work, Strangleman observes:

> There is a shared view . . . that capitalism has changed profoundly in terms of the speeding up of social and cultural change. Capital now demands greater flexibility and pliability . . . The kind of economy that

could provide a measure of stability for some through a 'job for life' is no longer possible, and those jobs that are relatively secure no longer provide meaning and identity for those lucky enough to have them. All of these accounts are united in the view that there is a process of individualization and fragmentation which spans the workplace and the wider communities in which individuals live. (Strangleman 2007: 87–88)

In this chapter I use a critique of Sennett's book to explore an inversion of this cause–effect line of argument. I propose that 'uncertainty' has always been a predicament of living, and that certain kinds of flexible work in part may have *proliferated* as a more recent *response* to this general predicament.[1]

The chapter is based on an ethnographic study of people working from home in rural Denmark via the internet, a practice known as telecommuting or teleworking (e.g. Ellison 1999; Garrett and Danziger 2007). Sennett indeed claims that this way of working belongs among the more extreme forms of flexible work (Sennett 1998: 58–59). And yet, what I found among teleworkers hardly resembled the scenario depicted by Sennett. It was not that something like uncertainty was absent from their lives. Rather, I found a more mundane and subtle sense of uncertainty, which my informants were better able to deal with than Sennett suggests.

My argument about this kind of uncertainty as a contributing cause for the proliferation of teleworking is based on what I propose is a related finding. As a result of my fieldwork, I became aware of a notable discrepancy between formal statistical surveys on the prevalence of telework in Denmark (e.g. Peters 1998: 9, 25–28) and what I could document around the rural villages where I lived for sixteen months to follow teleworkers' lives. A survey I conducted, aided by the familiarity I developed with the area, indicated that the prevalence of telework here, especially as part-time arrangements supplementing work away from home, was significantly higher than suggested by formal surveys (Kjaerulff 2010a: 57–59). Much of the telework I could document was not formalized, however, in ways that would readily be captured by larger-scale anonymous sampling. I believe there has been a striking lack of scholarly (and policy-related) attention to the possibility that telework predominantly may be practised *informally*, and that as such it may be much more prevalent than commonly assumed.[2] Where the wider, and certainly more influential, literature on the topic has approached the proliferation of flexible work in sweeping terms of 'top-down' driving forces of global change (e.g. Strangleman 2007: 92–100), the apparent prevalence of informal telework suggests that, in order to explain its proliferation, we need a better understanding of why people actively embrace this form of flexible work.

Sennett's book is an interesting point of departure from which to develop such an understanding. Most obviously, it is an influential discussion of the topic, which as yet has only received limited, sustained critical attention (e.g. Tietze and Musson 2002; Strangleman 2007). From the perspective of anthropology, the book further stands out in that Sennett claims inspiration from our discipline (Sennett 1998: 11). The book has even been acclaimed by an anthropologist of some standing (Ortner 2005: 43–46) as a particularly sensitive approach to the subjective experience of late capitalism. A critique of Sennett's book therefore is a suitable starting point for advancing a more nuanced anthropological approach to the experience of flexible work.

My main interest in Sennett's book, however, has to do with its theoretical core, which turns on the significance of 'routines' in social life (Sennett 1998: 32–45). This orientation resembles a wider range of social theory than Sennett acknowledges, in which cultural reproduction, change and something like uncertainty are themes which have been considered at length. Particularly well known in the latter regard is Bourdieu's attention to the temporal dimension of gift exchange, and his related move from 'rules to strategies' (Bourdieu 1977), both of which turn on an element of uncertainty as an inherent part of interaction. Sennett's affinity with such orientations is mostly implicit however, and on closer inspection it is clear that the way he executes this lead is inconsistent. I will suggest the latter shortcoming goes some way to account for his spectacular argument about 'the corrosion of character'. But more importantly, I aim to show how a more consistent approach in this regard opens up a different understanding of both uncertainty and flexibility. As for flexibility, I propose that the practices I could document partially converge with the kind of social and symbolic practice that Bourdieu saw entailed in the 'dialectics of strategy' (Bourdieu 1977), though I mainly draw on other orientations within the 'individualistic' branch of exchange theory (see Introduction, this volume).

In what follows, I first examine Sennett's book, especially the way he engages the notion of routine for theoretical leverage. I then situate this in terms of wider theoretical orientations which Sennett's approach resembles. This is followed by an ethnographic section, which I subsequently use to develop my argument about uncertainty and flexibility. The progression of the chapter is in part intended to convey a sense of how I arrived at the perspectives I develop through the experience of doing fieldwork. Lived experience comprises elements of surprise, and it is in this regard the theoretical orientations I draw on have particular strengths.

The Corrosion of Character Revisited

The full title of Sennett's book is *The Corrosion of Character: The Personal Consequences of Work in the New Capitalism*. For Sennett, 'the new capitalism' is all about flexibility: at the level of skills and learning to accommodate new kinds of production; in terms of decentralization and outsourcing to stay lean and mean; in terms of interaction to stay competitive; and variously in terms of the temporal and spatial dimensions of work (see esp. Sennett 1998: 46–63, a chapter entitled 'Flexible').

It is the social entailments of this pervasive regime of flexibility that Sennett is concerned with in the book. 'Character' in Sennett's use develops in the course of interaction with an environment: it has to do with the 'ethical value we place on our own desires and on our relations to others' (ibid.: 10), and it arises through 'loyalty and commitment' and 'the pursuit of long-term goals' (ibid.). For Sennett, the new practices of flexibility are fundamentally at odds with this, and produce instead a pervasive sense of uncertainty. As he notes: 'what's peculiar about uncertainty today is that it exists without any looming historical disaster; instead it is woven into the everyday practices of a vigorous capitalism' (ibid.: 31). Much of the book serves to make this concrete through longer narratives of a limited number of afflicted individuals. It is particularly in this regard that Ortner (2005) sees Sennett's approach as useful for appreciating postmodern subjectivity.

The theoretical core of the book however, on which Sennett builds these arguments, is a historical chapter entitled 'Routine' (Sennett 1998: 32–45), in which Sennett looks back at the emergence of industrial capitalism. It is here that he develops the argument about the social significance of routines, on which he rests the book's general argument about the corrosion of character. He does so by contrasting two perspectives on the transition to industrial work routines, those associated with Adam Smith and Diderot. What Sennett highlights in Adam Smith's *Wealth of Nations* are sections where Smith is anxious about industrial routines becoming, in Sennett's words, 'self-destructive, because human beings lose control over their own efforts; lack of control over work time means people go dead mentally' (ibid.: 37). Sennett observes that for this reason Smith saw the transition to industrial capitalism as 'crossing [a] great divide' (ibid.: 37). While sympathetic to Smith's concern, Sennett's hunch is to develop a different perspective. Inspired in this regard by Diderot's *Encyclopédie*, Sennett suggests that industrial routines also have benign dimensions. Sennett thus brings out how workers have in fact 'learn[ed] how to manipulate and alter each stage of the labor process' (ibid.: 34), and in later stages of industrialization they 'displayed a wide repertoire of techniques for sabotaging time–motion studies and, as a matter of course, ignored methods and process specifications whenever they got in the way or conflicted with their own interests' (ibid.: 41, reference omitted). On such grounds, Sennett therefore argues that 'metrics of time had become something other than an act of repression and domination practiced by management ... Routinized time had become an arena in which workers could assert their own demands, an arena of empowerment' (ibid.: 42–43). Sennett goes on to observes that, 'this was a political outcome Adam Smith did not anticipate' (ibid.: 43), and so, siding with Diderot against Adam Smith, the chapter's substantive conclusion is that, 'routine can demean, but it can also protect; routine can decompose labour, but it can also compose a life' (ibid.).

What interests me in Sennett's traverse through industrial history is the subtle shift of *analytical* perspective that he effectively also develops here, from a determinist perspective on routine and change (Adam Smith's) towards one which takes agency and reflection into account (with Diderot as its icon). Sennett is not very explicit about what the shift entails theoretically, but it is clear that, in the latter perspective, routine is a matter of ongoing development through engagements with a shifting environment. It is a process through which socio-cultural change comes about by way of practice, as the examples with time effectively suggest: new routines of timing, and timed routines, *became* socially significant, in terms *apart* from managerial ideals, a fact that management in turn had to reckon with (see Thompson 1967; cf. Whipp 1987; Ingold 1995; Glennie and Thrift 1996).

What is striking from this perspective is that the book's main argument about the contemporary demise of routine and the 'corrosion of character' effectively rests on a quite different theoretical approach than what Sennett alluded and embraced with Diderot. In Sennett's vision of contemporary flexible work, routines, agency and social practice appear to simply melt into the air. This is suggested in a number of ways on closer inspection, but an ominous passage concisely anticipates this direction of the book:

Diderot did not believe routine work is degrading; on the contrary, he thought routines beget narratives, as the rules and rhythms of work gradually evolve . . . Diderot's greatest modern heir, the sociologist Anthony Giddens, has tried to keep Diderot's insight alive by pointing to the primary value of habit in both social practices and self-understanding; we test out alternatives only in relation to habits which we have already mastered. To imagine a life of momentary impulses, of short term action, devoid of sustainable routines, a life without habits, is to imagine indeed a mindless existence. Today we stand at a historical divide on the issue of routine. The new language of flexibility implies that routine is dying in the dynamic sectors of the economy. (Sennett 1998: 44)

The 'historical divide' which Sennett is concerned about here bears more than a passing resemblance to the 'great divide' he states Adam Smith was concerned about (ibid.: 37).

Sennett's focus in the subsequent chapters is substantively on what in the above quote is phrased 'the new *language* of flexibility' (I add the emphasis). Aside from considering ideals of flexible management, most chapters are focused on narratives, which admittedly suggest apathy on the part of Sennett's interviewees. But as Evens and Handelman have also noted with reference to Sennett's book, what people say does not amount to what they do, that is, to practice (Evens and Handelman 2006: 7). Despite Sennett's claim to have found inspiration in anthropology, the narratives presented are not related much to what Sennett could observe for himself in terms of situated action. Moreover, Sennett's brief remark in the book's introduction – in effect, that these narratives, at least in part, are made up for his purpose – further compromise the narratives as compelling data. He thus states that he has resorted to 'occasionally compounding several voices into one or splitting one voice into many' (ibid.: 11), and goes on to observe: 'These disguises put demands on the reader's trust, but not the trust a novelist would seek to earn through a well-made narrative, for that coherence is now lacking in real lives' (ibid.). The latter presumably refers to his general argument about the 'corrosion of character', which in this reading would amount to a foregone conclusion imposed on his ethnography.

In sum, it seems that Sennett's inconsistent analytical approach, along with its methodological shortcomings, may account in significant measure for the spectacular claim that 'character is being corroded' as a consequence of flexible work.

At the same time, the book's theoretical core is worth considering further. Something like routine has had a more central place in social theory than Sennett acknowledges, not least in approaches aimed at understanding socio-cultural transformation.

Routine and Change: Wider Perspectives

To appreciate this, we can begin by briefly considering Marx. What among other things distinguished Marx's dialectical approach from Hegel's was his view that cultural and social forms developed from engagements with specific material and social environments (e.g. Marx 1990: 102; Nicolaus 1973: 24–44). For Marx, 'abstract labour' was a case in point, what we commonly call 'work' in a generic sense these days. Marx's view was that, historically, this notion of work took on significance only as a range of novel practices gained grounds (e.g. Marx 1973: 100–108; see also Godelier 1980). Briefly, the increasing organization of trade in terms of expanding markets, the associated increase in the use of money as a standard measure and intermediate medium of value and exchange, and the proliferation of production in terms of such developments were among the factors that contributed to a generic concept of work becoming 'true in practice', as Marx (1973: 105) put it.

Sennett's argument in the historical context resembles this dialectical or process aspect of Marx's writings. However, in the Maussian tradition of exchange theory with which Marx is commonly associated (see Introduction, this volume), this process orientation is not the most salient legacy from Marx (although it is not absent). It is instead the *type* of exchange and social relations Marx's wrote about which is especially highlighted here, that is, commodity exchange, compared to other types of exchange such as gift exchange, and the types of relations that such exchange entails (Sahlins 1972; Gregory 1982; see also e.g. Thomas 1991: 7–34; Graeber 2001: 23–47). To appreciate the theoretical significance of Sennett's historical argument, it is therefore useful to look to strands of exchange theory where the process orientation is more developed, namely those approaches to exchange commonly known as transactionalist, interactionist and practice-oriented approaches (e.g. Ortner 1984). Such approaches have paid more minute attention to socio-cultural process as a matter of interaction, often conceived of as exchange, entailing a more intimate actor-oriented perspective. Such approaches are often held to be incompatible with Maussian approaches due to the formers' alleged focus on 'individuals'. In my view, claiming such a fundamental divide is exaggerated, and seems in part rooted in the shortcoming (on both sides of the debate) of confounding two senses of the notion of 'individual'. Kapferer in his later work has acknowledged that what must be distinguished is 'the individual as culturally or ideologically valued' on the one hand, and 'the individual as an empirical unit' on the other (Kapferer 1988: 12; see also Macfarlane 1993: 2).[3] The former notion is central to exchange as conceived in economics. Here, individuals are largely seen as disembedded from wider social and cultural contexts, except implicitly in terms of the assumption of a utilitarian outlook (e.g. Kapferer 1976; Gregory 1982: 10–28; Macfarlane 1993; Wilk 1996: 1–13; Miller 2002). By contrast, an individual in the sense of 'an empirical unit' may indeed be socially embedded and socialized in whatever way, but seems (at least to me) an indispensable entity, if 'experience' is in fact to be taken seriously at the empirical level. This is not the place to engage at length in that discussion. The stronger emphasis on experience and process as a matter of situated action in the approaches I consider is what makes them relevant for my purpose, but I should state clearly that it is the latter notion of an individual that informs my approach.

Exchange in these strands of theory is often understood in an expanded sense, to also include items such as words and gestures. This is particularly the case in transactionalism (e.g. Barth 1981) and in interactionist approaches (e.g. Goffman 1959; Berger and Luckmann 1966), where I will begin. A measured interactionist influence can in turn be detected in Bourdieu's practice-oriented approach (Bourdieu 1977), and Bourdieu's work on exchange is in turn accepted as a contribution to Maussian exchange theory, thus bringing the interrelatedness of these approaches full circle.[4]

Berger and Luckmann's seminal work (Berger and Luckmann 1966) is a useful starting point because their notion of routine is so explicit, and because they distinguish between different levels of routine, as Sennett effectively does. At heart, Berger and Luckmann conceive of social life as a dialectical process involving what they distinguish as an internal (cognitive) and an external (material and social) world. They envision process as unfolding through interaction: exchanges of acts and gestures between actors, the meaning of which are both internalized and externalized, and so (re)produced to gradually form (and transform) a wider meaningful social environment. They summarize this process in an epigram that has since been widely quoted: 'Society is a human product. Society is an objective reality. Man is a social product' (ibid.: 58, quoted in e.g. Ortner 1984: 158). More specifically, they conceive of this ongoing process as a matter of what they call 'institutionalization' (Berger and Luckmann

1966: 45–85), and it is in developing this central concept that they distinguish between different levels of routine. Here I will outline three levels to highlight affinities with Sennett's argument.[5]

Berger and Luckmann's most basic level of routine is 'habitualization', which in some ways serves as an ersatz for animal motor-instincts, thus helping to uphold a most basic measure of liveable order (ibid.: 45–51). Habits are an important precondition and vehicle for more complex forms of routine in their scheme, a point also made more widely (e.g. Bourdieu 1977; Camic 1986; Young 1988).

At the second level of routine, Berger and Luckmann introduce the concepts 'institution' and 'institutionalization' (Berger and Luckmann 1966: 51 ff.). What distinguishes institutions from habits is that institutions are socially recognized and significant *as* 'routines' in a way that habits are not. Institutions arise and are reproduced in the course of interaction, and it is this process they call institutionalization. Institutions in the basic sense emerge as 'reciprocal typification[s] of habitualized actions' (ibid.: 51). A point of significance that Berger and Luckmann make here (ibid.: 53–54), is that an already existing habit (level one) can become objectified in a social environment, and so transmute into an institution, that is, into a socially significant routine (level two). Effectively, this is precisely the mechanism of change that Sennett invokes with Diderot in order to point to the benign side of industrial routines that Adam Smith did not appreciate. Strictly speaking, Berger and Luckmann in fact reserve the term institution for what I will distinguish as a third level of routine (as I will explain in a moment). At the second level I consider here, they speak merely of 'nascent institutions', which are more 'tenuous' than more fully developed institutions (ibid.: 55). The point is significant for my later discussion of uncertainty, which is why it bears mention here. Some scholars who make a similar distinction have used the term 'custom' for this second level of routine (e.g. Weber; see Camic 1986: 1044), and I will adopt 'custom' for this level in my discussion below (see also Otto and Pedersen 2005: 22–25).

The third level of routine may be labelled the level of 'tradition' (Berger and Luckmann 1966: 57 ff; cf. Otto and Pedersen 2005).[6] I will quote the way Berger and Luckmann introduce this level at some length, because the passage helps us appreciate the problem that lies at the heart of Sennett's theoretical project. Having developed their notion of 'nascent' institutions (customs), using paradigmatic examples of interactions between actors labelled A and B, Berger and Luckmann let A and B have children (Berger and Luckmann 1966: 55). This changes the quality of nascent institutions:

The institutional world, which existed *in statu nascendi* in the original situation of A and B, is now passed on to others. In this process institutionalization perfects itself. The . . . formations that until this point still had the quality of *ad hoc* conceptions of two individuals, now become historical institutions. [. . .] [I]n the process . . . the institutional world 'thickens' and 'hardens', not only for the children, but (by mirror effect) for the parents as well . . . Only at this point does it become possible to speak of a social world at all, in the sense of a comprehensive and given reality confronting the individual in a manner analogous to the reality of the natural world. (ibid.: 55, 56)

What is revealing in this passage is the way the dialectical approach itself begins to take on a reifying quality. In their eagerness to make a case for the hard reality of social worlds, Berger and Luckmann largely relegate the tenuous quality of institutions to an evolutionary morning of things, long since eclipsed by more rigid and completed traditions, where space for reflection and agency is more limited. Effectively, this is precisely what Sennett also reverts to, when he turns his attention from routines in the historical context of industrial work to contemporary practices of flexible work. It is from this perspective that flexibility in Sennett's judgment comes to shatter the very possibility of routine.

However, in other related theoretical orientations, such different levels of routine are seen as operating *simultaneously*. Otto and Pedersen (2000) capture this concisely in the context of debates that have ensued from Hobsbawm and Ranger's famous collection on 'the invention of tradition' (Hobsbawm and Ranger 1983). Otto and Pedersen suggest the concept of tradition should be seen as: 'embedded in and related to custom, even though it has to be distinguished from it. Tradition not only has a reflexive dimension, it is also intrinsically normative. By formulating and performing traditions, human beings make statements about desired behavior . . . Traditions can thus be seen as social devices for consciously monitoring customs' (Otto and Pedersen 2000: 7).

This brief excursus will suffice to cast Sennett's arguments in a different light. At heart, it is the social significance of routines that Sennett stresses in his argument about character. In making this point he shows, as it were, how the mechanical habitual behaviour introduced with industrialization transformed into socially significant routines or 'customs' among industrial workers. Sennett further brings out how, over time, such routines came to serve as normative references in industrial disputes, that is, in terms of how things 'should' be done, somewhat like tradition in Otto and Pedersen's scheme. But there is also a sense in which Sennett's own wider argument resembles an invocation of tradition. His normative reference to industrial routines in the course of his book has a nostalgic ring not dissimilar to how traditional ways are invoked in other contexts. Strangleman makes a similar point, when he suggests that there is an element of 'nostalgia at work' in much of the literature he reviews (Strangleman 2007: 88–95). Yet, as Sennett effectively demonstrates in his chapter on industrial history, such norms only developed through practice (Sennett 1998: 32–45). Similar perspectives on work as evolving 'tradition' have indeed been suggested more widely, both in European contexts and beyond (e.g. Dumont 1977; Joyce 1987; Kinzley 1991; Otto 2004).

When I embarked on my research, I merely envisioned exploring such dynamics in a more consistent fashion than Sennett. Uncertainty, as I approach it below, was only a dimension I began to pay more attention to in the course of my fieldwork. In what follows I briefly report on findings of relevance in this regard.

Telework in Practice

My interest in telework coalesced somewhat by happenstance as I was preparing a research project to focus on social and cultural change in contexts of paid work as they relate to uses of new information and communication technologies (ICTs). I had recently read Sennett's book when I happened to watch a story on TV which was to set the stage for my research. The story concerned a group of teleworkers in a Danish village, and the changes this form of work allegedly brought about. Backed by statistical material, it was claimed that telework would become much more prevalent in the not too distant future. The group of teleworkers portrayed was taken to suggest how working life and village life would change as a result. In contrast with a prevailing view of village life as something that has been deteriorating since the agrarian revolution (and perhaps well before; see Williams 1973), the story suggested that social life in the village had been reinvigorated as a result of the increasing number of people now present there during the working week.

A group had emerged between teleworking neighbours who routinely met once a week for 'work lunches', as they called these events, in part to counter a measure of social isolation that came with working from home. Anyone from the village working from home was welcome to join, and new social relations within the village were

allegedly taking shape this way. More than that, new sources of professional inspiration were allegedly emerging among these teleworking
villagers from very different professional backgrounds. Concretely,
the story indicated how, while having lunch, these people were 'discussing each other's projects', as one put it. On TV, the group was
depicted studying the drafts of an architect who was a member of the
group. His drafts were spread out on the lunch table, and the group's
members commented on and eagerly enquired about the work in
progress. Meanwhile, another member of the group, a psychologist,
said how discussions with a fellow teleworker, a journalist, had given
him entirely new perspectives on certain aspects of his own specialized work. Thus, not only village life but also working life was seemingly changing as the practice of telework became more prevalent.

What intrigued me was the contrast this story provided to that in
Sennett's book. Above all, it hardly seemed that routines were 'dying'
among these teleworkers. More in line with Sennett's approach in
the historical context, the story on TV seemed to indicate that these
teleworkers had developed new routines of some cultural and social
significance, as suggested by the way these neighbours had seemingly
transformed into 'colleagues'. Interestingly – whereas there appeared
to be some resonance between Sennett's arguments and the story
about these people, in as much as they felt a measure of social isolation
– these people had evidently acted, seemingly somewhat successfully, to ameliorate their state of affairs. Such action seemed largely
absent from Sennett's account. It was such discrepancies which first
made me reconsider Sennett's arguments, and in particular the conceptual framework by which he develops them, as I have outlined it
above.

I ended up doing sixteen months of fieldwork in the villages portrayed on the TV programme, with the lunch group as my point
of departure. When I embarked on fieldwork I simply envisioned
extending the analytic perspectives outlined in Sennett's historical discussion. As it turned out, these ambitions were frustrated as
I gradually found many discrepancies between the story I had seen
on TV, and that which I observed as I participated in the lunches
on a weekly basis. For one thing, I was surprised by the extent to
which the lunches seemed in practice not to be much about 'work'.
I certainly never saw the architect's drawings on the lunch table, nor
anyone else's projects. In the course of my informal interaction with
the group, some members of it indicated that the story on TV had
been an exaggeration, that they in fact did not consider each other
'colleagues', and that the group was just engaged in 'commonplace

socializing' (*almindeligt menneskeligt samvær*). At other times, however, the very same individuals would point out that the group was occasionally and in some ways about 'work' after all, in the sense that they could exchange occasional tips – about such things as tax issues and IT trouble shooting – and meet up with like-minded people in the middle of the working day.[7]

It was not just I who was confused. So (it gradually appeared) were they. For example, they occasionally reprimanded one another for serving food that was 'too lavish' and extravagant, rather than being affordable and 'work-like', and for inviting fellow villagers to the lunches who were unemployed, and so ostensibly did not 'belong' there. While the lunches clearly comprised elements of routinized behaviour – in terms of such things as timing and the consumption of food – their routinization seemed at best a matter of degree, and the cultural significance of the lunches as a 'work' routine was certainly less than straightforward, as even my informants effectively acknowledged. In short, the concept of 'routine' as an analytic category began to appear increasingly simplistic, all the more so as I looked beyond the narrow context of these lunches.

My intention had never been to focus exclusively on this lunch group. Indeed, the story on TV had concerned the village as a whole, in a sense of 'society writ large'. As part of my effort to engage with people working from home in the villages and who were not members of the lunch group, I carried out the survey I referred above. Although a main purpose of the survey was simply to create a starting point for further contact with a broader range of informants, the results it yielded were significant to the subsequent direction of my research. Of the entire stock of respondents to my survey, only two had a teleworking arrangement formally designated as such, in the sense of a written agreement with their workplace. I found this quite remarkable given the extent of written regulations and contracts in the world of work. At the same time, the survey suggested that the sheer number of people practising de facto or informal telework ('using internet for purposes at work from home') far exceeded what had been suggested on TV with reference to the said statistical material. This highlighted the importance of looking at the motivations and agency of people practising this form of flexible work to adequately explain its prevalence.

As my fieldwork progressed, I sought to achieve an in-depth understanding of how telework was in fact practised, the context in terms of which practice was situated, and how this motivated people to embrace this form of flexible work. Even though I only worked with a couple of villages as my point of departure, I gradually found not only a staggering diversity in terms of how telework was practised, but also a considerable complexity in terms of how such practice was situated and motivated, reflected in the substantial flux in the practices of telework that I could document. In the latter regard, I gradually came to realize that a significance of 'telework' lies not just in the active engagement with work from home in front of the computer. Merely 'having' a telework arrangement at hand for potential use was also widely perceived as an asset with tangible effects.[8] I came to realize that 'having' a telework arrangement may both 'fill a gap and cut a Gordian knot' as it were, in that it can animate a sense of prospect and aspiration at a social canvass of moral judgement where diverse aspirations in terms of work and family are often experienced as in conflict, being difficult to reconcile or fulfil.

While these dimensions of telework were prevalent across a broad range of my data, I want to provide a more concrete sense of these dimensions by briefly accounting for the telework experience of just one individual, here called Edward. During my fieldwork, Edward was the head of a branch of a large multinational computing company, with considerable responsibilities (see Kjaerulff 2010a: 92–122). He had started teleworking as an informal arrangement in connection with a promotion, which he had accepted on condition that he would be allowed to take care of overtime from home via the company's intranet and the internet. When I first encountered Edward, he informed me that he had had this informal arrangement for three years, but that he had made a firm decision to abandon it half a year prior to my arrival in the village, as it had intruded unduly on his family life. Edward and his wife explained to me how, during these years, work and even just the potential of engaging in work-related matters had preoccupied Edward more often than not, due to the telework arrangement. The family had found it difficult to 'read his behaviour' as they put it, and never felt quite sure if he was 'mentally present', or if 'his brain was in the computer'. That way of practising parenting and partnering was not what they had wanted, and so telework was 'kicked out'.

However, as I became better acquainted with the family during my village-based research, I found that Edward had never informed his work place of his decision to end telework as a means of handling overtime. Indeed, I began to realize he was at some pains to keep his colleagues in the dark in this regard. It was only at this point that I began paying more focused attention to Edward and his family. In the candid conversations which ensued, he cogently reflected on what he called his 'flex-flex' way of teleworking, that is, his 'flexible' way of practising flexible work, to the effect of alleviating himself from flexible work in substance. On formal grounds he did nothing wrong, but he felt uncertain and somewhat anxious about whether his colleagues might interpret his decision to end teleworking as 'slack' in terms of the work hours they thought he continued to deliver from home, and so set social dynamics in motion with tangible and unfortunate consequences for his career. Hence the relative secrecy regarding his decision to terminate actively teleworking as far as his workplace was concerned. In a real sense then – a social sense – I realized that he could still be perceived as 'teleworking'; that is, working in part from home to take care of overtime issues. Indeed his telework equipment remained in the household throughout my fieldwork.

As I became yet further familiar with this household through regular informal interaction, I gradually found that he also still actively teleworked in the conventional sense on an occasional basis, despite his stated rejection of this option. These engagements fluctuated and were mostly carefully negotiated with his wife as a matter of 'making exceptions to the rule', as they put it. But Edward would sometimes also telework when his significant others were not at home (as I came to realize through unannounced visits to the household). He downplayed this, and above all saw this continued teleworking as a way of dealing with a wider and continuous problem he struggled with, of making things 'work out', as he and his wife often put it (*få det til at gå op*).

Rethinking Uncertainty and Flexibility

On the one hand, my fieldwork amply suggested that socially relevant routines persist among teleworkers. In line with Sennett's discussion of the historical context, but in contrast to his wider argument, it also seems that new routines of tangible social significance continue to proliferate, as is brought out both by the 'work' dimensions to the lunches, and by Edward's experiences in contexts of both work and family.

Yet fieldwork made me acknowledge that much routine-like behaviour involves an element of what I here call 'uncertainty', although it is a more subtle and manageable kind of uncertainty than that portrayed in the wider literature on flexible work.

The context of telework might suggest such uncertainty arises from the novel circumstances in terms of which work was practised, and this is undoubtedly part of the picture. Yet the prevalence of such uncertainty far exceeds the narrow context of telework. Behavioural flux and struggles to 'work things out' were indeed readily detectable across a much broader spectrum of the lives that I followed, though often less spectacularly brought out than in Edward's case. Telework quite aside, I suspect such dimensions are simply part of living an unfolding life, inherently comprised of complex social arenas and multiple schemes of cultural interpretation. In the course of practical living, people try to work things out through twists and turns, and by embracing various and shifting means. They may indeed be partially successful in such endeavours, but most successes are limited in duration, and people may change their outlook, agendas and course of action. Even the limited material I have presented brings this out as a core feature, at a rather miniscule level of commonplace interaction. As it turned out, the cultural and social significance of the lunches was, in the course of practice, a matter of *partially* shared meaning as to what the lunches 'were about', and in this way their routinization to degree remained unsettled. Or consider Edward's ongoing struggle to 'work things out' as reflected just in his telework trajectory: one salient dimension to this is his continued concern about how his family and colleagues judged his behaviour, quite apart from how he might judge it himself.

It was in part to engage such mundane uncertainties that Bourdieu proposed moving from 'the mechanics of the model' to 'the dialectic of strategies' (Bourdieu 1977: 3). Bourdieu's point of departure for this move was Lévi-Strauss's approach to kinship and marriage alliance (see Lévi-Strauss 1969). In its day, Lévi-Strauss's approach was widely recognized as an innovation in exchange theory, in that he conceived of marriage as a form of gift exchange, involving the exchange of women between kinship groups, and he used it in order to examine social structure in terms of the dynamics of different exchange forms (see Gregory 1994: 925–928). Bourdieu's point, widely regarded as another important contribution, was that Lévi-Strauss's structuralist approach overlooked the 'objective' reality of experience in such exchanges. As he observes: 'Any really objective analysis of the exchange of gifts, words, challenges, or even women must allow for the fact that each of these inaugural acts may misfire, and that it receives its meaning, in any case, from the response it triggers off, even if the response is a failure to reply that retroactively removes its intended meaning' (Bourdieu 1977: 5). This aspect of Bourdieu's work is commonly referred to in terms of a temporal dimension to exchange and interaction. But the shift really turns on ambiguity and uncertainty as integral features of transaction, not unlike Berger and Luckmann's point about 'nascent institutions'. For Bourdieu (more than Berger and Luckmann), this perspective entailed conceptualizing cultural models (such as traditions of kinship) as a matter of continued reflexive engagement and representation at the level of interaction, through which routines ('habitus' for Bourdieu) are dialectically reproduced (ibid.: 5–9, 30–71).

While Bourdieu's work is widely known, I will draw on a somewhat different approach to advance my general argument. This is in part because Bourdieu's rather rigid notion of 'habitus' (e.g. Jenkins 1992: 66–102) encumbers an analytical engagement with the experience of uncertainty, a problem which is also reflected in the notable absence of a temporal dimension in some aspects of Bourdieu's work (see e.g. Gell 1992: 276–79; Munn 1992: 106–8). The extent to which Bourdieu develops his notion of strategy in terms of self-interested calculation and 'capital' is also a limitation in his approach (see e.g. Graeber 2001: 26–30; Narotzky, this volume). This is somewhat ironic, given how widely Bourdieu's work has been embraced relative to the interactionist and transactionalist approaches which in particular have been taken to task on this account.

As a subtler alternative, I have found Fredrik Barth's more recent work useful. Barth has conventionally been seen as an arch transactionalist on the basis of his publications in the 1950s and 1960s, which are still often taken to represent excesses of economism in anthropological thought. Perhaps for this reason, his more recent and rather more profound work seems somewhat overlooked (see Kjaerulff 2010b). Strongly stated, one could say that where some notion of routine, structure or order is a premise both in practice-based orientations such as Bourdieu's (e.g. Ortner 1984), and in Maussian exchange orientations, Barth's premise is the exact opposite.[9] As he has put it, he wishes to: 'start with a heuristic assumption of a *disordered* assembly and then, by modeling the way people interact, and the cumulative, formative effects of such action, to *generate* trends toward linkage and coherence . . . thereby to identify processes that build [the observed] degree of order' (1993a: 340, original emphasis). More concretely, Barth has developed a model of cultural reproduction as unfolding through situated social action, where he makes a key distinction between 'events' and 'acts'.[10] The concept of event refers to 'the outwards appearance of behaviour', while act refers to 'the intended and interpreted meaning of that behaviour' (Barth 1992: 21–24; 1993a: 158–60 et passim). The same event – such as a lunch or an event of telework – may be interpreted differently by different individuals, as the ethnography above makes concrete. In this way, events tend to be 'underdetermined', as Barth has put it (Barth 1993a: 5), and may well be 'at variance with the intentions of individual actors' (Barth 1989: 134; cf. 1993a: 286–304). Briefly put, one edge this approach has over Bourdieu's is in the way cultural sharing and routine, and indeed cultural reproduction, are here seen as an inherently *partial* matter. In turn, emphasis is then shifted to an enquiry about the upholding of partial order through continuous (re) thinking and (re)action, not least its wider material and social dimensions. A somewhat similar orientation is also found in so-called actor-network theory, but it would exceed my purpose to consider that here.

What is important is the way uncertainty from this perspective comprises a significant *momentum* for ongoing (re)action and reflection. Consider again the trajectory of Edward's telework experience: He and his wife originally envisioned the arrangement as an attractive way of meeting simultaneous requirements and desires in terms of work and family. In the course of events they both got more first-hand experience with this way of working, but it also turned out to be different from what they had hoped. At the same time, Edward got to know what he called the 'flex-flex' potential of the arrangement. Based on the knowledge he acquired from the experience of teleworking, he then decided to terminate the arrangement. But despite no formal wrong doing, Edward was uncertain about how this act might be interpreted by his colleagues, and the 'flex-flex' dimension became more important to him. As it turned out, contrary to what he stated and presumably intended, he also continued to work from home on an occasional basis despite his decision, something that was a potential source of disagreement and uncertainty in the domestic context. The whole ordeal may be seen as a continuous struggle to 'work it out', as Edward and his wife put it, to impose a workable measure of order which was not given, but a matter of continuous intervention.

It is important to appreciate that, despite the criticism often levelled against Barth (usually his earlier work, in ignorance of his later work), it is not that events and actions in this perspective are not embedded in a wider social context, or informed in culturally specific or diverse ways. In fact, quite the contrary: in Barth's view, there is rather a 'surfeit of culture' (Barth 1993a: 339), that is, too much culture and context to be 'put together in one cohering structure or one person's practice to be universally and equally shared' (ibid.: 5; cf. Schlecker and Hirsch 2001). It is precisely this, in Barth's view, that is an important contributory factor to the experience of uncertainty in its own right, a perspective which has lead Barth to think of uncertainty in more specific terms of situated 'concerns' (Barth 1993a: 286–304, 330–33, 341–53; 1993b: 39–46). For Barth, 'concerns' reflect recurring experiences of 'trying to cope in a complex, unpredictable, and imperfectly known world' (Barth 1993a: 343). Concerns arise in part from 'the legitimate and illegitimate wishes, demands, pressures, and general coercion emanating from other people' (ibid.: 330). Uncertainty, from this perspective, is evidently culturally and historically specific, and emerges from the experience of socially embedded action (cf. Jackson 1996; Whyte 1997: 19; Werbner 2002: 14).

Barth describes how people in Bali deal with such concerns, in part at the level of representation. But the practice of representation is for Barth informed more subtly than in Bourdieu's scheme of strategic calculation, and its enactment and effects bear closer affinity to so-called actor-network theory than to Bourdieu, in the way Barth understands the complex entanglement of its material and social dimensions.

These perspectives serve to cast the flexibility yielded by telework in a different light. There is no doubt that an important attraction of telework from this perspective is the flexibility it offers in the conventional sense: it helps people deal with uncertainties in the shape of unforeseen turns of events, such as when family members fall ill, when the roads get buried under snow, when deadlines collide with regular work hours and so on. This is in its own right a major reason why telework should have broad appeal, even as an informal arrangement, and many teleworkers indeed point this out themselves.

But from the perspective I have outlined, there seems to be yet another attraction in telework, which is less commonly recognized. It is this dimension that I take Edward's 'flex-flex' practice of telework to bring out in the material I have presented (see also Kjaerulff 2010a: 123–47). In that context I noted how, through Edward's teleworking trajectory, he had a continuous concern about how his family and colleagues judged his behaviour, quite apart from how he might judge it himself, and the material I presented suggested how the 'flex-flex' dimension to his telework variously made a tangible difference in this regard. When he first discovered it, it allowed him to leave his office when the formal work day was over, despite the need for overtime, while still entertaining ideals of 'working hard' and 'doing his part' among his colleagues. This social image was of course important for Edward, not only in terms of his everyday social life at work, but also in tangible terms of his continued career. A similar scenario was at issue at home, though in terms of quite different cultural ideals and social dynamics of parenting and partnering, and of 'flex-flex-ing' the kids and the wife, so to speak. It was precisely the latter which had brought Edward and his wife to reflect on a discrepancy between ideal and practice, so that Edward eventually abandoned his telework. But as it turned out, they continued to 'work out' the issue, also at the level of representation, by carefully framing Edward's occasional work from home as 'exceptions', i.e. to the extent that his family was in the house when he did work from home.

The expanded sense of flexibility I here point to, as a symbolic practice, must as I see it be appreciated in light of the concerns, that is, the various pressures arising from participating in social contexts of both work and family, which, telework quite aside, are widely reported as domains of life that are often difficult to reconcile. Indeed, others have reported on symbolic ways of dealing with such experiences of conflicting demands and aspirations in the context of work and family (e.g. Hochschild 1997; Townsend 2002: 77–79; cf. Williams 1973: 297). Telework only seems like a novel, but potent, symbolic device among many others, arguably because it underpins desirable prospects in both domains simultaneously, and in that all it really takes as an informal arrangement is a networked computer.

In a quite different context, Miller and Slater have reported findings that resonate to a degree with my own regarding networked computers. They observe that internet engagements in Trinidad are informed in part by a quest for what they call 'expansive realization' (Miller and Slater 2000: 10–13). Here, the 'internet is viewed as a means through which one can enact – often in highly idealized form ...what one thinks one really is ... [C]ontradictions concerning one's ability, in practical life, to be who one thinks one is seem capable of being resolved on the expanded scale and terrain of the internet' (ibid.: 10–11). However, I believe the attraction of the flexibilities of telework I have here considered only truly emerges from the perspective on uncertainty to which I have sought to link it.

Conclusion

I have suggested a need for a more nuanced approach to understanding the experience and practice of flexible work. As an acclaimed 'qualitative' study inspired by anthropology, Sennett's book is misleading. I have tried to show that one merit of Sennett's book, nonetheless, is in the theoretical orientation at the heart of Sennett's argument. Because this orientation is largely implicit and not executed consistently, the book obscures important dimensions of work as a dynamic and evolving domain of cultural tradition and social practice (Kjaerulff 2010a).

Complementing Neveling's argument (this volume), I have shown that such tradition, understood as 'long term' ideals (cf. Bloch and Parry 1989), entails a measure of 'uncertainty' at the level of lived experience. In this way I have developed a perspective which complicates and so complements, rather than falsifies, the more widely suggested connection between flexibility and uncertainty. Against the widely propounded view that flexible work effects attenuated experiences of uncertainty, I have argued that it may also be the other way around, at least in contexts of teleworking, highlighted in the wider literature as among the more extreme forms of flexible work. Uncertainty as I have approached it is an inherent dimension of social life, and informal telework may have proliferated in part as a recent response to this more fundamental predicament. At least this perspective would go some way to account for the proliferation of telework as an informal and partially symbolic practice of 'flexibility', dimensions to telework which seem salient, although to date they have been largely ignored in the wider literature.

Obviously teleworking is just one kind of 'flexible' work, and I should make quite clear that I do not claim to have uncovered a mechanism in its own right explaining the proliferation of any kind of flexible work. It is also conceivable that the wider 'Danish' context of my study, not considered in this chapter, be it in terms of cultural tradition or welfare policies pertaining in contexts of work, may make my study a somewhat unusual case relative to other countries where telework is practised. But I fail to see how such dimensions would fundamentally affect the core dynamics and arguments I have pursued. In fact, Edward, whose case I have considered here, was not a Danish citizen; he did not grow up in Denmark, and the company in which he worked was an international one with many identical policies across its branches. On the other hand, I note a degree of resonance with what I have sought to advance in the arguments of Garsten and Knox (both this volume) about flexible work entailing respectively dimensions of 'liminality' and 'potential'. The symbolic practices I have considered as a form of 'flexibility' can be said to concern a kind of 'potential' similar to that which Knox considers in a different context, where ICTs 'extending' sociality is also at issue.[11] Likewise, the kind of uncertainty I have discussed bears some affinity with what Garsten considers in terms of 'liminality', a concept which indeed is taken from radically different contexts having nothing to do with flexible work.

Above all, there seems to be a need for more complex understandings of the social significances of flexible work (cf. Strangleman 2007), and as I see it, this includes a need to take experience, as it is concretely situated in social and material terms, more seriously as an empirical phenomenon. It is in part in this regard that the theoretical legacy I have engaged seems to complement Maussian approaches to exchange.

Notes

1 I stick with the terms 'flexibility' and 'uncertainty' here, although a variety of terms are used across this literature, often interchangeably, to substantially similar effects. Strangleman thus notes how Ulrich Beck 'stretches his notion of the risk society to incorporate the uncertainty over work', an uncertainty which Beck sees as 'both a product of, and contribut[ing] to, the "risk society"' (Strangleman 2007: 84). Strangleman similarly notes how social relations are seen as becoming 'increasingly fugitive and ephemeral' as workers are required to be more 'mobile and flexible' (ibid.: 85). In the course of this chapter I will clarify my usage of the terms in the context of my argument about their inverse relation.

2 Of course, this is related to the problem of defining telework (Garrett and Danziger 2007; Kjaerulff 2010a: 57–59).

3 Kapferer has been among prominent critics of so-called individualistic exchange orientations, but in the work cited here he notes: 'The empirical statement that all societies are composed of individuals, separate biologically integrated behaving units, is generally unproblematic. It becomes problematic when it is stated as a cultural value or it is assumed that all societies, for example, carry dominant conceptions of the primacy of the individual in society or of the autonomy of the individual in society that are essentially the same despite superficial cultural differences' (Kapferer 1988: 12–13).

4 More recently, there has been some convergence between so-called actor-network theory and Strathern's version of a Maussian approach (e.g. Law 1999), and actor-network theory contains a measure of interactionist inspiration: see e.g. Callon (1998), who is most explicit in his use of Goffman.

5 The following outline owes more to Otto and Pedersen (2000, 2005) than is indicated here, notably the distinction between 'three levels' of

routine, which Otto and Pedersen in turn develop drawing especially on Berger and Luckmann.

6 The term 'tradition' derives from Latin *tradere*, meaning 'to hand down or deliver' (Williams 1983: 318–20), a connotation which is suggestive in the interactionist context I consider here.

7 The lunches were usually at 12 noon on Wednesdays, for which reason they were known among members as 'the Wednesday lunches'.

8 Cf. Knox's argument about 'potential' (Knox, this volume).

9 Contrary to what is often assumed, socialization is not absent here, but rather seen as a matter of degree which needs to be explained. The approach is above all a heuristic methodological stance, rooted in Barth's insistence on what he calls 'naturalism', a strong empirical grounding which has long distinguished his work (e.g. Barth 1981: 33; 1987: 8; see also Kjaerulff 2010b: 222).

10 Barth refers to Weber as an inspiration for this distinction (e.g. Barth 1993a: 158), but it is also suggestive of phenomenological influence, notably Alfred Schutz's work (e.g. Schutz 1973: 24 ff.). Indeed, Barth's interest in 'knowledge' throughout much of his later career (e.g. Barth 2002) seems to bear some affinity with Schutz's thought (which in turn was partially cast as a critical engagement with Weber). Schutz was also a major influence on Berger and Luckmann.

11 See also Grétarsdóttir (this volume), drawing on Munn and Miller in this regard.

References

Barth, F. 1981 [1966]. 'Models of Social Organization: I', in *Process and Form in Social Life: Selected Essays*, Vol. 1. London: Routledge and Kegan Paul, pp. 32–47.

——— 1987. *Cosmologies in the Making: A Generative Approach to Cultural Variation in Inner New Guinea*. Cambridge: Cambridge University Press.

——— 1989. 'The Analysis of Culture in Complex Societies', *Ethnos* 54(3/4): 120–142.

——— 1992. 'Towards a Greater Naturalism in Conceptualizing Societies', in A. Kuper (ed.), *Conceptualizing Society*. London: Routledge, pp. 17–33.

——— 1993a. *Balinese Worlds*. Chicago: University of Chicago Press.

——— 1993b. 'Are Values Real? The Enigma of Naturalism in the Anthropological Imputation of Values', in M. Hecter et al. (eds), *The Origin of Values*. New York: de Gruyter, pp. 31–46.

——— 2002. 'An Anthropology of Knowledge', *Current Anthropology* 43(1): 1–18.

Berger, P., and T. Luckmann. 1966. *The Social Construction of Reality: A Treatise in the Sociology of Knowledge*. New York: Doubleday.

Bloch, M., and J. Parry. 1989. 'Introduction: Money and the Morality of Exchange', in J. Parry and M. Bloch (eds), *Money and the Morality of Exchange*. Cambridge: Cambridge University Press, pp. 1–32.

Boholm, A. 2003. 'Situated Risk: An Introduction', *Ethnos* 68(2): 157–158.

Bourdieu, P. 1977. *Outline of a Theory of Practice*. Cambridge: Cambridge University Press.

Callon, M. 1998. 'An Essay on Framing and Overflowing: Economic Externalities Revisited by Sociology', in M. Callon (ed.), *The Laws of the Market*. Oxford: Blackwell, pp. 244–269.

Camic, C. 1986. 'The Matter of Habit', *American Journal of Sociology* 91(5): 1039–1087.

Dumont, L. 1977. *From Mandeville to Marx: The Genesis and Triumph of Economic Ideology*. Chicago: University of Chicago Press.

Ellison, N.B. 1999. 'Social Impacts: New Perspectives on Telework', *Social Science Computer Review* 17(3): 338–356.

Evens, T.M.S., and D. Handelman. 2006. 'Introduction: The Ethnographic Praxis of the Theory of Practice', in T.M.S. Evens and D. Handelman (eds), *The Manchester School: Practice and Ethnographic Praxis in Anthropology*. Oxford: Berghahn Books, pp. 1–11.

Garrett, R.K., and J.N. Danziger. 2007. 'Which Telework? Defining and Testing a Taxonomy of Technology-mediated Work at a Distance', *Social Science Computer Review* 25(1): 27–47.

Gell, A. 1992. *The Anthropology of Time: Cultural Constructions of Temporal Maps and Images*. Oxford: Berg.

Glennie, P., and N. Thrift. 1996. 'Reworking E.P. Thompson's "Time, Work-discipline and Industrial Capitalism"', *Time and Society* 5(3): 275–299.

Godelier, M. 1980. 'Work and its Representations: A Research Proposal', *History Workshop Journal* 10: 164–174.

Goffman, E. 1959. *The Presentation of Self in Everyday Life*. New York: Doubleday.

Graeber, D. 2001. *Toward an Anthropological Theory of Value: The False Coin of Our Own Dreams*. New York: Palgrave.

Gregory, C. 1982. *Gifts and Commodities*. London: Academic Press.

———— 1994. 'Exchange and Reciprocity', in T. Ingold (ed.), *Companion Encyclopedia of Anthropology*. London: Routledge, pp. 911–939.

Hobsbawm, E., and T. Ranger (eds). 1983. *The Invention of Tradition*. Cambridge: Cambridge University Press.

Hochschild, A. 1997. *The Time Bind: When Work becomes Home, and Home becomes Work*. New York: Metropolitan Books.

Ingold, T. 1995. 'Work, Time and Industry', *Time and Society* 4(1): 5–28.

Jackson, M. 1996. 'Introduction: Phenomenology, Radical Empiricism, and Anthropological Critique', in M. Jackson (ed.), *Things as They Are: New Directions in Phenomenological Anthropology*. Bloomington: Indiana University Press, pp. 1–50.

Jenkins, R. 1992. *Pierre Bourdieu*. London: Routledge.

Joyce, P. 1987. 'The Historical Meanings of Work: An Introduction', in P. Joyce (ed.), *The Historical Meanings of Work*. Cambridge: Cambridge University Press, pp. 1–30.

Kapferer, B. 1976. 'Introduction: Transactional Models Reconsidered', in B. Kapferer (ed.), *Transaction and Meaning: Directions in the Anthropology of Exchange and Symbolic Behavior*. Philadelphia: Institute for the Study of Human Issues, pp. 1–22.

——— 1988. *Legends of People, Myths of State: Violence, Intolerance, and Political Culture in Sri Lanka and Australia*. Washington: Smithsonian Press.

Kinzley, W.D. 1991. *Industrial Harmony in Modern Japan: The Invention of Tradition*. London: Routledge.

Kjaerulff, J. 2010a. *Internet and Change: An Anthropology of Knowledge and Flexible Work*. Hoejbjerg: Intervention Press.

——— 2010b. 'A Barthian Approach to Practice and Media: Internet Engagements among Teleworkers in Rural Denmark', in B. Brauchler and J. Postill (eds), *Theorising Media and Practice*. Oxford: Berghahn Books, pp. 213–231.

Law, J. 1999. 'After ANT: Complexity, Naming and Topology', in J. Law and J. Hassard (eds), *Actor Network Theory and After*. Oxford: Blackwell, pp. 1–14.

Lévi-Strauss, C. 1969 [1949]. *The Elementary Structures of Kinship*. London: Eyre and Spottiswoode.

Macfarlane, A. 1993. 'Louis Dumont and the Origins of Individualism', *Cambridge Anthropology* 16(1): 1–28.

Marx, K. 1973. *Grundrisse*. Harmondsworth: Penguin.

——— 1990 [1867]. *Capital*, Vol. 1. London: Penguin.

Miller, D. 1998. 'Conclusion: A Theory of Virtualism', in J.G. Carrier and D. Miller (eds), *Virtualism: A New Political Economy*. Oxford: Berg, pp. 187–215.

——— 2002. 'Turning Callon the Right Way Up', *Economy and Society* 31(2): 218–233.

Miller, D., and D. Slater. 2000. *The Internet: An Ethnographic Approach*. Oxford: Berg.

Munn, N.D. 1992. 'The Cultural Anthropology of Time: A Critical Essay', *Annual Review of Anthropology* 21: 93–123.

Nicolaus, M. 1973. 'Foreword', in K. Marx, *Grundrisse*. Harmondsworth: Penguin, pp. 7–63.

Ortner, S.B. 1984. 'Theory in Anthropology Since the Sixties', *Comparative Studies in Society and History* 26(1): 126–166.

——— 2005. 'Subjectivity and Cultural Critique', *Anthropological Theory* 5(1): 31–52.

Otto, T. 2004. 'Work, Wealth and Knowledge: Enigmas of Cargoist Identifications', in H. Jebens (ed.), *Cargo, Cult and Culture Critique*. Honolulu: University of Hawaii Press, pp. 209–226.

Otto, T., and P. Pedersen. 2000. 'Tradition between Continuity and Invention: An Introduction', *Folk* 42: 3–17.
——— 2005. 'Disentangling Traditions: Culture, Agency and Power', in T. Otto and P. Pedersen (eds), *Tradition and Agency: Tracing Cultural Continuity and Invention*. Aarhus: Aarhus University Press, pp. 11–49.
Peters, J. 1998. *På Job – Hjemme*. Copenhagen: Fremad.
Sahlins, M. 1972 [1965]. 'On the Sociology of Primitive Exchange', in *Stone Age Economics*. New York: Aldine de Gruyter, pp. 185–275.
Schlecker, M., and E. Hirsch. 2001. 'Incomplete Knowledge: Ethnography and the Crisis of Context in Studies of Media, Science and Technology', *History of the Human Sciences* 14(1): 69–87.
Schutz, A. 1973 [1953]. 'Common-sense and Scientific Interpretation of Human Action', in *Collected Papers*, Vol. 1. The Hague: Nijhoff, pp. 2–47.
Sennett, R. 1998. *The Corrosion of Character: The Personal Consequences of Work in the New Capitalism*. New York: Norton.
Strangleman, T. 2007. 'The Nostalgia for Permanence at Work? The End of Work and its Commentators', *Sociological Review* 55(1): 81–103.
Thomas, N. 1991. *Entangled Objects: Exchange, Material Culture and Colonialism in the Pacific*. Cambridge, MA: Harvard University Press.
Thompson, E.P. 1967. 'Time, Work-discipline, and Industrial Capitalism', *Past and Present* 38: 56–97.
Tietze, S., and G. Musson. 2002. 'When "Work" Meets "Home": Temporal Flexibility as Lived Experience', *Time and Society* 11(2/3): 315–334.
Townsend, N.W. 2002. *The Package Deal: Marriage, Work, and Fatherhood in Men's Lives*. Philadelphia: Temple University Press.
Werbner, R. 2002. 'Postcolonial Subjectivities: The Personal, the Political and the Moral', in R. Werbner (ed.), *Postcolonial Subjectivities in Africa*. London: Zed Books, pp. 1–21.
Whipp, R. 1987. '"A Time to Every Purpose": An Essay on Time and Work', in P. Joyce (ed.), *The Historical Meanings of Work*. Cambridge: Cambridge University Press, pp. 210–236.
Whyte, S.R. 1997. *Questioning Misfortune: The Pragmatics of Uncertainty in Eastern Uganda*. Cambridge: Cambridge University Press.
Wilk, R. 1996. *Economies and Cultures: Foundations of Economic Anthropology*. Boulder, CO: Westview Press.
Williams, R. 1973. *The Country and the City*. London: Chatto and Windus.
——— 1983. *Keywords: A Vocabulary of Culture and Society*. London: Fontana.
Young, M.D. 1988. The Metronomic Society: Natural Rhythms and Human Timetables. London: Thames and Hudson.

9

Afterword

Exchange and Corporate Forms Today

Keir Martin

As I write, the world is waking up to what seems like the hundredth banking industry scandal to emerge since the near collapse of the global economy in 2008. Just over a week ago, *Rolling Stone* published a piece by their excellent financial correspondent Matt Taibbi entitled 'Why Is Nobody Freaking Out about the LIBOR Banking Scandal?' (Taibbi 2012). A week is a long time in global economic Armageddon, and if nobody in the US was freaking out back then, they sure are now. Today's UK press reports that the crisis that has gripped the UK political classes for the past two weeks is about to go global, as, 'the investigation into the LIBOR interest rate-rigging in the United Kingdom becomes a financial scandal of tsunami-like proportions' (Nye 2012) that is set to rock the USA and other countries. At its heart, the LIBOR scandal is a remarkably simple one. LIBOR is the interest rate at which banks lend to each other, and has consequently become the yardstick for most commercial lending around the world, making it one of the fundamental instruments that underpins every aspect of global finance. In theory, LIBOR is supposed to be a neutral and objective economic measurement, a status that is ensured by a strict separation between bankers who set the rates and the traders who make deals, based at least in part upon the rates that the bankers set. But now e-mails released by regulators reveal that – surprise, surprise! – back in 2006, at the height of the bubble that was about to burst, there was an ongoing breach of this *cordon sanitaire* at one UK bank, Barclays. The implication now is that many other banks and elements of the UK government were actively engaged in

the conspiracy, or at best complicit through their silence, and the fear
is that the resulting panic that this revelation has caused may yet push
the teetering global financial system over the brink.

When the scandal first broke in the UK a few weeks ago with the
publication of the Financial Services Authority report fining Barclays
for rate fixing (FSA 2012), there was one theme running through
the e-mails that particularly struck a nerve with commentators and
the public. In an e-mail dated 26 October 2006, an external trader
e-mails 'Trader G' at Barclays, saying that he needs a lower three-
month US dollar LIBOR submission. 'If it comes in unchanged, I'm
a dead man', he tells Trader G. Trader G promises to 'have a chat'
with the persons responsible, and sure enough Barclay's submission for the rate comes in at half a point lower than the previous day.
The external trader's response to this news is unsurprising: 'Dude. I
owe you big time! Come over one day after work and I'm opening
a bottle of Bollinger' (ibid.: 19). In another message dated 10.52 AM,
7 April 2006, Trader C asks one of the bank's employees responsible
for submitting its proposed LIBOR rates for lower one-month and
three-month US dollar LIBOR submissions: 'If it's not too late low
1m and 3m would be nice, but please feel free to say "no" . . . Coffees
will be coming your way either way, just to say thank you for your
help in the past few weeks'. Later in the day the Submitter responds
to Trader C's e-mail with the message, 'Done . . . for you big boy'
(ibid.: 13).

Many commentators were struck by the difference in scale
between the enormous sums of money that rode on LIBOR rates
– anthropologist turned financial journalist Gillian Tett (cited in
Smith 2012) estimates that $350 trillion worth of contracts glob-
ally have been underwritten by LIBOR – on the one hand, and the
paltry offerings made in return for their manipulation on the other.
Certainly, these gift offerings make no sense if conceived of as simple
one-off bribes. Given the amount of money that the traders stood
to make and the risks that the Submitters ran from manipulating the
rates in these ways, it seems unlikely that many people would accept
an outright bribe of such low value, least of all people as notoriously
hard-headed and economically shrewd as City bankers. Instead, what
these examples illustrate is the continuing importance of ongoing
relations of trust and obligation, often made concrete through the
offering and exchange of gifts, in even the seemingly most financial-
ized and depersonalized sectors of our global economy. It's hard to
imagine that these are isolated examples. After all, they merely illustrate what so many recent ethnographies of finance have illustrated;

namely, that in order to achieve things and get things done on Wall Street and in the City, people need to cultivate these kinds of relationships and to engage in the kinds of exchange and offerings that create and sustain them (Abolafia 1996; Hertz 1998; Zaloom 2006; Ho 2009; Tett 2009; Ourossoff 2010).

As Karen Ho (2009: 6) observes in her ethnography of Wall Street, much of the impetus towards deregulated and flexible labour globally over the past two decades has come from financial centres such as Wall Street and the City of London. And just as the financial instruments that drove these processes were driven in part by subterranean practices of gifting and relationships of long-term mutual obligation, the deregulation that they inspired, far from simply removing these kinds of relationships from the workplaces that they restructured, led in many contexts to their intensification. The small gifts of coffee and champagne, hidden from regulators and managers, by which City traders save their skins on the virtual trading floor bear a remarkable similarity to the exchange and offer of gifts of food, smuggled into work and discouraged by management, by which workers in an Indian diamond factory gain informal access to the materials and skills that they need to survive on the shop floor (Cross, this volume). The two groups of people may live very different lives and inhabit very different places in the global political economy, but for both groups informal gift relationships remain key to the actual process of securing a living.

The question is: What kind of sense are we to make of the role of these kinds of relationships in the world of neoliberalized flexibility that we inhabit? The kind of flexibility that is under consideration has two fundamental aspects: an increased flexibility of labour practices, and an increasingly flexible way of describing the organization and culture of many workplaces and business organizations. These two aspects are often seen as being mutually reinforcing, so that a global economy that rewards flexible organizational forms also rewards those workers who are flexible enough to continuously recreate themselves to adapt to their ever changing environment (see Knox, this volume). At the lower end of the labour market, however, it is often the case that the flexibility that is required of workers is the ability to adapt to ever-more rigid forms of control within workplaces. In these cases, flexibility, rather than being a term that might describe a two-way process, seems to carry a highly evaluative inflection, in which the assumption is that what needs to be made more flexible is the practices of shop-floor workers rather than the often highly inflexible systems within which they work.

Exchange and Long-term Obligation in Anthropology

What is at issue is the role of long-term relationships of mutual reciprocal obligation in the contemporary global political economy. Such relationships, although not always relying on the exchange of physical gifts, very often do rely upon them, and the role of gift exchange in creating and maintaining such relations has been a key concern of anthropological theory for almost a century. In the past within anthropology, gift exchange theory often acted as an external critique of the concept of Western 'economic man' operating from the position of the non-Western 'Other' who showed us that our understanding of our way of being was culturally specific and not universal. Certain areas of the world, in particular Melanesia, have been particularly associated with the logic of the gift within the discipline of anthropology, and here I will draw upon examples both from my own field research among Tolai people of Papua New Guinea and the wider regional literature to illustrate points of comparison with the issues raised in this volume. But my intention in doing so is not to draw a contrast between different societies that have different logics of exchange. As is by now well established, this is a position that, whilst well intentioned, always carried the danger of romanticizing non-Western societies whilst totally dehumanizing Western society at the same time (Appadurai 1986). But what the examples gathered in this collection might suggest is that our response should be not to discard the idea of forms of exchange that are radically opposed to the ideal of commodity exchange altogether (as some have suggested), but instead to reposition the critical purchase of the Gift as a central aspect of the form and function of exchange in the twenty-first-century global political economy. What the promised cups of coffee that threaten to bring down a nation's banking industry tell us is that it has never been more important to understand the social effect of gifting relationships and other ties of long-term mutual obligation not as the structuring logic of non-capitalist societies, but as a fundamental part of the social fabric that makes possible the large-scale commodity exchanges that we see reported in the news and financial press.

Indeed, it is worth pointing out that many of the most influential uses of the idea of the gift in contemporary anthropology are based upon an attempt to understand the ways in which gifting can be caused by and help to sustain global flows of commodity exchange. Gregory's *Gifts and Commodities* (1982), for example, is an attempt to explain why the integration of Papua New Guinea into a global capitalist economy did not lead to the disappearance of ritual gift exchange as many had predicted, but instead led to its efflorescence. Drawing on the analyses of Meillasoux (1981) and Fitzpatrick (1980), this 'gift economy' in the village is then described as sustaining and subsidizing the cost of production of commodities in Papua New Guinea, thus making gift exchange a part of the global production of commodities that we began with. Gregory is largely talking about a rural economy based upon gift exchange that is physically separated from the commodity production in town or plantations that it then subsidizes. In many respects this is very different from the exchange of food in an Indian factory (or even the offer of coffee at Barclays), but in both kinds of example a hidden economy of gifting is described as being part of the social fabric that makes the large-scale production and circulation of commodities in the marketplace possible.

The initial scheme that Gregory outlines sometimes seems to imply that there are two spheres of exchange – the gift economy and the commodity economy – and that, at any one point, any object or relationship can be categorized as belonging to one or the other, regardless of its potential to move between them. However, one of the themes arising from the ethnographic examples collected in this book is that it is often precisely the ambiguous nature of exchange or relationships that makes them simultaneously both so potentially productive yet also unsettling for those working in regimes of flexible labour (e.g. Garsten, Kjaerulff, Knox, Neveling, Wood, this volume). Indeed such is the centrality of ambiguity to flexible labour relations once they are subjected to close ethnographic examination, that Narotzky (this volume) suggests that we need to move our starting point from one of 'distinct confronted realms of value creation' to one of 'an ambivalent value realm . . . highly arbitrary and morally shifting and contradictory'.

Moral Economies and Moral Evaluations

What room is there for such 'discrete, differentiated abstractions' (Narotzky, this volume) as gift versus commodity, reciprocity versus non-reciprocity, or long term versus short-term relationships in this schema? In his later work, Gregory (1997: 48) is keen to stress how the sharp conceptual division between gift and commodity is a way of making sense of a real world of messy ambiguity, much as a distinction between the absolute categories of light and dark is what enables us to describe the subtle differences between different shades of grey (see also Introduction, this volume). And it is in the way in which the people working in regimes of flexible labour use sharply opposed categories of moral evaluation as part of an ongoing attempt to shape its ambiguity that we perhaps see the continued relevance of discrete abstractions, even if, like Narotzky, we do take ambivalence to be our theoretical starting point.

Perhaps the earliest, and still one of the most famous, ethnographic examples that would pave the way to the building of the gift/commodity distinction is the one that Malinowski describes Trobrianders drawing between *kula* and *gimwali* (Malinowski 1922: 95–96). As used to be widely known within anthropological circles, *kula* is the gift exchange circuit par excellence, setting up ongoing and indissoluble ties between men on different islands, whilst *gimwali* is a form of barter that, in sharp contrast to *kula*, is motivated by an attempt to get the best deal possible and maximize one's gains. The two kinds of exchange are motivated by different value systems, the one being an archetype for the anthropological concept of the gift, and the other looking much closer to the economic ideal of commodity exchange that the gift would go on to be contrasted with. Yet Malinowski's description of the two concepts is not one of two discrete spheres of value whose boundaries are clear to all Trobrianders. Rather, they are introduced as concepts designed to morally evaluate exchanges that are open to conflicting categorization. 'Often when critcising . . . they will say: 'He conducts his Kula as if it were *gimwali*' (ibid.: 96). In Malinowski's description, Trobrianders are well aware that transactions are ambiguous with regard to the kinds of relations that they value, and are open to conflicting interpretations. But, in order to make sense of what kinds of obligations are legitimately acknowledged and honoured by particular ambiguous transactions, they make use of discrete and sharply opposed categories of moral evaluation. And in doing so, they hope to shape the 'ambivalent value field' that they inhabit, using particular categorizations to exert social pressure upon persons and practices of which they disapprove.

Such sharply divergent evaluations of morally ambiguous relations and transactions remain central to the world in which we live. In my own fieldwork in Papua New Guinea in the early 2000s, the word *kastom* ('custom') seemed omnipresent. It was a word that described, among other things, adherence to an ethic of respecting obligations based on ties of gifting and ongoing reciprocal interdependence. As such it was often contrasted with conceptual opposites, such as 'business' or even 'not *kastom*', and was fundamentally a term of moral evaluation. 'That's the right way to do things in our *kastom*'; 'That's not proper *kastom*'; 'That's not *kastom*, that's a business', and so on. As such, the distinction between *kastom* and its opposites, like the distinction between *kula* and *gimwali*, was at least as much an attempt to shape social relations that were inherently ambiguous as it was an attempt to describe separate spheres of social life. But like the *kula/gimwali* distinction, it was an attempt to shape an ambiguous social field that rested upon conflicting descriptions that depicted that field as being ideally capable of being divided in such a manner. And although *kastom* was broadly associated with ongoing ties of reciprocal interdependence that we associate with gift exchange and was most often positively evaluated, it was not the case that it was simply a term used to describe an indigenous gift exchange economy to be contrasted with the negative and amoral commodity exchange that had been introduced first by colonialism and then by neoliberal globalization. On some occasions, *kastom* could be a negative moral evaluator, used dismissively to denigrate those who appealed to ties of kinship or gift obligation in contexts where they were considered inappropriate, such as the workplace or in public service. Although Malinowski does not mention examples, it is clear from his ethnography that a Trobriander who conducted *gimwali* as if he were doing *kula* would be as likely to be subject to a negative evaluation (albeit that the response would perhaps be one of pity rather than moral outrage). *Kastom* did not simply represent an indigenous gift-based moral economy to be defended against the impact of commoditization. As Neveling (this volume) points out, such a description would run the risk of romanticizing things, and it might fail to reveal the ways in which long-term gift and short-term commodity descriptions have always been a part of the construction of an ambiguous social field. There is a complex interaction of different ways of evaluating exchanges, and the same exchange can be praised (or denigrated) as *kastom* or one of its conceptual opposites such as business in different contexts. *Kastom* as a shifting signifier marks the limits of claims that can be made on the basis of reciprocal interdependence: to say something is or is not *kastom* can act as a means of accepting or denying claims made on this basis. Its very flexibility as a term is precisely what enables Tolai to negotiate and contest what kinds of obligations are considered suitable in some kinds of business ventures but unsuitable in others.

Exchange, Obligation and Flexible Labour

Likewise, it is the ongoing interplay of gift and commodity idioms for describing the moral appropriateness of different kinds of relations (rather than the interplay of transactions that can be unambiguously described as being in one category or the other) that is at the heart of shaping the ambiguous social fields of flexible labour and flexible business organization described in this collection. Although the wage-labour relationship is one that is often described ideally as a stand-alone commodity transaction, as we have seen it is often reliant upon a variety of longer-term reciprocal relationships that threaten that neat categorization. It has often been observed that managers and capitalists have an interest in removing these long-term elements of obligation from the way in which the labour relationship is understood, whilst workers often resist their removal.

The Indian diamond workers described by Cross (this volume), who attempt to preserve elements of gift-based ongoing reciprocity in their relationship with their employers, carry echoes of the South American miners described by Taussig (1980), who also wish to preserve a gift element in their employment. The diamond-workers' complaint is that their wages do not in themselves amount to adequate reciprocal recognition of their collective labour. Their remark that 'we are giving production but we are not getting anything back' likewise brings to mind Mauss's observation that a society that refuses its workers demands for reciprocal recognition does so at its own peril: 'The producer-exchanger feels now as he has always felt – but this time he feels it more acutely – that he is giving something of himself, his time and his life. Thus he wants recompense, however modest, for this gift. And to refuse him this recompense is to incite him to laziness and lower production' (Mauss 1966: 75).

But as the chapters in this collection show, context is everything. The same workers who try to preserve reciprocity in their labour relations are quick to condemn it when they feel it is pushed too far to gain unfair advantage. 'Soaping' becomes a pejorative designed by Cross's diamond-workers to police the appropriate limits of such reciprocal interdependence, much as the claims that some old men in my field site were *paulim* or *bagarapim* (spoiling) *kastom* by extending claims based on ongoing reciprocal interdependence into contexts where they were not appropriate. As Garsten (this volume) observes, flexibility is likely to encourage a more transactional attitude towards labour in some contexts (workers losing any sense of ongoing loyalty to a long-term employer) whilst encouraging a more personal long-term orientation in others (such as the cultivation of such relationships with particular individuals in employment agencies).

Likewise, whilst managers often try to remove gift-like elements from the labour process in search of a pure commodity transaction with no ongoing obligations, there are many contexts in which they do not only acknowledge such elements, but instead positively encourage them. The description by Wood (this volume) of the use of share options in the Canadian oil industry as a means of securing the loyalty of workers in a field known for rapid mergers and acquisitions serves as a case in point. As Garsten observes, flexibility is in this context itself a remarkably flexible term, encompassing phenomena as seemingly opposed as the intensely Taylorist management of poorly paid workers in factories in deregulated enterprise zones, to relatively privileged creative workers in the IT industry in the USA and UK (Garsten, Knox, this volume). In such industries, as Garsten observes, the trend is often for management to encourage the cultivation of long-term ties of reciprocity between people in the industry. Today it is a commonplace amongst many management consultants and gurus that the major problem of twentieth-century US business was a dysfunctional organizational culture, based upon Taylorist scientific management, that encouraged short-term sectional competition aimed at hitting targets at the expense of the overall picture or the final product. And what is interesting is that these prescriptions for fixing dysfunctional organizational cultures very often centre on their tendency to prioritize the hitting of short-term targets at the expense of the development of ongoing ties of mutual reciprocal interdependence within organizations that are considered productive of innovation and creativity.[1]

Exchange, Obligation and Flexible Corporate Forms

Mauss's interest in the kinds of social obligations engendered by different categorizations of exchange was matched by an interest in different conceptions of the person as a social entity, and in particular the kinds of relations that made it possible to conceive of persons as discrete individuals, as they have frequently been presented in Western political thought (Mauss 1985). The concern with mapping the relationship between different idioms of exchange and different categorizations of the nature and boundaries of persons has become a central concern of anthropological theory, as evidenced by the ongoing influence of books such as Marilyn Strathern's *Gender of the Gift* (1988). Strathern's work starts from a comparison between an individual person conceived of as being prior to the commodity exchanges that they enter into who is typical of Western social theory, and a 'dividual' person made up of the gift relations that constitute them, typical of what she imagines a rival Melanesian social theory might look like. Strathern is at pains to point out that this contrast is an analytical fiction and should in no way be taken as a template for how all Melanesians think at all times (a caveat that seems to have passed the attention of many of her disciples). Regardless of the virtues of such thought experiments that divide the world into distinct cultural areas,[2] Strathern's book has been useful in highlighting the relationship between gift idioms of exchange and flexible boundaries of persons and other entities on the one hand, and commodity idioms of exchange and more discretely bounded individual entities on the other. But what both contemporary Melanesian ethnography and the examples collected in this book illustrate is that perhaps a more useful starting point than an ideal Melanesia versus an ideal West is an examination of the creative and contested tension between different ways of categorizing exchanges, and how these are constitutive of the relative boundedness of entities as diverse as Melanesian landholder groups, American IT companies and nation-states.

In Melanesia, there is now a large body of evidence suggesting there are strong tendencies to increasingly prioritize 'exclusive' rights of access to resources such as land as opposed to 'inclusive' rights (Lea 1997). In other words, the kinds of overlapping rights of access shared by different persons and groups linked by ongoing gift relationships is increasingly replaced by the idea of a unitary landholder (be that a person or a collective group) whose ownership is less open to challenge and not reliant upon their recognition of ongoing mutual obligations. These tendencies are often linked in ethnographic descriptions to the pressures brought about by engagement with global networks of commodity exchange. Jorgensen (1997), for example, describes the way in which, among Telefolmin people of Sandaun Province, Papua New Guinea, the *tenuum mit*, a very loose cognatic descent group, has increasingly been referred to as an exclusively patrilineal descent group in the years since large-scale mining arrived in the area. In part this is local people organizing themselves in ways that they know they need to be organized in order for powerful actors responsible for distributing royalties, such as mining companies and the nation-state, to recognize them. In addition, it drastically reduces the number of people who can claim affiliation to a named *tenuum mit* from almost anyone in the community to a small number who can claim exclusively patrilineal descent from a single founding figure.

By contrast, the Tolai people of Papua New Guinea's East New Britain Province, amongst whom I conducted my fieldwork, have always had exclusively matrilineal descent groups. But here too, similar tendencies could be observed. The old men that I mentioned earlier were accused of 'spoiling' custom by arguing for the most inclusive possible definition of shared kinship as the basis of ongoing gift exchange between two groups that most others were adamant should be considered as separate entities. Likewise, the relationship between matrilineal clans (*vunatarai*) and their 'children' (that is, children of male members of the clan) was much more fraught then it was described for previous generations. Children of the clan were much more likely to be kicked off the land upon their father's death than in previous generations, a time when showing willingness to honour ongoing gift obligations to their father's clan would have been likely to secure permission to stay. In response, men were more likely today to buy land from their own clan (that of their mother) in order to secure their children's rights to remain, a transaction that had clearly become increasingly 'commoditized' over the past thirty years, and increasingly constructed both nuclear families and clans as more discrete individual social units (Martin 2006). These changes were universally described as a response to cash cropping for the global market, which turned land into a potentially valuable commodity.

Such examples speak of a profound ongoing transformation in Melanesian sociality, and in particular of the role of business and production for the global market in that transformation. By themselves, however, they may give a misleading picture of the nature of the relationship between commercialization and a tendency towards more discrete unitary forms of social organization, implicitly presenting a teleological image in which commoditization leads inexorably to ever less fuzzy and ever more rigid boundaries. This would amount to another replay of the 'destruction of the indigenous moral economy' narrative, in which the institutions of that moral economy were not destroyed, but instead transformed from fluid relational forms into fixed, bounded, property-owning and commodity-trading entities. Instead, what the examples gathered here show us is that, just as there is an ongoing tension over the extent of gift-like obligation at the heart of the flexible economy of labour, there is likewise an associated ongoing tension over the extent to which the entities that organize such labour processes can be conceived of as discrete bounded corporate individuals.

Take the main kind of social formation that organizes labour globally: corporations or limited companies. As is well known, in US and UK commercial law, the corporation is viewed as a legal person with most of the rights and obligations that other persons hold when they enter into transactions. It is clear that the establishment of this legal personality in the nineteenth century entailed the drawing of clear boundaries around this new entity. Most notably, it entailed drawing a line around the kinds of liabilities that shareholders might have, protecting them from liability in the case of bankruptcy by making that liability primarily the individual responsibility of the new corporate person. The chain of relationships along which debts might be chased was cut short, and the corporate person faced its debtors as a unitary entity separated from the investors whose mutual relationship as shareholders had made its existence possible. In the UK, two landmark moments marked the formation of this new legal personality: the Companies Act of 1862 that set these provisions in law, and the legal case of *Salomon* v. *A. Salomon and Co.* in 1897 that provided the first major test of these provisions.[3] *Salomon* v. *Salomon* finally established that, '[t]he company is at law a different person altogether from the subscribers', as Lord Macnaghten put it in his summing up. The precedent established by this case has been far reaching in the UK and most of its former colonies, and would on the surface appear to be part of an unambiguous trend towards the creation of bounded corporate entities that are separated from the relations that go into their creation, a trend that might seem to connect a company set up by a Victorian East London shoemaker with the *tenuum mit* of postcolonial Papua New Guinea.

But once again, the picture is a little more complex than this single trajectory. The final judgment by the House of Lords in the Salomon case overturned an earlier judgment by the Court of Appeal, which had ruled the other way on the basis that A. Salomon's company was a sham and a, 'corporation created for an illegitimate purpose', whose other shareholders were, 'mere puppets' set up to protect Salomon from liability.[4] This was an understandable suspicion given that A. Salomon owned 20,001 of the 20,007 shares issued, the other six shares being held individually by six members of his family. The Court of Appeal ruling in other words sought to evaluate the moral legitimacy of the kinds of relations that went into making up the company, and found them wanting. It did so on the basis that, far from being legitimate commercial investments, that the six individual shareholdings were based on family loyalty. Family and kin relations are where ties of affection, ongoing mutual obligation and gifting continue to be most publicly acknowledged and validated in modern society. What the Court of Appeal ruling in essence argued was that, just as the family needed to be kept free of commercialism, so too must the corporate person be kept free of these kinds of ties. If the corporate person were built on these kinds of relationships, then its integrity was fatally compromised and it was exposed as a sham.

Although the nature of interpersonal relations within the Salomon family is now lost to history, it is perhaps not hard to imagine Aaron Salomon sealing the deal with his relatives with a gift of food or drink. Much like the gifts of coffee offered by City bankers a couple of miles away and 109 years later, although such a gift would not in any way match the value of the financial protection that he gained by their agreement, it would act as an acknowledgment of the longer relations of obligation within which it was embedded. Whether such gifts were offered or not, it is the way in which Aaron Salomon relied upon motivations that the Court of Appeal evaluated as being established from ongoing personalized ties of mutual obligation and affection, rather than from legitimately commercial motivations that led to their initial negative judgment of Salomon's company.

In establishing what Lord Denning was later to refer to as the 'veil over the personality of the limited company',[5] the final judgment in the House of Lords created the company as a discrete person. But in doing so it also helped to enshrine the ability to install relations that could easily be evaluated as morally illegitimate by virtue of their basis in non-commercial reciprocal interdependence at the heart of a commercial entity, safe from scrutiny or appraisal. Even this judgment that led to the establishment of the company form as we know it in the UK did not lead in a singular direction. Just as there has not been a single movement from a moral economy based on reciprocity to a commercial economy, likewise there has not been a simple move from permeable and flexible non-commercial social entities to commoditized and bounded ones. Rather, there has always been an ongoing tension over the extent to which different kinds of boundaries and relations are evaluated and considered appropriate in which contexts. A central part of this tension is the way in which moves to create more bounded entities designed to enter into commercial transactions actually encourages relationships that might be very differently evaluated when viewed from non-commercial perspectives.

These kinds of non-commercial relationships that new commercial forms encourage at their heart are often hidden. So just as the kinship relations at the heart of Salomon's company were hidden by a 'corporate veil', so too are the gift relations at the heart of flexible labour in Cross's discussion of the Indian diamond factory. But this is not always the case. What the examples in this collection show is that current moves towards flexibility often encourage the more open appearance of enduring ties based upon long-term obligation and reciprocity. As we have seen, Garsten and Knox both show this with regard to various parts of the IT industry. And sometimes more permeable boundaries and flexible social formations are openly encouraged as well. Grétasdóttir observes that the nation-state form that has been so associated with the industrial age often appears more flexible in recent accounts, and shows how the presentation and acceptance of a gift can be part of the process by which this increased flexibility occurs.

The current trends towards increased flexibility in some areas of labour relations and business organization are accompanied by seemingly opposite trends in other contexts. What the chapters collected here illustrate is that an understanding of these dynamics still rests to a large extent upon an understanding of the dynamics of different modalities of exchange that have been a mainstay of anthropological theory since the days of Malinowski and Mauss. Such modalities are perhaps best understand not as the forms of exchange for different societies or even for different (moral) economies co-existing within the same society, but as ways of describing kinds of moral evaluations of the limits of ongoing reciprocal obligation in different social contexts. The era of flexibility seems to throw up challenges about the extent of such obligations and concerns that they either extend too far or not far enough, dependent upon the context in question and the perspective of the person evaluating them. In that respect, it is similar to what has gone before and whatever is likely to face us in the future.

Notes

1 See e.g. top US management consultant Steven Covey, who claims that too often work relationships are 'essentially transactional', but that the greatest business achievements come from nurturing ongoing relationships that are 'transformational', by virtue of being built on ongoing interdependence: 'It's not a function of efficiency. It's a function of the exchange of understanding, insights, new learnings and excitement around those new learnings' (Covey, Merill and Merrill 1994: 27).

2 See Carrier (1992) for a discussion of the potential dangers of this approach.
3 *Salomon* v. *A. Salomon and Co.* [1897] AC22, 51.
4 *Salomon* v. *A. Salomon and Co.* [1895] 2 Ch. 337.
5 *Littlewoods Mail Order Stores Ltd* v. *IRC*; *Same* v. *McGregor* [1969] 1 WLR 1241.

References

Abolafia, M. 1996. *Making Markets: Opportunism and Restraint on Wall Street*. Cambridge, MA: Harvard University Press.

Appadurai, A. (ed.). 1986. *The Social Life of Things: Commodities in Cultural Perspective*. Cambridge: Cambridge University Press.

Carrier, J. (ed.). 1992. *History and Tradition in Melanesian Anthropology*. Berkeley: University of California Press.

Covey, S., A. Merrill and R. Merrill. 1994. *First Things First: Coping with the Ever-increasing Demands of the Workplace*. London: Simon and Schuster.

Fitzpatrick, P. 1980. *Law and State in Papua New Guinea*. London: Academic Press.

FSA. 2012. 'Final Notice Delivered to Barclays Bank', Financial Services Authority. Retrieved 12 July 2012 from: www.fsa.gov.uk/static/pubs/final/barclays-jun12.pdf

Gregory, C. 1982. *Gifts and Commodities*. London: Academic Press.

——— 1997. *Savage Money: The Anthropology and Politics of Commodity Exchange*. Amsterdam: Harwood Academic.

Hertz, E. 1998. *The Trading Crowd: An Ethnography of the Shanghai Stock Market*. Cambridge: Cambridge University Press.

Ho, K. 2009. *Liquidated: An Ethnography of Wall Street*. Durham, NC: Duke University Press.

Jorgensen, D. 1997. 'Who or What is a Landowner? Mythology and Marking the Ground in a Papua New Guinea Mining Project', *Anthropological Forum* 7(4): 599–628.

Lea, D. 1997. *Melanesian Land Tenure in a Contemporary and Philosophical Perspective*. Lanham, MD: University Press of America.

Malinowski, B. 1922. *Argonauts of the Western Pacific: An Account of Native Enterprise and Adventure in the Archipelagoes of Melanesian New Guinea*. London: Routledge and Kegan Paul.

Martin, K. 2006. 'Land, Customary and Non-customary in East New Britain', in J. Weiner and K. Glaskin (eds), *Customary Land Tenure and Registration in Australia and Papua New Guinea: Anthropological Perspectives*. Canberra: Australian National University Press.

Mauss, M. 1966. *The Gift: Forms and Functions of Exchange in Archaic Societies*, trans. I Cunnison. London: Cohen and West.

———— 1985. 'A Category of the Human Mind: The Notion of the Person; the Notion of the Self', in M. Carrithers, S. Collins and S. Lukes (eds), *The Category of the Person: Anthropology, Philosophy, History*. Cambridge: Cambridge University Press, pp. 1–25.

Meillasoux, C. 1981. *Maidens, Meal and Money: Capitalism and the Domestic Community*. Cambridge: Cambridge University Press.

Nye, J. 2012. 'LIBOR Scandal Set to Rock US as Experts Warn It Could Be "the Biggest Consumer Fraud in History"', *Daily Mail*, 12 July.

Ouroussoff, A. 2010. *Wall Street at War: The Secret Struggle for the Global Economy*. Cambridge: Polity.

Smith, R. 2012. 'Rigging LIBOR: Banking Scandal Hits Home (Literally)', *National Public Radio* (US) 6 July. Retrieved 12 July 2012 from: www. npr.org/blogs/money/2012/07/06/156371620/rigging-libor-banking-scandal-hits-home-literally.

Strathern, M. 1988. *The Gender of the Gift: Problems with Women and Problems with Society in Melanesia*. Berkeley: University of California Press.

Taibbi, M. 2012. 'Why Is Nobody Freaking Out about the LIBOR Scandal?' *Rolling Stone*, 3 July.

Taussig, M. 1980. *The Devil and Commodity Fetishism in South America*. Chapel Hill: University of North Carolina Press.

Tett, G. 2009. *Fools' Gold: How Unrestrained Greed Corrupted a Dream, Shattered Global Markets and Unleashed a Catastrophe*. London: Little Brown.

Zaloom, C. 2006. *Out of the Pits: Traders and Technology from Chicago to London*. Chicago: University of Chicago Press.

Notes on Contributors

Jamie Cross is Senior Lecturer in Social Anthropology at the University of Edinburgh. His research brings together wide-ranging interests in economic anthropology and the anthropology of international development. He is the author of *Dream Zones: Anticipating Capitalism and Development in India* (2014) and has published widely on the lived economies of industrial work and labour in contemporary South Asia.

Christina Garsten is Professor of Social Anthropology the Department of Social Anthropology, Stockholm University, and Chair of the Executive Board of the Stockholm Centre for Organizational Research. She is also Professor of Globalization and Organization at Copenhagen Business School. She researches globalization processes in corporations and markets, and has focused on transnational organizational culture, organizational visions of transparency and accountability for transnational trade, and policy changes towards flexibility and employability in work life. She is currently studying the role of think tanks in the construction of policy-relevant knowledge and in setting agendas for global governance.

Tinna Grétarsdóttir is an anthropologist. Her research focuses on art, cultural politics and competing discourses of creativity in the neoliberal regime. She has been involved in curatorial works, taught courses at the University of Iceland and the Icelandic Art Academy, and is currently involved in interdisciplinary art-based research at a former NATO base in Iceland. Her most recent writings are 'Run for Your Life' in *Scarcity in Excess: the Built Environment and the Economic Crisis in Iceland* (2014), and 'Creativity and Crisis' in *Gambling Debt: Iceland's Struggle with the New World Order* (2014).

Jens Kjaerulff is a social anthropologist, and research fellow at Aalborg University. He has previously been lecturer in social anthropology at the University of Manchester, and taught at Simon Fraser University and the University of Victoria. Among his publications on economic practice and contemporary change is the monograph *Internet and Change: an Anthropology of Knowledge and Flexible Work* (2010, Intervention Press).

Hannah Knox is Lecturer in Digital Anthropology and Material Culture at University College London, and an affiliate of the ESRC Centre for Research on Socio-cultural Change at the University of Manchester. She has published widely on the anthropology of technology, infrastructure and social change. Her books include *Objects and Materials: A Routledge Companion* (2013) and *Roads: An Anthropology of Infrastructure and Expertise* (forthcoming 2015).

Keir Martin is Lecturer in Social Anthropology at the University of Oslo. Previously he was Research Fellow at the University of Aarhus and a recipient of the Royal Anthropological Institute's Sutasoma Award for work likely to make an outstanding contribution to social anthropology. He is the author of a number of academic and media publications on Papua New Guinea and the global economy.

Susana Narotzky is Professor of Social Anthropology at the Universitat de Barcelona and currently holds the Fellowship ICREA-Academia awarded by the Generalitat de Catalunya (2016–2021). Her research project 'Grassroots Economics: Meaning, Project and Practice in the Pursuit of Livelihood' (European Research Council Advanced Grant) addresses social reproduction under austerity policies. Work and Livelihoods – History, Ethnography and Models in Times of Crisis, Routledge, 2017, a co-edited volume, was awarded the Society for the Anthropology of Work book prize in 2017. Her more recent publication is "Rethinking the concept of labour", Journal of the Royal Anthropological Institute, Vol.24 (S1):29–43.

Patrick Neveling is Senior Researcher at the Historical Institute, University of Bern and Associate Researcher at the Department of Anthropology, University of Bergen. Patrick has published widely on capitalism from historical, anthropological and critical political economy perspectives and is currently finishing a book on the global history and political economy of special economic zones.

Caura Wood is an anthropologist and former energy executive writing on the intersections of oil and gas capital markets, assetization, energy futures and energy transition in western Canada. Wood resides in Calgary, Alberta where she is completing a manuscript entitled: 'Depletable Worlds: Formulas of a Resource Economy'.

Index

commodity (*cont.*)
  commodity form, 2, 4, 5, 178, 192,
    241
  morality, 5, 16, 19–22, 27, 141,
    264–74
  relation, 2, 5, 16, 18, 19–22, 27, 33,
    61–63, 96, 105–11, 139, 151, 160,
    191–92, 195–96, 212, 241, 264–74
    (*see also* alienation)
  See also exchange
Companies Act 1862, 272
consumption, 12, 17–19, 46, 47, 51,
  55, 67, 87, 93, 120, 158, 187,
  190–96, 217–23, 247
contract, 28, 29, 31, 45, 47, 57, 60, 94,
  96, 97, 98, 106, 111, 126, 137, 139,
  140, 148, 166, 175, 176, 178, 182,
  185, 186–87, 188–89, 191, 199n15,
  199n18, 211, 214, 262
  'social contract', 9, 15, 181
  See also sub-contracting
'corporate veil', 273–74
corporations, 27, 50, 70, 73, 98, 101,
  108–9, 117–22, 128, 130–31,
  133–41, 216, 218, 224, 248, 272
  as legal persons, 272–74
cosmic order. *See* ontological order
crises, 6–7, 35, 178, 207–8, 211–13,
  261
custom, 56, 105, 183, 186, 193, 196,
  199n15, 243–44, 256n5, 266, 271.
  See also routine

Denmark, 33, 235–60
development, 95, 119, 146–47, 149–69,
  178–84, 196–97, 197n2, 198n7,
  208–9, 213, 215–23, 230. *See also*
  transformation

economics. *See* exchange theory: in
  economics
economy
  in anthropological exchange theory,
    1–5, 11–22 (*see also* exchange
    theory)
  'economy of connection', 25, 26,
    46, 68, 93–115
  moral (*see* moral economy)

political (*see* political economy)
  See also exchange
embeddedness, 2, 11–14, 179–80,
  183–84, 188–89, 192–95, 242,
  252–53
employment, 3, 8, 17–18, 27–28, 31,
  45, 50, 57, 59–60, 94, 96–99,
  102–11, 116–22, 126–38, 154,
  158–68, 180, 185, 213–22, 224,
  228, 247, 268–69. *See also* work
ethnography, 1, 8, 19, 21–22, 27, 29,
  32, 35–36, 44, 45, 47–48, 68,
  94–95, 109, 116–18, 122, 151,
  173–74, 179–80, 185, 188, 193,
  236–38, 240, 245, 249, 262–63,
  265–67, 270–71
European Union (EU), 8, 28, 69, 146,
  153, 155, 186, 187
evolution, 14, 15, 174, 178, 244. *See*
  also transformation
exchange
  'agonistic' (*see* competitive gift
    exchange)
  as 'total social phenomena', 1, 15,
    139, 198n11
  barter, 12, 200n25, 209, 266
  commodity, 16–19, 46, 47, 61–63,
    96–97, 105–11, 116–17, 122,
    139–40, 151, 163, 185–89, 195–96,
    211–14, 228, 241, 264–74 (*see also*
    commodities: labour)
  competitive gift exchange, 15–16,
    17, 26
  forms of, 11, 15–16, 18, 96–97, 105,
    195, 241, 250, 264, 274 (*see also*
    exchange: principles of)
  gift, 16–19, 21, 23–25, 46–48, 49–50,
    56, 57, 61–63, 67–69, 83–88,
    96–97, 105–11, 116–18, 122,
    139–40, 151, 183, 200n25,
    209–10, 212, 222, 229, 237, 250,
    264–74
  interest in, 15–16, 26, 46, 71, 86–88,
    97, 105–12, 121, 140, 157–58,
    164–65, 167, 175–76, 179–80,
    183–86, 189, 222–23, 239, 242,
    250–51, 261–62, 268–69 (*see also*
    value)